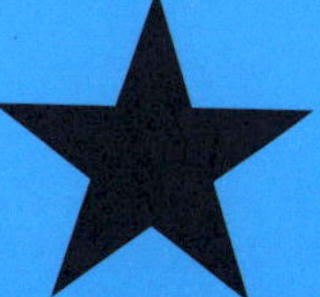

Brittany Colombo
Olan Prenatt

Model
Skater / Actor / Painter

Santa Monica
Venice

Jasmine Benjamin
City of Angels. A Book About L.A. Style

Photographs Copyright © 2024 Jasmine Benjamin
Foreword Copyright © 2024 Chioma Nnadi
Cover & Design © 2024 Kilo Kish Studio

Published by Damiani Books srl
info@damianibooks.com
www.damianibooks.com

Printed in December 2024, Italy

ISBN 978-88-6208-835-0

CITY OF ANGELS

A BOOK
ABOUT L.A. STYLE

PHOTOGRAPHS
BY

JASMINE
BENJAMIN

My Brother Joshua,
you taught me everything I know about style.

My Mother EdnaSarah and Father Richard,
you taught me everything about music and culture.

Los Angeles you forever inspire me.

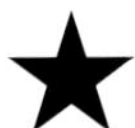

"In Los Angeles, everyone is a star."
Denzel Washington, viral quote, 2000s.

CONTENTS

INTRODUCTION
1

CITY OF ANGELS A BOOK ABOUT L.A STYLE is an exciting visual survey highlighting a diverse group of authentic Los Angeles creatives. 80% of the subjects in the book are LA born-and-bred, and all are shot on locations across their vast city.

Los Angeles is a place of magic and myth. Envisioned by outsiders as a Paradise City of palm trees, pools and posing celebrities, those truly 'in the know' have always been drawn to the currents that run just below the surface of its patchwork of clashing street grids. Barely 100 years since rancho borders became roads and movie cameras rolled in to take advantage of 300 days of annual sunshine, these dusty canyons are now home to the biggest broadcasting production line on the planet. A direct connection to the past is the popular abbreviation "City of Angels," the original name given to the Spanish colonial settlement (the remains of which now lie beneath Union Station) "En 1781: "El Pueblo de Nuestra Señora la Reina de Los Angeles de la Porciuncula" - "The City of Our Lady the Queen of the Angels of la Porciuncula."

It's been a lightning-fast glow-up, and today the town claims an inordinate amount of cultural currency, far greater than that of many cities with thousands of years of history. A town so ubiquitous it is internationally recognized by its initials, "L.A."

From Beverly Hills 90210 to Baywatch, Moesha to Clueless, Boyz n the Hood to The Fresh Prince of Bel Air, from Jackie Brown to Pulp Fiction L.A. is perhaps the most transmitted location in the world, beaming out the shifting moods and tropes of an endlessly evolving zeitgeist, forever imprinting itself deep into the global imagination. Despite the ubiquity of the city on screens of all sizes, no-one seems to be able to truly grasp the style of the real L.A., a place often considered to have no inherent aesthetic other than the paid-product-placement parades of red-carpet dressing. This misunderstanding has been pushed by the media for decades.

As a woman of color deeply invested in the issues of the society in which I live, I have a particularly nuanced perspective on Los Angeles fashion and style. I was born and raised on the West Coast, with both of my parents artistically and politically involved in many aspects of California counter-culture. Over the past 20 years, I've built a successful career as a stylist and creative director, building worlds within my own generation's visual culture. This project comes from a place of genuine interest in the lives of the people around me and the desire to show the world that not only do we have style in Los Angeles, but that it is a strong and vital force. I believe that a serious reevaluation of that style is long overdue.

This book was conceived and created wholly independently. Drawing on my wide network of friends and industry contacts, **CITY OF ANGELS** presents an insider view of who and what is happening, right here, right now. Several of my subjects are globally famous and/or icons in their fields. Some are local icons and others are new discoveries, whose personal style reflects the city and its incredible subcultures.

CITY OF ANGELS features 120+ portraits of daring, expressive Los Angeles creatives shot in locations across the length and breadth of this massive metropolis. It's a megacity called home by participants in a myriad of subcultural scenes, and I have set out to represent as many of these as I can. On these pages you'll meet iconic streetwear creators, surf and skate kids in Venice Beach, edgy Echo Park hipsters, Los Feliz vintage aficionados, shopgirls, shopboys and the wonderful variety of Chicanos, K-Town cuties, Hollywood royalty, LGBTQAI fashion designers, Laurel Canyon bohemians, Black musicians and artists from South Central and Inglewood as well as from the affluent suburbs of Baldwin Hills and historic Leimert Park. I shot from Watts to Electric Avenue, Boyle Heights to Sunset Boulevard, Westside to Eastside, pavement to hilltop, alleyway to open field. I wanted to juxtapose beauty with idiosyncratic, glamor and urban grime to create a document that requires the viewer to do more than rely on cliché and tabloid distortion when considering "L.A. Style."

In my photography, I decided to use the straight up format. I was very inspired by Japanese street photographer and founder of Fruits magazine Shoichi Aoki. The legendary Fruits magazine was founded in 1997 and chronicled the style of the different groups of young people that often hung out in the Harajuku neighborhood of Tokyo.

In January 2023, couture bible Italian Vogue reviewed the cultural impact of their own 70 page mega-editorial 'Hollywood Style' cover story by Steven Meisel that rocked high fashion in 2005. Presented in the form of a tabloid exposé, with long-lensed paparazzi shots of ultra-casual models getting Starbucks in sweats and exposed thongs, it was a critique that in fact celebrated everything about the typical L.A. low-key thrown-together look. Today, the original issue is a collector's item and L.A. street style is firmly entrenched as the touchstone of cool. Instead of blind obedience to any international fashion runway you will see that, for these tastemakers, it's all about repurposing, customizing and remixing codes as a rebellious and creative act.

Los Angeles is often, and aptly, called the City of Stars because this land is blessed - and cursed - with a magnet that pulls in a constant stream of hopefuls with big dreams looking to make their mark and become stars themselves. In my opinion, however, it's not the transplants but the local residents who really make this place worth coming to, and I've found that they are often overlooked when people consider the culture of L.A. That's why mostly everyone included in this book was either born or raised in Los Angeles County or greater California or contributed to the overall zeitgeist of the inside culture. These are the true denizens of this precarious city, who wake each day prepared for earthquake, wildfire, smog, violence and vice; they are committed to their hometown long-term, ride-or-die. Counter to the prevalent media narrative, you won't find them in "Real Housewives" gated communities or Calabasas McMansions. Nor will you find my stylish subjects flocking to peacock in one convenient, central location. There is no center here, no Times Square or Avenue Montaigne. If you want to see what's up you've got to make the effort to drive out to each special spot. Complaining about traffic in L.A. is a favorite sport, but visitors who stick to the fastest routes and freeways miss much. Putting together this project, I've learned every turn on the map and put many miles on the odometer while meeting my chosen subjects in their residential neighborhoods. Some are shot in areas I know well, others I had never been to before. Or I'd head over to emblematic locales such as Downtown dive bar La Cita or the Sunset Strip's Saddle Ranch as well as other iconic locations. My aim was to give real streets and the real people that live in them, the limelight they deserve. To shoot in these raw environments, there could be no big crew or fuss. Instead, it's just me, rolling up in my car, and the talent styling themselves in their own clothes. It was all D.I.Y, and the results are exceptional.

I've had a front-row seat to many of the subcultural cycles specific to this city over the past 20+ years. Through the process of building my own career, I've been able to meet and collaborate with the best and the brightest talents, who were carving out their own creative spaces. Arriving as a young person in the early 2000s, the very practical fact that I had to work to support myself led not just to a double, but what could be described as a triple life. In 2003, while a student at

FIDM, (the Fashion Institute of Design and Merchandising) in Downtown L.A. I was also interning at Interscope Records in the urban marketing department, serving as a production assistant on music videos, working as a salesgirl at the hip Kitson Boutique on Robertson Blvd, and manning the door evenings at cool Eastside as well as Westside bars.

On any given afternoon at Kitson Y2K's hottest celebutantes; Britney Spears, Paris Hilton, Lindsey Lohan, Nicole Richie and a young Kim Kardashian would swing by to deck themselves out in all the latest trends, while paparazzi waited on Robertson Blvd to get candids of the girls shopping. Being at the epicenter of this zeitgeist-capturing moment was undoubtedly exciting. But while the whole world saw glossy privilege, diamanté flip-phones, over-baked spray tans and little dogs in handbags and thought this is LA, it exposed to me the paradox of this place. That's because, at night I was immersed in an entirely different scene, working the door at soul music speakeasy clubs Temple Bar, Little Temple and Zanzibar, where I would usher in superstar musicians such as Prince, J Dilla, Bilal, Erykah Badu, and Andre 3000. Homegrown performers who are now internationally successful — artists like Flying Lotus, Miguel, J* Davey, Anderson .Paak, Thundercat, Madlib, and Aloe Blac —were passing through, all just starting out like I was.

It was during these night shifts that I encountered SA-RA Creative Partners, a major foundational L.A. group who created a new genre and have had a long-lasting effect on the L.A. sound, as well as its fashion. Now they're all Grammy-winners under their own names, but I remember witnessing SA-RA's first show, at which TAZ ARNOLD performed in an unforgettable look: huge black angel wings, hair curly and cut on a slant, like a hi-top Gumby with a twist. I had never seen anything like it. Later, others clued into his special magic. Artist Kanye West and Virgil Abloh were directly inspired by him. The original Black L.A. hipster, he's a true hometown style hero who's been rocking the scene since he was just a kid, so it was essential to include him in this book.

CITY OF ANGELS is full of similarly significant characters, all with their own distinct personal styles. I wanted to give pages to everyone I've met over these years who have inspired me and continue to do so. Here is a brief rundown of a few notables I have photographed and interviewed so far: Artist LAUREN HALSEY, who recently installed an imposing monument on the roof of the Metropolitan Museum in New York; a 22-foot-high temple structure featuring Afro-futurist Sphinxes and concrete tile hieroglyphics that riff on graffiti tags. This, and all of Halsey's output, is imbued with the collective energy and imagination of the L.A. community where she was born, raised and continues to work. I photographed her at the nerve center of it all, her South Central studio. A large-scale Lauren Halsey photo-collage mural covers the interior wall of Neighbors Skate Shop on Degnan Blvd in Leimert Park, a street that is also home to the artist Mark Bradford's Art + Practice initiative as well as many Black-owned businesses. This is where I shot TRÉ, the influential founder of the store, who mentors many young people in the area. Three-time Grammy award-winning THUNDERCAT started making music while still a student at Locke High School in Watts and now crafts psychedelic jazz funk that is as colorful as his look, as seen in the portrait I took of him. The daughter of a true Hollywood bohemian, director and photographer Autumn de Wilde, ARROW DE WILDE started her own band, Starcrawler, at 16 years old. Fascinated with the seedy, seamy side of music culture, onstage the young rock star is a whirlwind of long limbs, with a stage presence some have likened to Iggy Pop. As I sought to make imagery strong enough to convey the creativity, ingenuity, cunning, and courage that are the ingredients behind the best examples of eclectic L.A. style. Through my images, I wanted to show my respect for all of those people who have carved out their own platforms to adapt and exist in a tough town, surviving and thriving without the need for mainstream approval.

Looking back over L.A.'s social history, it's clear that, over many decades, deliberate redlining policies, systemic racism, segregation, and discrimination conspired to create tight, ethnically concentrated communities. I would argue that the same constrained circumstances that spawned street gangs also spawned street style. Cult L.A. streetwear brand Born x Raised is quite literally that - made for, produced and worn by those proud of being "born and raised" within city limits. Founders Alex Erdmann aka 2TONE and Chris Printup aka SPANTO, both born in Venice beach, were two very important personalities for me to include in **CITY OF ANGELS**. Since the making of this book Spanto has passed away and I am very honored to have known him and to have been able to honor him with his portrait in my book. He was a true hero to Los Angeles. I've never known anyone who has loved L.A. as much as Spanto did and the city loved him the same in return.

What happens in Los Angeles does not stay in Los Angeles. L.A. style culture, high and low, attracts attention from the biggest of global brands. In recent seasons, top European creative directors have been jetting in to source California-infused vibe, spending their time and budgets staging fashion extravaganzas on location here. Former Gucci designer ALESSANDRO MICHELE took over (and cleaned up) Hollywood Boulevard for an all-star klieg bulb-lit show dedicated to the feather and sequin-embellished glamor of the Golden Age of Hollywood. ANTHONY VACCARELLO exploited the moody sands and crashing tide of moonlit Malibu at night for his atmospheric YSL menswear show of 2020. During his memorable tenure at Saint Laurent, HEDI SLIMANE made L.A. his forever muse, his street-scouting eye informing all aspects of the historic Parisian brand's revamped new look. Under Hedi's tutelage, skinny Viper Room rockers turned into YSL campaign models for a wild show-gig-party at the legendary Palladium. As creative director of Celine, he staged a similar event for the house at The Wiltern in December 2022. Christian Dior's British creative director KIM JONES sought out the multi-talented local ELI RUSSELL LINNETZ, whose core aesthetic is about luxuriating the eccentric, low-key vibe of Venice Beach, for the Dior x ERL SS23 collaboration. Windward Avenue was transformed from boardwalk to catwalk, with Linnetz subsequently invited to be the guest designer at Pitti Uomo, the prestigious menswear showcase in Florence, Italy, for the June 2023 edition. It seems you just can't keep any current creative director away from Paradise City - in August 2023, Balenciaga's Demna Gvasalia announced that he will be showing the controversially revamped brand's fall 2024 men's and women's collections here in early December. Even designers from L.A. make their way back to draw upon the multitude of stylistic statements that emerge from this city's seething cauldrons of creativity. Dark master RICK OWENS, who grew up just north of Bakersfield, launched what was to grow into his half-billion dollar fashion venture Owenscorp in 1994. While he later moved operations to Paris to be closer to his European manufacturers, his Angeleno undercurrent can be readily identified in the relaxed ease of his artfully cut t-shirts and sweats in cool, neutral colors, as well as in the Mayan Revival angles of his bold architectural silhouettes.

To me, that's what Los Angeles style is all about: hybrid practices that travel far beyond the fashion narrative into visual art, cinema, music and social activism. The entire **CITY OF ANGELS** project is about this way of seeing, and asks readers to see past the clichés and stereotypes to re-engage the city and entertain new possibilities and ways of seeing the beautifully complex and eternal city of Los Angeles in an active struggle against preconception and entertain new possibilities in all senses. **CITY OF ANGELS** is a true-to-life, positive, and inspiring portrait not just of clothing or style but of the diverse, dazzlingly eclectic character of this captivating city.

References:

1.Taylor Hanes, "On the colonial settlement of L.A," Last Modified June 2019: https://theculturetrip.com/north-america/usa/california/articles/how-los-angeles-got-its-nickname-the-city-of-angels/

2. Victoria Bernal, "A walk along L.A.'s original borders reveals surprising remnants from the city's past," Last Modified April 27th 2021: https://www.kcet.org/shows/lost-la/los-angeles-original-borders

3. "Los Angeles: the Making of a City," Los Angeles History Project, 1988: https://www.films.com/id/2640/Los_Angeles_The_Making_of_a_City.htm

4.Various Authors, "Navigating LA," L.A. History Archive, Last Modified June 2011: https://www.lahistoryarchive.org/resources/Navigating_LA/

5. Giulia Di Giamberardino, 'Hollywood Style'on the Vogue Italia January 2005 editorial, Last Modified April 2024: https://www.vogue.it/moda/article/hollywood-style-vogue-italia-del-gennaio-2005-celebrities-paparazzi

6. Antwaun Sargent, "Social Works" in Gagosian Magazine, Last modified Summer 2021: https://gagosian.com/quarterly/2021/06/16/essay-notes-social-works/

7. Antwaun Sargent, "The Future Will See You Now: The Private Worlds of Black Desire," in "Utopia," Aperture no 241, Last Modified: Winter 2020: https://issues.aperture.org/article/2020/4/4/the- future-will-see-you now also https://aperture.org/exhibition/the-new-black-vanguard/

8. Darnell Hunt and Ana-Christina Ramón (eds), "Black Los Angeles: American Dreams and Racial Realities," 2010 NYU Press: https:// nyupress.org/9780814737347/black-los-angeles/

9. Brian Galindo, "27 reminders that Kitson was the hottest celebrity spot of the 00s," Buzzfeed, Last Modified August 2016: https://www.buzzfeed.com/briangalindo/27-photos-that-take-you- back-to-the-glory-days-of-kitson

10. Zainab Jama, "Sa-Ra Creative Partners, Nuclear Evolution: The Age of Love," Factmag, Last Modified June 2009: https://www.factmag.com/2009/06/26/sa- ra-creative-partners-nuclear-evolution-the-age-of-love/

11. Tracey William Cohen, "Don C Talks Iconic Paris Fashion Week Pic of Him, Kanye West, Virgil, Taz Arnold, and More," Complex, Last Modified March 2018: https://www.complex.com/style/a/ tracewilliamcowen/don-c-looks-back-on-kanye-west-paris-fashion- week-photo-with-virgil-abloh-taz-arnold

12. Holland Cotter, "Lauren Halsey at the Metropolitan Museum, Met's roof garden draws on ancient Egypt and South Central L.A.," Last Modified April 2023:https://www.nytimes.com/2023/04/16/arts/design/lauren-halsey-met-roof-garden-monument.html

13. Cerise Castle on Neighbors Skate Shop, "Skating can be a bridge in L.A. These 3 crews show how bonds form on four wheels," Los Angeles Times, Last Modified September 2021: https://www.latimes.com/lifestyle/image/story/2021-09-16/these-1- a-skate-crews-show-you-how-bonds-form-on-four-wheels

14. Miki Hellerback, "Thundercat, I'm still here and I'm alive!" Notion magazine, Last Modified September 2021: https://notion.online/thundercat-still-here-exclusive-interview/

15. Thomas Clausen,"Arrow De Wilde, the most exciting woman in rock music right now," L'Officiel magazine, Last Modified August 2022: https://www.lofficiel.at/en/lifestyle/glamour-danger-arrow-de-wilde-is-the-most-exciting-woman-in-rock-music-right-now

16. Spanto of Born x Raised, Mister Cartoon and Willy Chavarria, "The Influence of Chicano Culture in Fashion as Told by Leading Latino Pioneers in the Industry," Hypebeast, Last Modified February 2017: https://hypebeast.com/2017/2/chicano-influence-in-fashion

17. Layla Ilchi, "Chris Spanto Printup founder of Born x Raised," WWD, Last Modified June 2023: https://wwd.com/fashion-news/ fashion-scoops/born-x-raised-chris-spanto-printup-died- obituary-1235717600/

18. Merle Ginsberg, "House of Gucci Invades Hollywood Boulevard With Starry Runway," LA Mag, Last Modified November 2021: https://www.lamag.com/culturefiles/house-of-gucci-invades- hollywood-boulevard-with-starry-runway/

19. Matt Sebra, "Saint Laurent's Big Malibu Fashion Show Brought Out Keanu Reeves and Some Wavy New Menswear," GQ, Last Modified June 2019: https://www.gq.com/story/ saint-laurent-malibu-keanu-reeves

20. "Hedi Slimane's love affair with L.A. culture," i-D magazine, https://i-d.vice.com/en/article/xwxk34/exploring-hedi-slimanes- love-affair-with-la-through-the%20ages

21. "Hedi Slimane's Saint Laurent show at the Hollywood Palladium," W Magazine, Last Modified February 2016: https://www.wmagazine.com/story/saint-laurent-hedi-slimane-fall-2016- palladium-los-angeles

22. "Eli Russell Linnetz," BoF, Last Modified 2022: https:// www. businessoffashion.com/community/people/eli-russell-linnetz

23. Booth Moore, "Rick Owens Returning to L.A. for First Time in 16 Years," WWD, Last Modified November 2019: https://wwd.com/feature/rick-owens- returning-to-l-a-for-first-time-in-16-years-1203362234/

24. Miles Soca, "Balenciaga Will Show in Los Angeles in December 2023," WWD, Last Modified July 2023: https:// wwd. com/fashion-news/fashion-scoops/balenciaga-los-angeles-fashion- show-la-1235756116/

FOREWORD
2

Chioma
Nnadi

If I had to name the single biggest influence on my personal style, I'd undoubtedly say it was London, where I was born and raised. Even after 20 years of living in the States, the scrappy, creative spirit of my hometown stayed deep in my bones. It is, I suspect, why I've always been drawn to places with a distinctive flavor, places where getting dressed is an expression of local pride.

And yet I admit that I wasn't always hip to the subtleties of Los Angeles. Like most people, I imagined LA through the prism of celebrity culture, rarely looking beyond the gloss of Hollywood. Back in the early aughts, what I knew about style in the city revolved largely around the reality TV-fueled craze for Juicy Couture tracksuits, bedazzled Von Dutch trucker hats, and designer denim. (Like every other fashion obsessive at the time, I coveted a pair of distressed True Religion jeans.) What I didn't know was that the really good stuff was hiding in plain sight.

I have Jasmine Benjamin to thank for opening my eyes to the city. When I befriended her in New York, she was an aspiring stylist, a West Coast transplant filled with boundless energy and sunny optimism that was a refreshing antidote to the city's toughness. We quickly bonded over a mutual fascination with youth subcultures. While my personal style was forged by the UK's nascent rave scene, she'd come of age just as indie hip hop was beginning to explode in California.

At the time we met, a new generation of musicians was coming out of LA; artists like the Internet and Thundercat, whose look—cool yet entirely unstudied— was quickly becoming just as influential as their sound. Of course, Jasmine was the first to introduce me to the scene. I was quickly hooked. It wasn't long before she'd convinced me to take a trip to Los Angeles to experience it all first hand. I'd been to LA before, but never really strayed from Hollywood. And since I worked at a music magazine, I could practically write the experience off as research. Standing in the middle of the crowd at a small music festival on the Eastside, and I couldn't help but stop and stare: the kids here dressed with so much verve, pulling from a smorgasbord of sartorial references—skate, surf, goth, you name it. I was totally spellbound.

Many of those exquisitely dressed people can be found in the pages of this book, starting with the truly talented Syd, lead singer of the Internet, who I was lucky enough to see perform that night. Pictured on page 42, visual artist Lauren Halsey has the kind of riotously colorful and bombastic style that speaks to the spirit of South Central, where she's from. Then there's the rapper YG, buttoned up in his black leather vest and matching leather gloves, the embodiment of Compton Swagger. And if you're an out-of-towner like me and you've never been to Leimert Park, then the stylish local characters in the neighborhood are every reason to visit. Though I've been to Los Angeles several times since, I have yet to fully grasp its sprawling geography. So frankly I consider this book to be something of a key to the city.

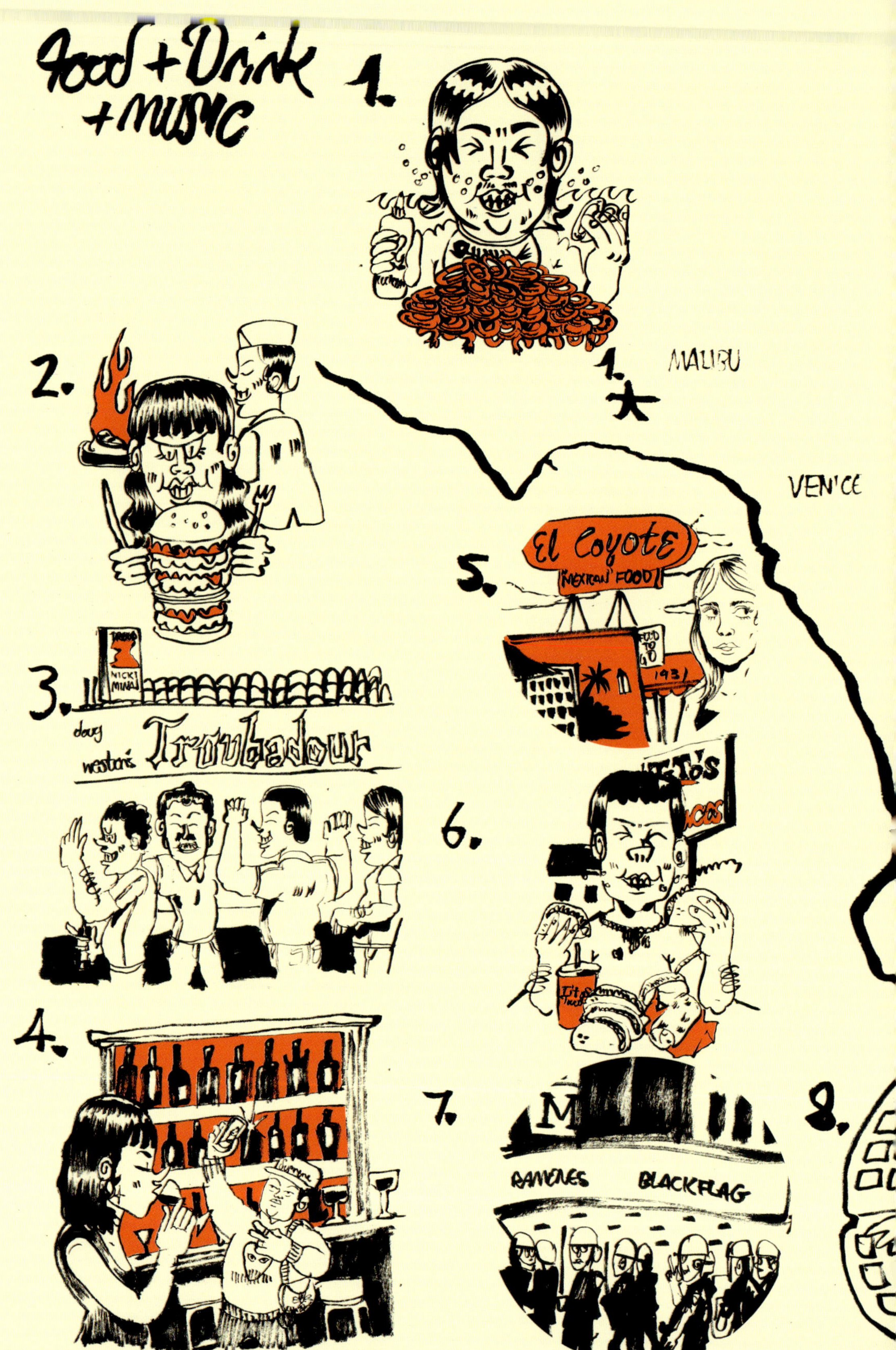

food + Drink + MUSIC
1.
MALIBU
VEN'CE
1.
2.
3.
doug weston's Troubadour
NICKI MINAJ
5.
El Coyote
MEXICAN FOOD
FOOD TO GO
1931
6.
TITO'S TACOS
Tito's Tacos
4.
7.
RAMONES
BLACK FLAG
8.

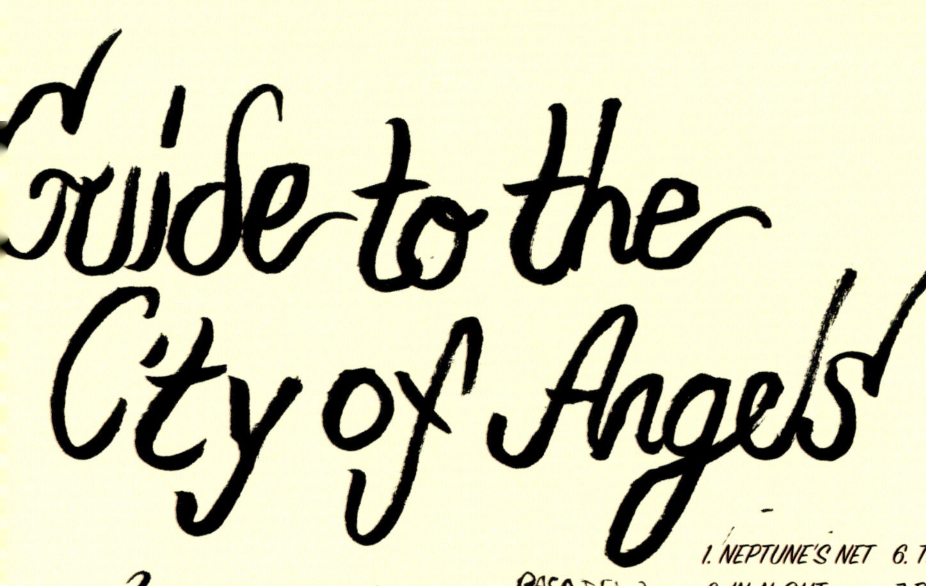

Guide to the
City of Angels
PASADENA
HOLLYWOOD
2.
3.
4.
5.
6.
7.
8.
9.
10.
11.
INGLEWOOD
DTLA
EAST LA
HAWTHORNE
SOUTH CENTRAL
1. NEPTUNE'S NET
2. IN-N-OUT
3. TROUBADOUR
4. THE DIME
5. EL COYOTE
6. TITO'S TACOS
7. PALLADIUM
8. ROSCOE'S
9. DRAWING ROOM
10. THE ECHO
11. LA CITA

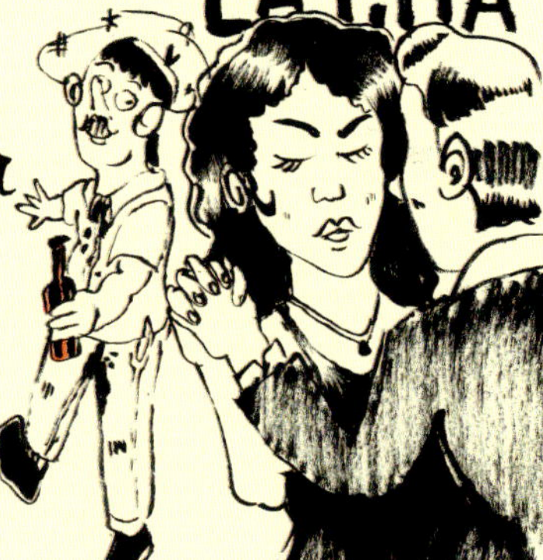

LA CITA

LONG BEACH

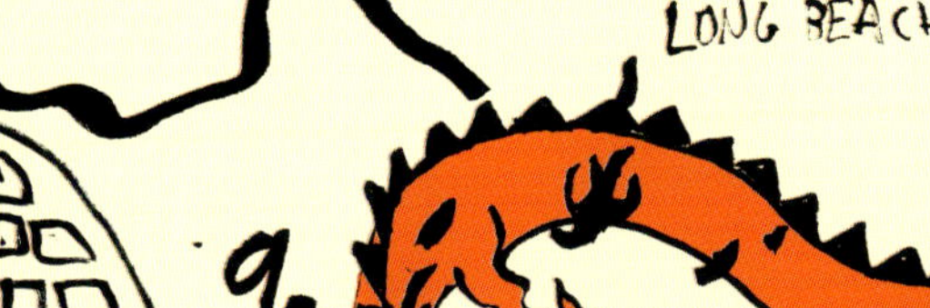

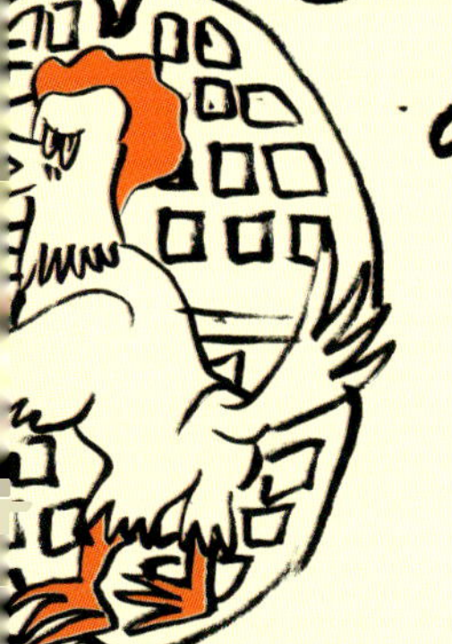

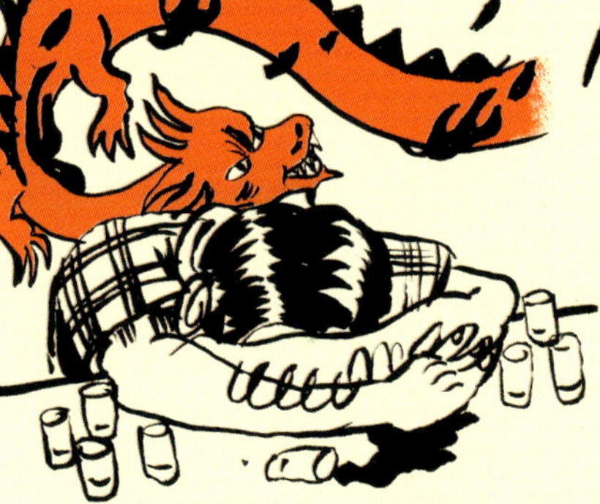

9.

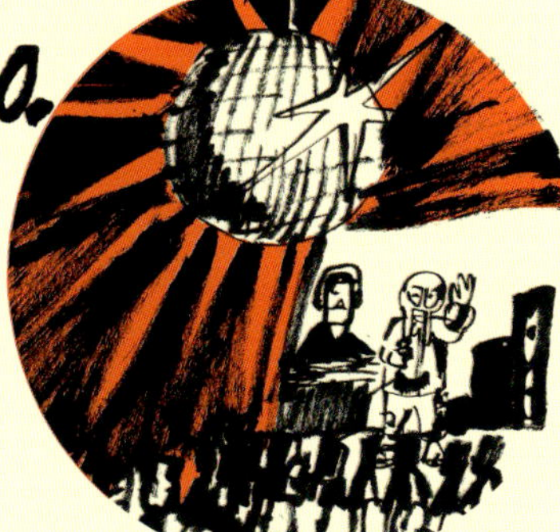

10.

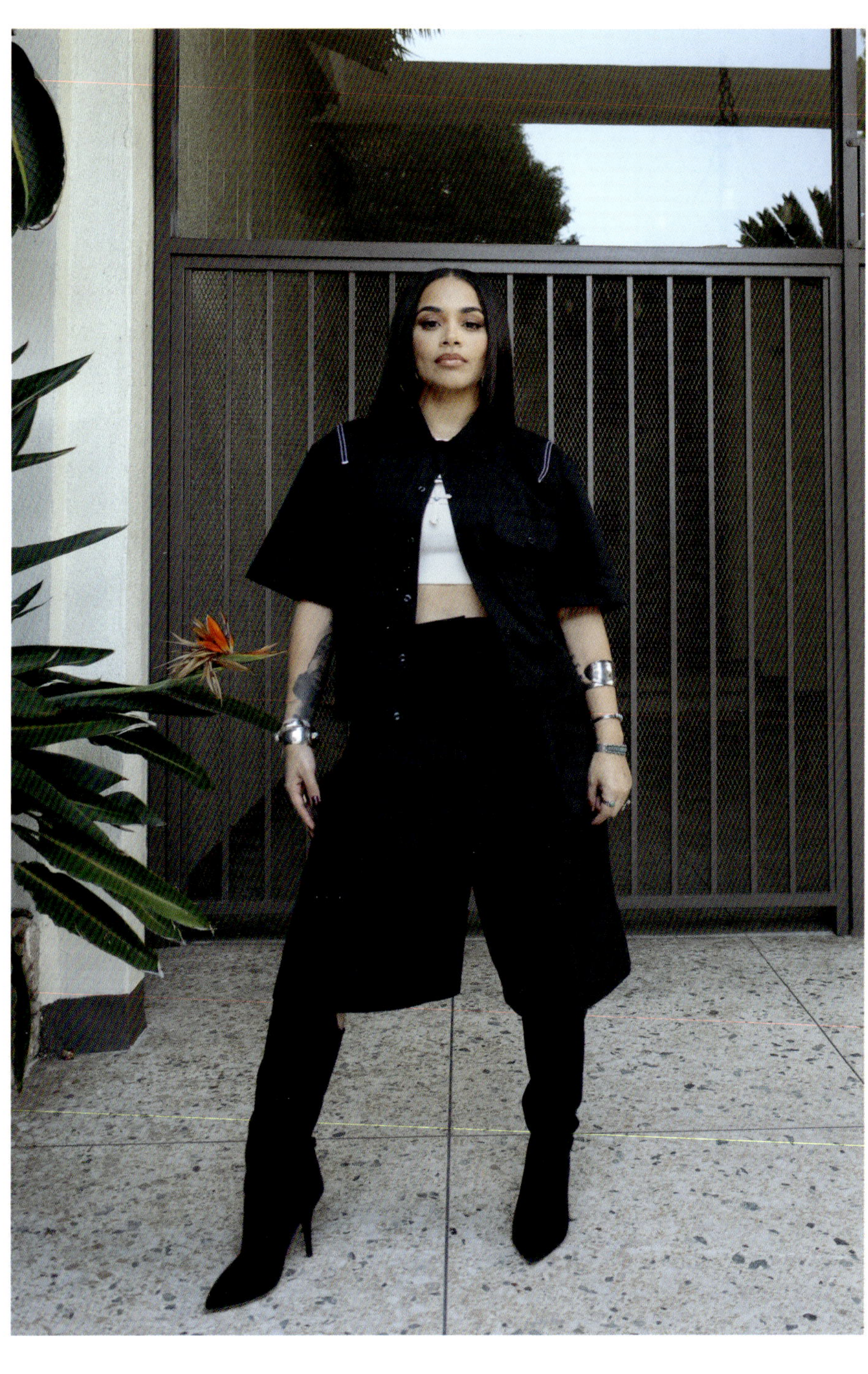

Lauren London

Actor / Creative Director / Entrepreneur

West L.A.

LAUREN LONDON

Name

Lauren London

Occupation?

Actor / Creative Director / Entrepreneur

Where in Los Angeles are you from?

West L.A.

What do you love most about LA?

That L.A. is a big melting pot of all kinds of cultures and people.

Where do you like to hang?

Crystal shops and the beach.

What would you tell someone who has never been to LA before?

Just because it's a neighborhood with a lot of nice houses doesn't mean it's not dangerous. Venture away from the tourist spots and really go meet the people from L.A. because we are pretty special.

What about LA inspires your personal style?

I love the classic LA style. Like, Chucks, Puma Suedes, Dickies pants, any type of white tee and jeans is crackin. These pieces are simple and never go out of style.

First childhood memory of LA style?

Starter jackets and Chucks.

What is the one thing people get wrong about LA?

That it's fake and Hollywood and it's not at all. The people who are from here are not like that at all.

Create your soundtrack for LA in 1-3 songs

Hustle in the House -Nipsey Hustle
Never Leave Me Alone -Nate Dogg
Why You Bullshittin -Suga Free
We Can Freak It -Kurupt

West L.A.

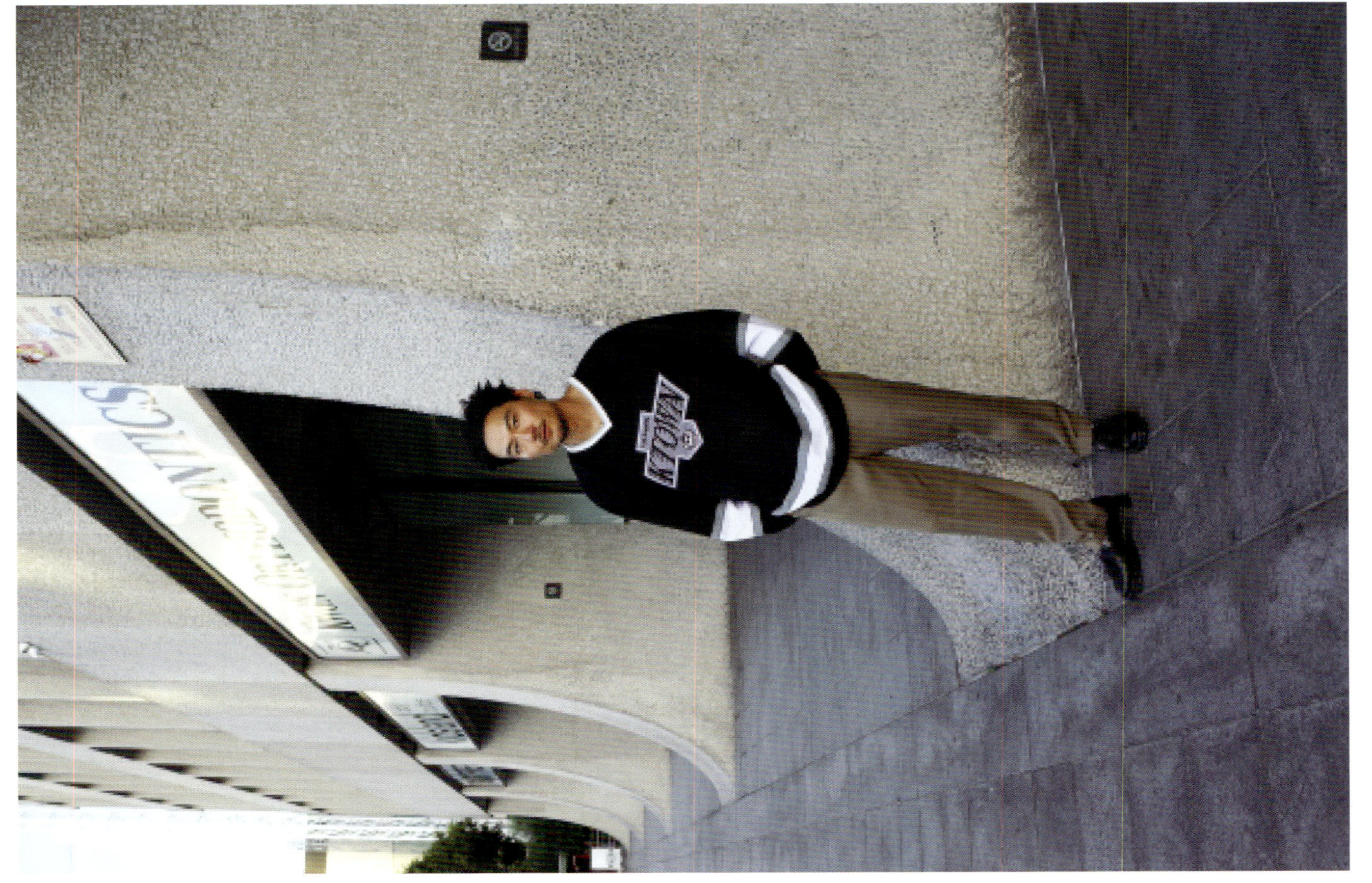

CITY OF ANGELS

DUMBFOUNDED

Name

Jonnie "Dumbfoundead" Park

Occupation?

Rapper / Actor / Writer

Where in Los Angeles are you from?

Koreatown

What do you love most about LA?

I love that every block is different from the next. It's like a pack of jelly beans with random flavors. Some are nasty and some are fantastic, such is life.

Where do you like to hang?

Koreatown Plaza Food Court, the Comedy Store, Runyon Canyon (I don't care what yall say, it's a nice quick hike) but far as areas I love: Ktown, Echo Park/Silverlake, Leimert Park.

What would you tell someone who has never been to LA before?

We have the best food in the world. We do EVERY culture's food very well. I stand on this wholeheartedly, you're wrong.

What about LA inspires your personal style?

It's hard to look fly when you live in weather where you can have your shirt off everyday. The hardest part is having layers on without being sweaty. I think these challenges have helped me find my style.

First childhood memory of LA style?

Going to work with my father in Downtown LA and roaming around the swap meets that sold Dickies and Pro Clubs. I still incorporate a lot of the workwear I grew up around into my everyday style.

What is the one thing people get wrong about LA?

That it's "fake". This is a real place with real people and when reality hits you, you'll feel it.

Create your soundtrack for LA in 1-3 songs

Never Leave Me Alone
-Nate Dogg ft. Snoop Dogg

Koreatown

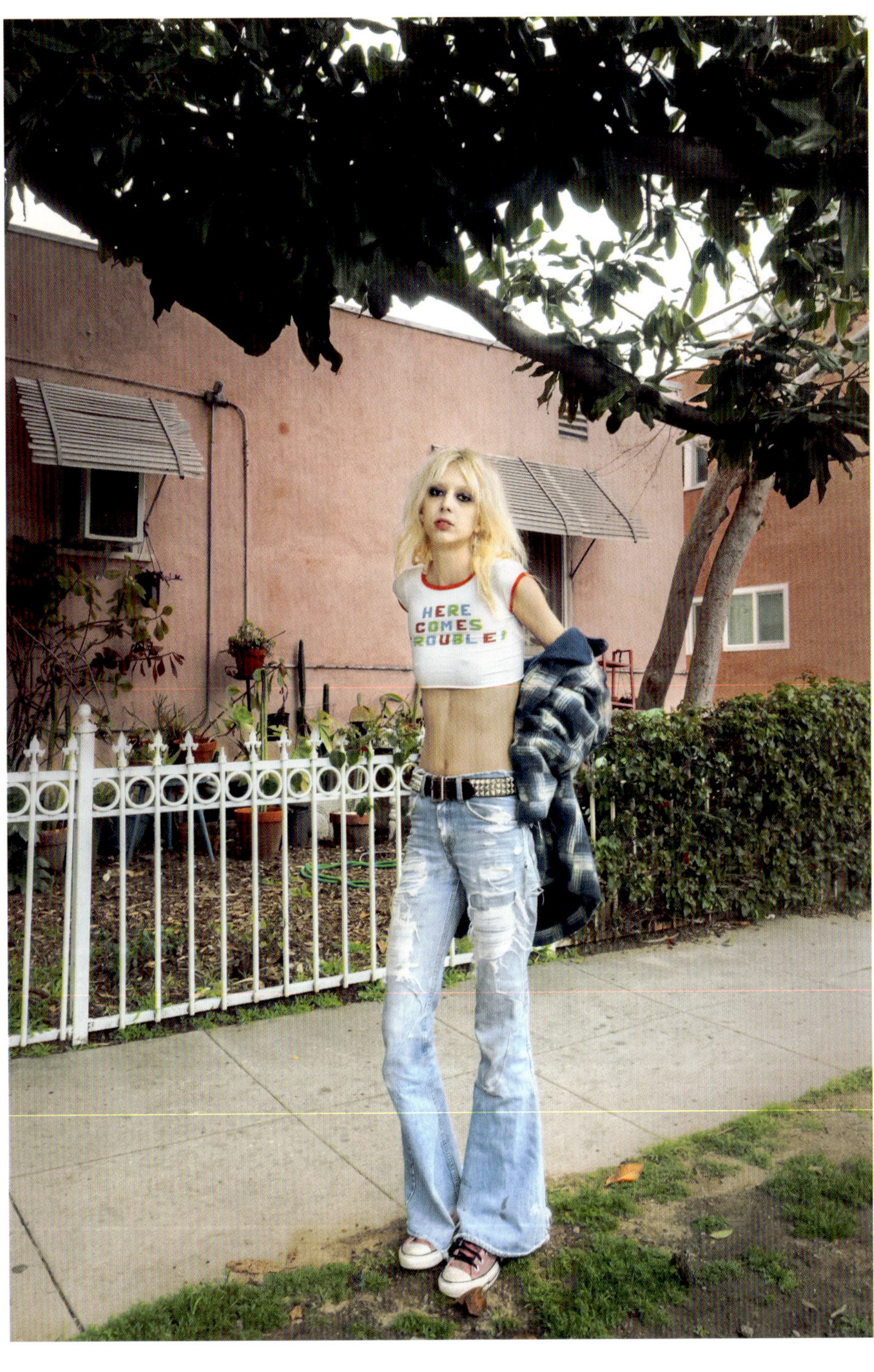

ARROW DE WILDE

Name

Arrow de Wilde

Occupation?

Singer in Starcrawler.

Where in Los Angeles are you from?

I grew up mainly in Echo Park, but also in the Hollywood/Beachwood area. My grandparents on my moms side have lived in Los Feliz since 1970, and my dad's side of the family is from the Altadena/Pasadena area so I kind of grew up hopping all around (the east side).

Where do you like to hang?

I live in Los Feliz now, and honestly love chilling around here. I like pretty much all parts of LA though, except for like West Hollywood. Even then there's some cool shit over there, I just hate how long it takes to get there and all the influencers roaming around.

What do you love most about LA?

The food, the culture, I love how even on the nastiest & dirtiest streets there are still flowers and fruit trees growing everywhere. I love the palm trees and the tragic tackiness of Hollywood Blvd. I love the smoggy sunsets and the smell of jasmine. I love the old locals like Angelyne that still roam the streets doing their thing. I love everything that makes LA what it is, but I guess to me it's the stuff that most people don't necessarily think twice about.

Describe your personal style.

I'm either in jeans, a T-shirt and Vans, or I'm completely decked out in some crazy shit. It's kind of hard to describe what my personal style is I guess, but when I go out at night I always feel like I need to make a statement. Also the less clothing the better.

What would you tell someone who has never been to LA before?

Don't trust your friend who moved here for college and claims they "know the spots". They don't.

First childhood memory of LA style?

Probably the Chicana girls at my elementary school. They used to tie scrunchies around the bottom of their jeans to make them kind of puffy, with clean white tube socks and K-Swiss sneakers. I begged my grandma to take me to the mall and buy me a pair of K-Swiss. Eventually she did, but of course when I wore them to school I got made fun of. Also the goths I would see walking around Hollywood Blvd in those huge chunky platform buckle shoes with tons of face piercings. I guess that one isn't specifically LA, but it definitely made an impact on me.

What is the one thing people get wrong about LA?

Pretty much everything.

Create your soundtrack for LA in 1-3 songs

We're Desperate -X
Kiss Me LA -Angelyne
Stop -Jane's Addiction

Echo Park

Sara Fernandez

Model / Educator

Highland Park

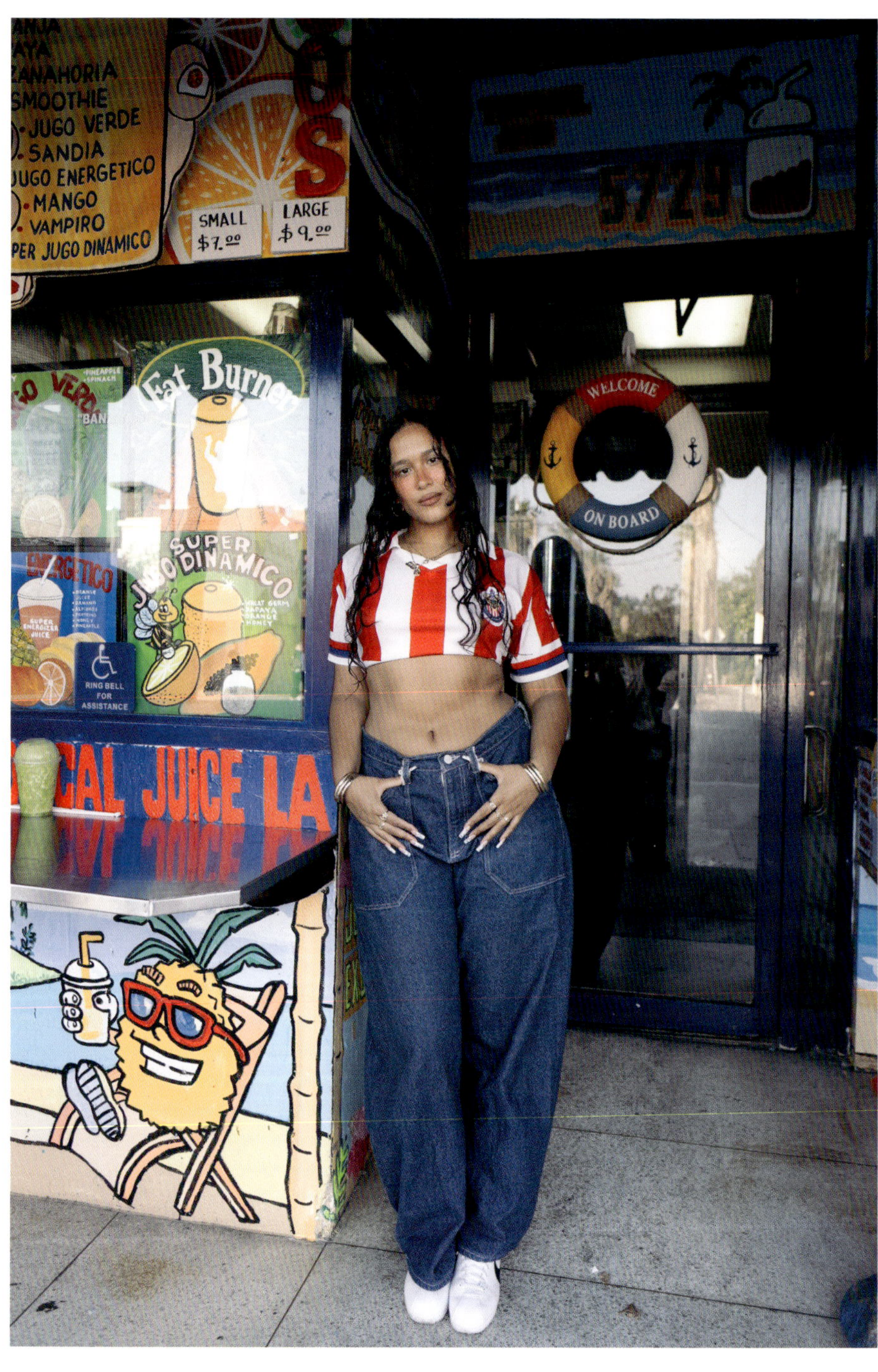

SARA FERNANDEZ

Name

Sara Fernandez

Where in Los Angeles are you from?

I am from northeast Los Angeles. Highland Park.

What do you love most about LA?

I love that I can close my eyes at night and hear all the norteñas, cumbia, and just all of our music. When I hear that, that's how I know I'm home.

Where do you like to hang?

My favorite place is the Mount Washington view. You can see all of north east LA, Pasadena, and Downtown. It's been my favorite spot since I was little. Never been to LA before? Been here my whole life!

What about LA inspires your personal style?

LA is extremely vibrant. I see endless amounts of colors and patterns everywhere. Also, a lot of the different styles that are prominent in Los Angeles come with a lot of history. Everyone dresses very intentionally because of that.

First childhood memory of LA style?

My first prominent memory of LA style is of when I would see my sisters and tias get ready when I was little. I would see that they would dress very Chicana: they had the nails, the eyebrows, the gold jewelry. I was always in awe by how detailed they were with their style, it definitely influenced my own style today.

What is the one thing people get wrong about LA?

That people from LA are fake. Not everyone in LA County is fake. It is a generalization that people who are not from here make and they are usually referring to other people who are not actually FROM here.

Create your soundtrack for LA in 1-3 songs

Backstrokin -Fatback Band
Suavecito -Malo
Hair Down -Sir

Highland Park

Jesse Rosenthal

Student / Model

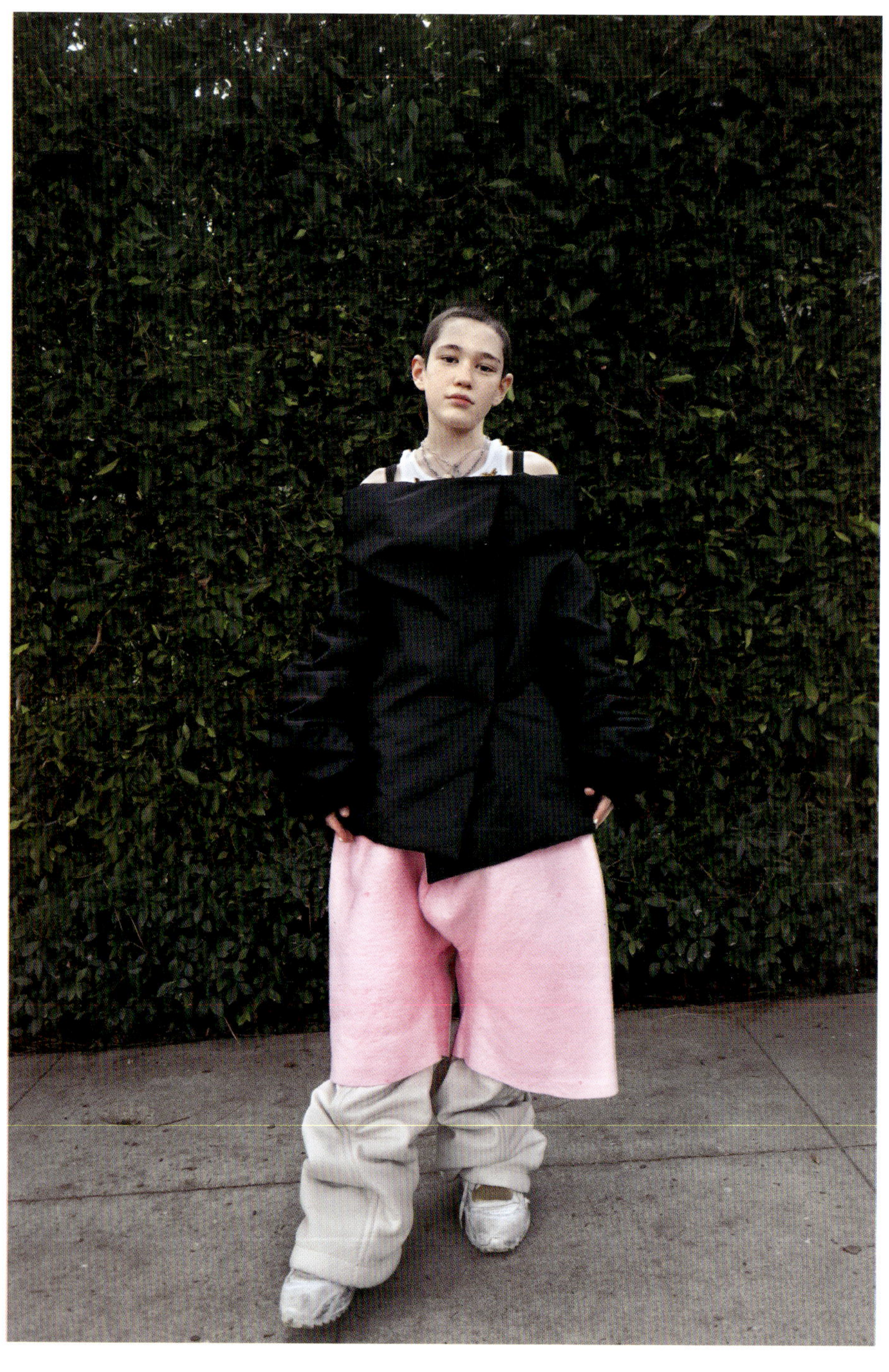

Santa Monica

JESSE ROSENTHAL

Name

Jesse Rosenthal

Where are you from in Los Angeles?

Santa Monica

Where do you like to hang?

Fairfax, Supreme/Golf Wang. The Palisades.

What do you love most about LA?

Diversity of people. No matter what your interests are you can find your clique.

What about LA inspires your personal style?

Silhouettes in LA, the mountains, the buildings, the architecture, a lot of the street style.

What would you tell someone who has never been to LA before?

Come here with an open mind. Don't base LA off of a certain group or place. It's so vast and so diverse.

Create your soundtrack for LA in 1-3 songs

Honey -070 Shake
Waves -Kanye West
Nights -Frank Ocean

Santa Monica

Kasey Elise

Filmmaker

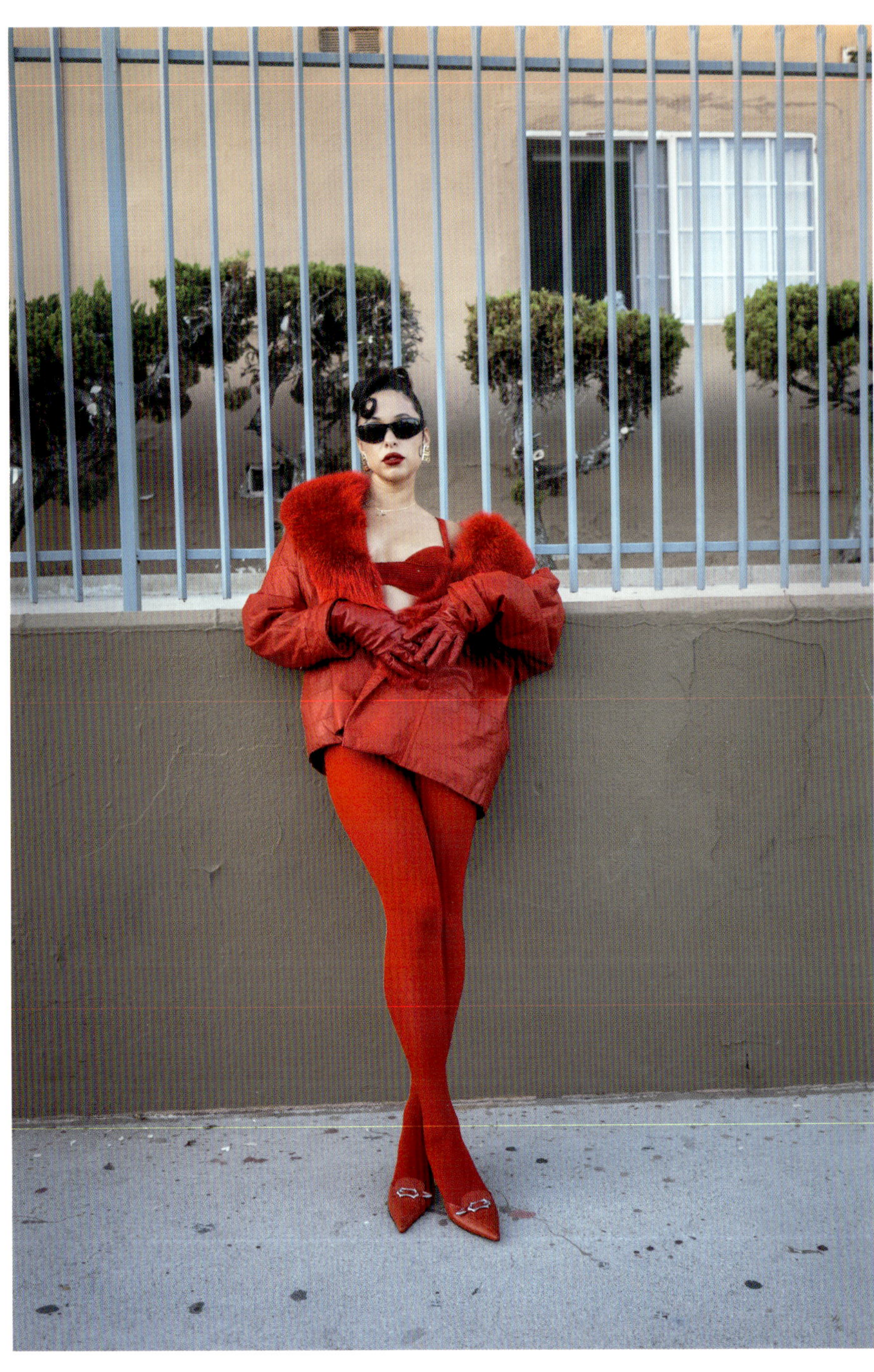

Baldwin Hills

KASEY ELISE

Name

Kasey Elise

Where in Los Angeles are you from?

Baldwin Hills

What do you love most about LA?

I love that it's easy to get to the beach, mountains, nature, and the city. You get a little bit of everything. You can drive an hour to hot springs. You can be anyone you want to be. No restrictions! So many diff types of ways to make your dreams come true.

What about LA inspires your personal style?

The community I grew up in, I spent my teen years in South LA with all different kinds of people. The diff personalities. Nobody is the same as everyone. Pulled a lot from my glamorous mother and grandmother. The 1980s and 1990s with my aunts and mom and grandmothers. My family. The lifestyle of my community. I like to rep where I'm from. Where I came from and where I wanna go. Everybody wants to get on. There is this dramatic element to become more and move up in your class! You feel more worthy with dressing "up". Dress the part. It's really important to my dad that you look clean and together. You take pride in your appearance. I grew up with a beauty salon in my house. My dad built my mother her beauty salon. My family spent hours getting ready. My dad is crispy and clean and glamorous. They like to floss. They are flossy.

Describe your personal style?

Glamorous. Bold colors. Class. Regal. Feminine. Boomerang film ref meets Working Girl.

What would you tell someone who has never been to LA before?

LA is about the people! It's about the people you know, that can change your experience! I'm plugged into so many diff crowds and people, versatility and the streets. I would hang in the palisades to south central. I feel so filled with history and culture.

First childhood memory of LA style?

In preschool, parents were picking up students and my mom walked in with, black curly hair and long red nails and Reebok Classic. I was like my mom is so fly! I understood style at that moment. I like how she stood out. She was so effortless. That's who she was!

Create your soundtrack for LA in 1-3 songs

Return of the Mack -Mark Morrison
Be Your Girl -Teedra Moses
I'd Rather Be Your Ni**a -Tupac

Baldwin Hills

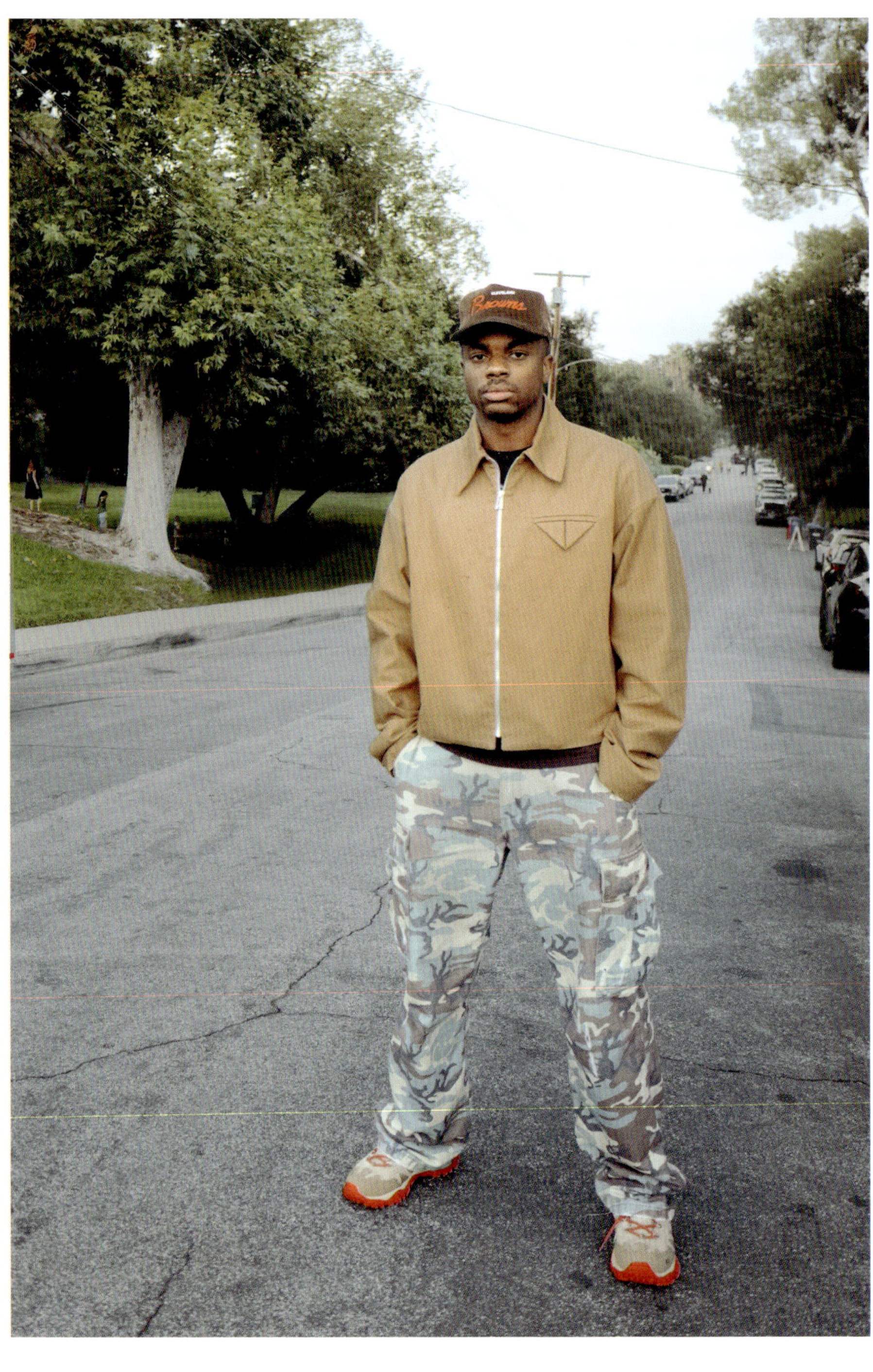

Vince Staples

Artist

Long Beach

VINCE STAPLES

Name

Vince Staples

Where in Los Angeles are you from?

Long Beach

What do you love most about LA?

The familiarity

What would you tell someone who has never been to LA before?

Have an open mind and explore the diaspora of LA County.

What about LA inspires your personal style?

You are what you know. It is very diverse and you can find your pockets. You won't get judged, LA allows expression.

First childhood memory of LA style?

Church and funerals. The coordination, you have to dress up to attend funerals. I remember seeing a lot of those "In Memory Of" t-shirts that are airbrushed growing up.

What is the one thing people get wrong about LA?

It's not as dangerous and vain as people say. It's in between both. You have to find the sweet spot.

Create your soundtrack for LA in 1-3 songs

Dream Chasers -Murs
If You Don't Know Me By Now -The Blue Notes
Cali is Active -Doggpound

Long Beach

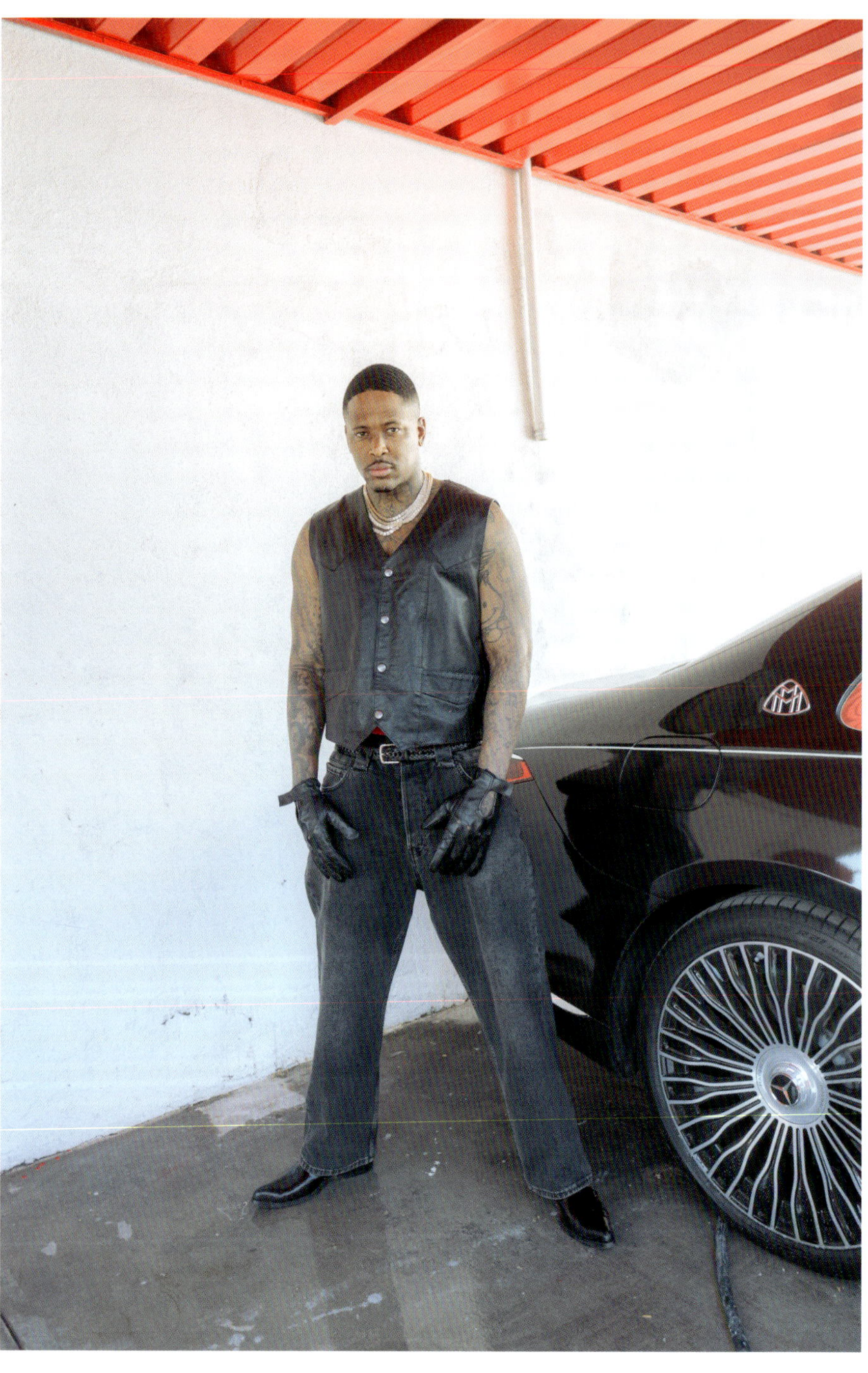

YG

Name

YG

Where in Los Angeles are you from?

Compton

What do you love most about LA?

You take a 20 min drive and you are in a whole different world.

What would you tell someone who has never been to LA before?

I would tell people to get outside of Hollywood. Do not judge LA if you are north of Pico. You gotta be south of Pico. Your experiences have to be south of Pico if you are gonna speak on LA.

What about LA inspires your personal style?

Gang culture of LA from the 80s/70s.

First childhood memory of LA style?

Snoop Dogg. I was born in the 1990s. So the Snoop was big and I was paying attention.

What is the one thing people get wrong about LA?

That there is no culture, period.

Create your soundtrack for LA in 1-3 songs

California Love -Tupac
To Live and Die in L.A. -Tupac
Bpt -YG

Compton

Music Producer

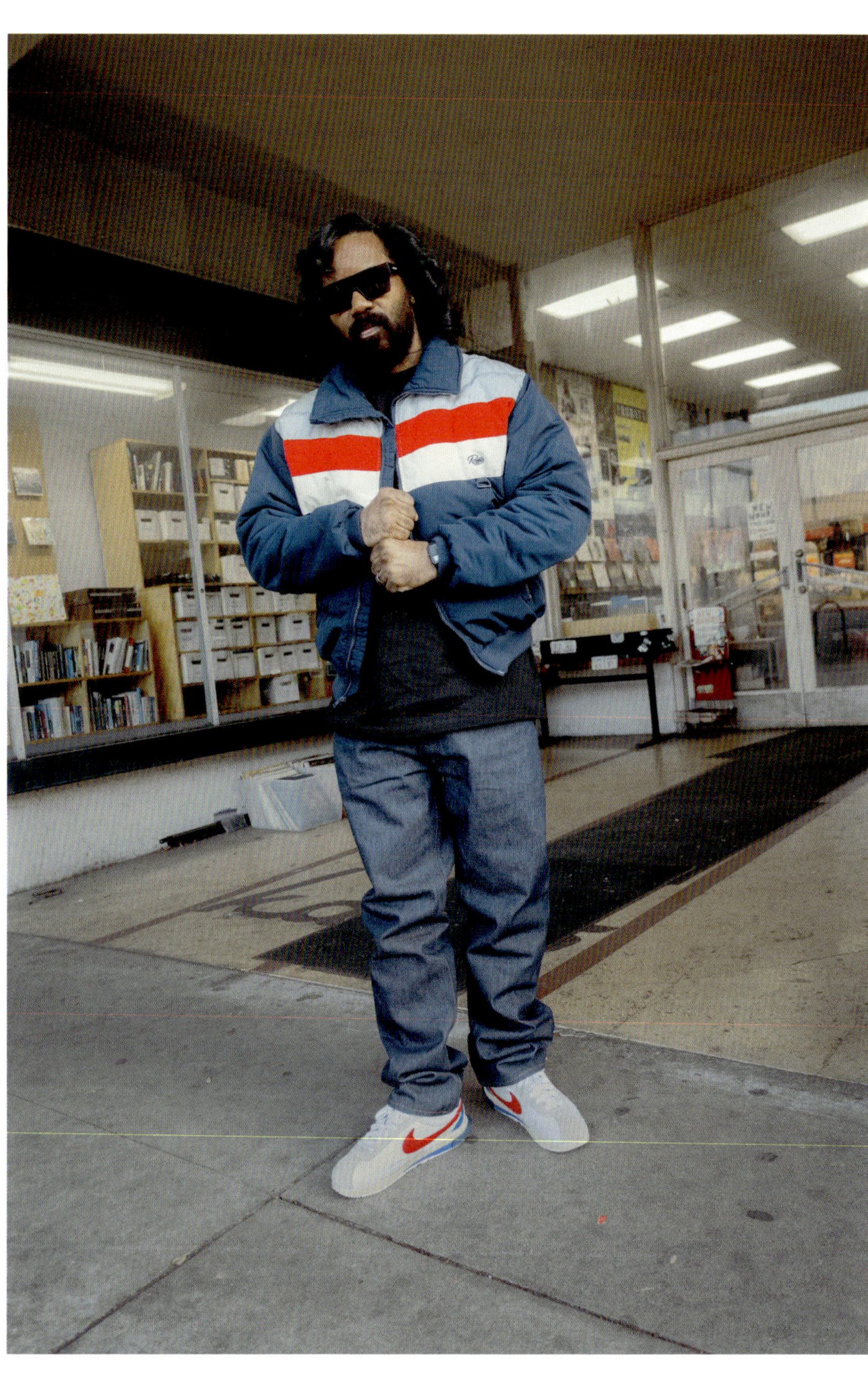

Culver City

DAM FUNK

Name

Dam Funk

Where in Los Angeles are you from?

Pasadena, born in Culver City.

What do you love most about LA?

The sunsets. The weather.

What about LA inspires your personal style?

The comfort and freedom and the temperature. Casual aesthetic and feel of the city. The street wear. The eclectic ways to shop.

Describe your personal style.

Sophisticated funk.

What would you tell someone who has never been to LA before?

Mingle with the natives, check out diff haunts that aren't on the radar. Have a positive outlook on the history of the city. Diff ethnicities. The fact it feels like a small town at night time. A country vibe.

First childhood memory of LA style?

Levi's 501s, without shrinking to fit. Cords creased with starch. Ironing all the clothes. We even ironed our money. Ironing is an important aspect of Southern Cali clothes especially if you were Latino or Black. The house shoes. The Pro Club shirts gotta have a tight neck. Neck can't be loose. Things need to be crispy.

Create your soundtrack for LA in 1-3 songs

More Bounce to the Ounce -Zapp
Knee Deep -Funkadelic
10 West -Dam Funk

Culver City

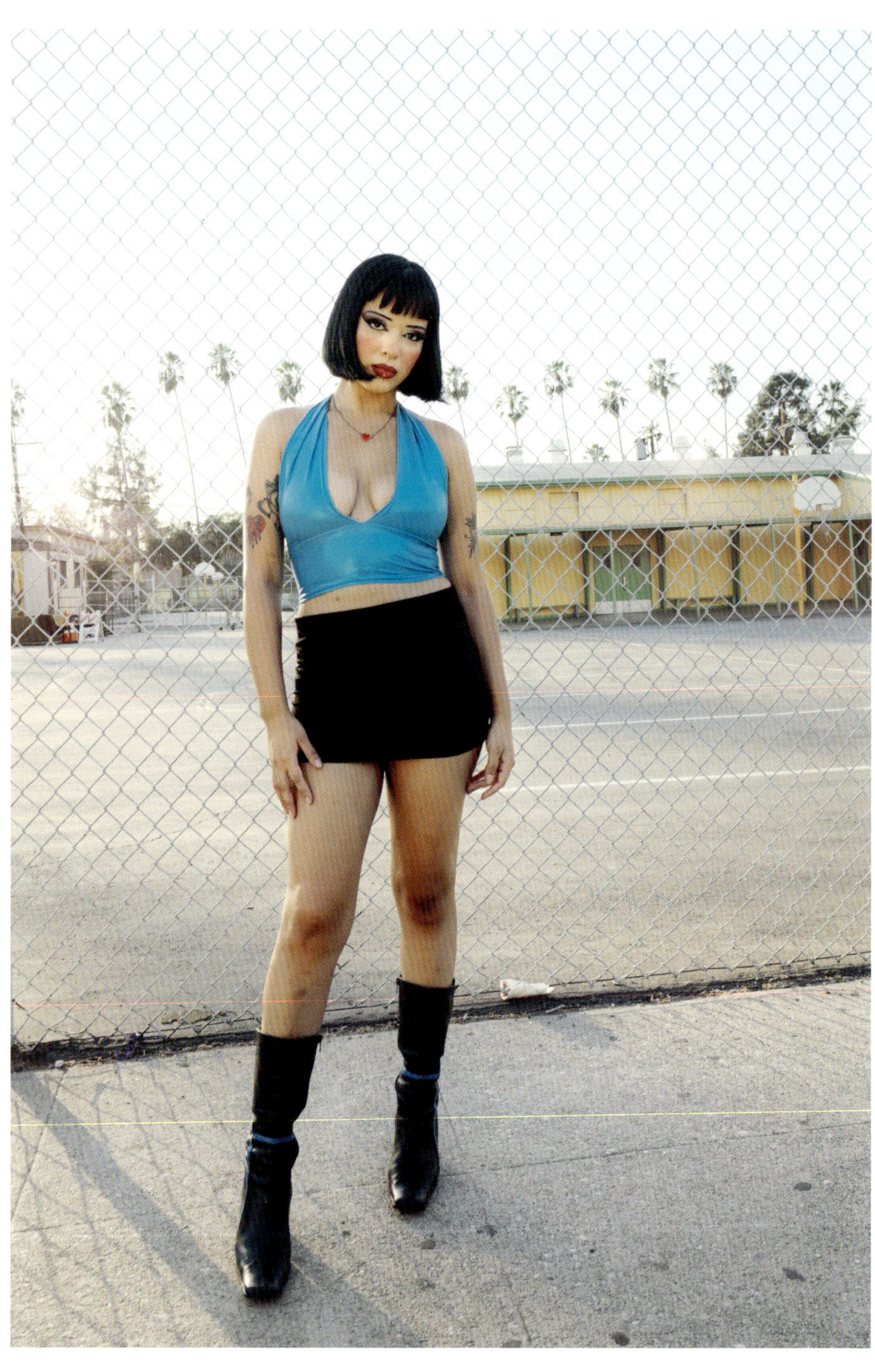

GISSELLE HIDALGO

Name

Gisselle Hidalgo

Where in Los Angeles are you from?

Boyle Heights/El Monte.

Where do you like to hang?

The Holiday Bar.

What do you love most about LA?

Everything, literally everything even the bad I love, LA is my forever home. But my favorite thing is the endless opportunities and the amazing people.

What about LA inspires your personal style?

The classics. Old classic Hollywood, the staple LA Latina aesthetic that is forever timeless.

Describe your personal style?

Mod, Retro, with a mix of classic 90s.

What would you tell someone who has never been to LA before?

To stay on the Eastside. That's where the real LA is and a prime example of our culture.

First childhood memory of LA style?

Admiring my mom and tias 90s/early 2000s makeup and clothing style that is still relevant today, they are the blueprint.

What is the one thing people get wrong about LA?

The tired take that LA people aren't genuine, which is a fabricated perception made solely by transplants that are in the wrong areas. This place is rich with good souls and the best people you will ever meet.

Create your soundtrack for LA in 1-3 song

Westcoast Poplock -Ronnie Hudson
Memories of El Monte -The Penguins
Why U Bullshittin -Suga Free

Boyle Heights

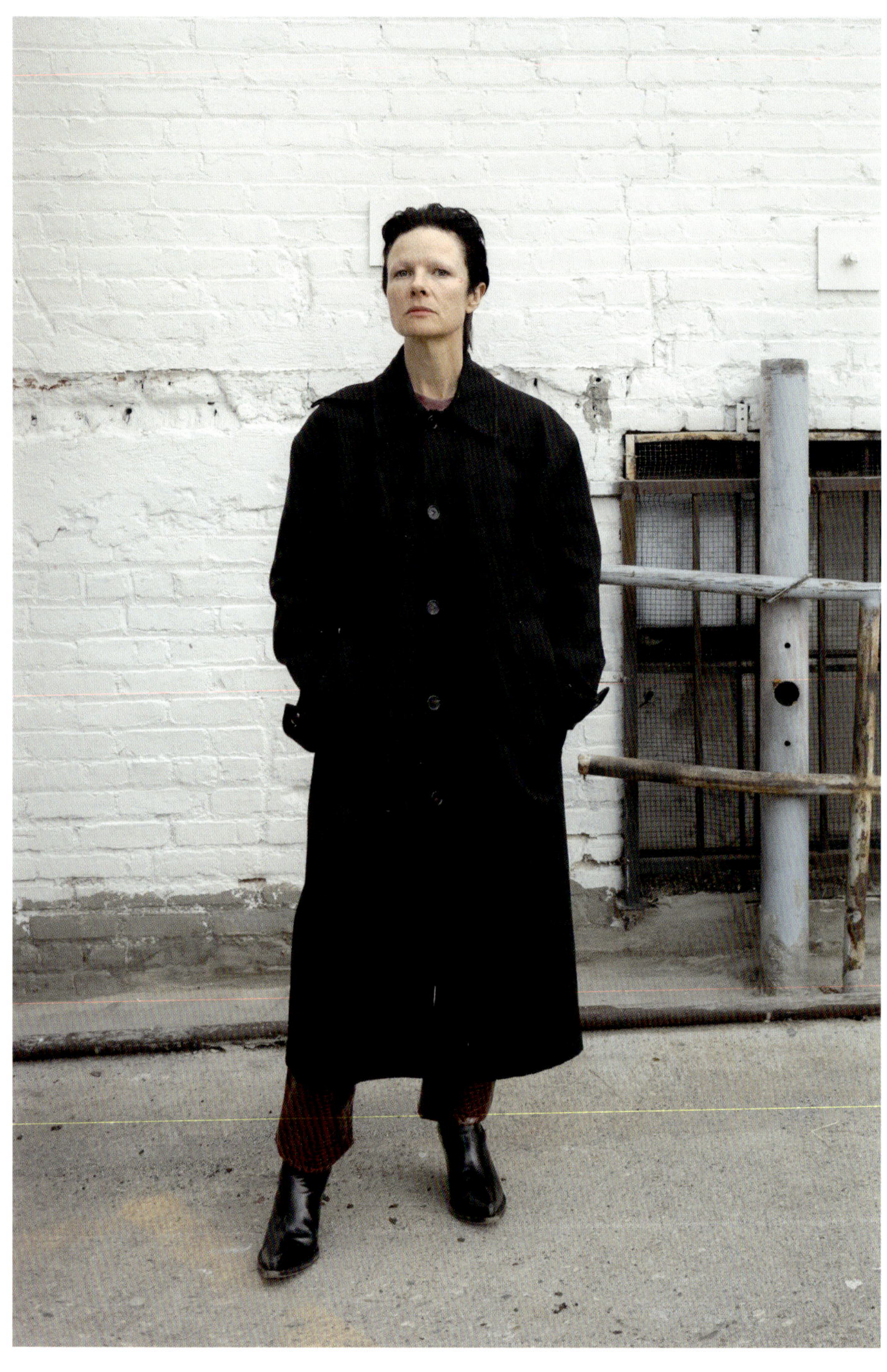

Isabelle Albuquerque

Artist

Santa Monica

ISABELLE ALBUQUERQUE

Name

Isabelle Albuquerque

Where in Los Angeles are you from?

Santa Monica, grew up in Culver City, moved to Malibu.

What do you love most about LA?

The only city other than Mumbai that has wild animals living amongst us. We have coyotes, snakes, deer, lions, etc.

Where do you like to hang?

MacArthur Park. My community is the ducks. There is a thriving bird community. Hawks, Egyptian geese, Mandarin ducks, swans, pelicans, night herons.

What would you tell someone who has never been to LA before?

It's ok to feel lost. That's part of it. Don't be afraid of that feeling.

What about LA inspires your personal style?

The sleaze.

First childhood memory of LA style?

My dad used to wear cut off jean shorts on Venice Beach.

Create your soundtrack for LA in 1-3 songs

Under the Bridge -Red Hot Chilli Peppers

Santa Monica

The Architect of the Game

South Central

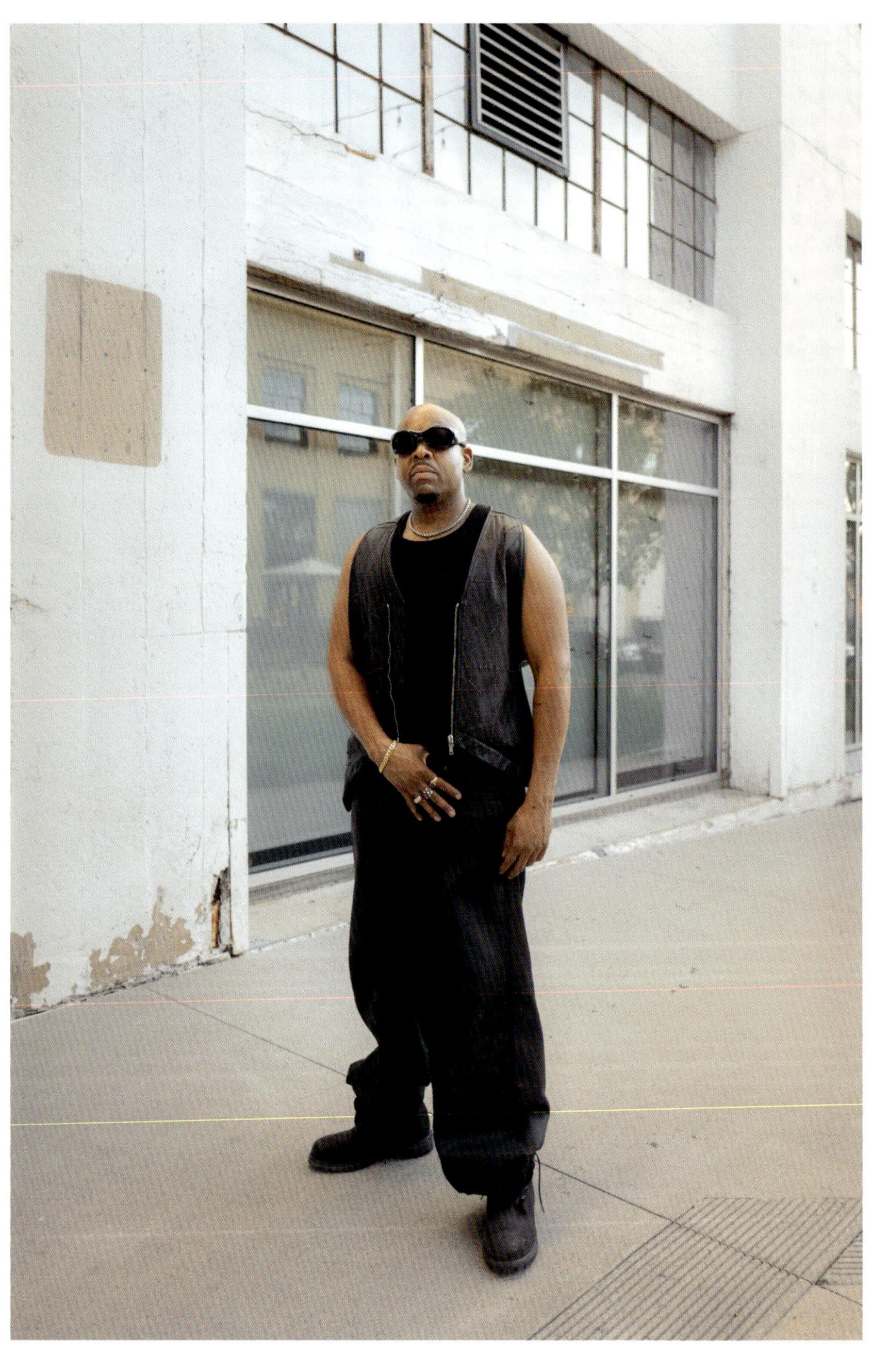

JAY 305

Name

Jay 305

Where in Los Angeles are you from?

South Central LA.

What do you love most about LA?

The culture. Everything transcends and merges. From Malibu to Big Bear in 1 day.

Where do you like to hang?

Silverlake. The Jungles. Malibu.

What would you tell someone who has never been to LA before?

Pay attention to the palm trees and people's front yards and that will tell a lot about the city. You will not see a lot of native plants and trees. You will see a cactus, a wild bush and a palm tree all in the same yard. That will tell you right there about the illusions of the city. Because then, when people say LA doesn't look dangerous, they are easily fooled. Things happen real quick.

What about LA inspires your personal style?

The lifestyle. A hot day and a cold night.

First childhood memory of LA style?

Being poor helped push my creativity. I couldn't afford the things that I wanted. So I had to figure out how to get those things and also how to create the things I want, which helped with my vision in style. It started with my mom setting me up by dressing me in the ghetto.

What is the one thing people get wrong about LA?

That we are fake. That we can't dress and that it's always sunny and safe here. We have so many scenes you have to tap in with the right people.

Create your soundtrack for LA in 1-3 songs

I Don't Give a Fuck -Nipsey Hustle
We Still Party -DJ Quik
Hollywood (remix) -Sa-ra

South Central

Jesse Jo Stark

Artist

Malibu

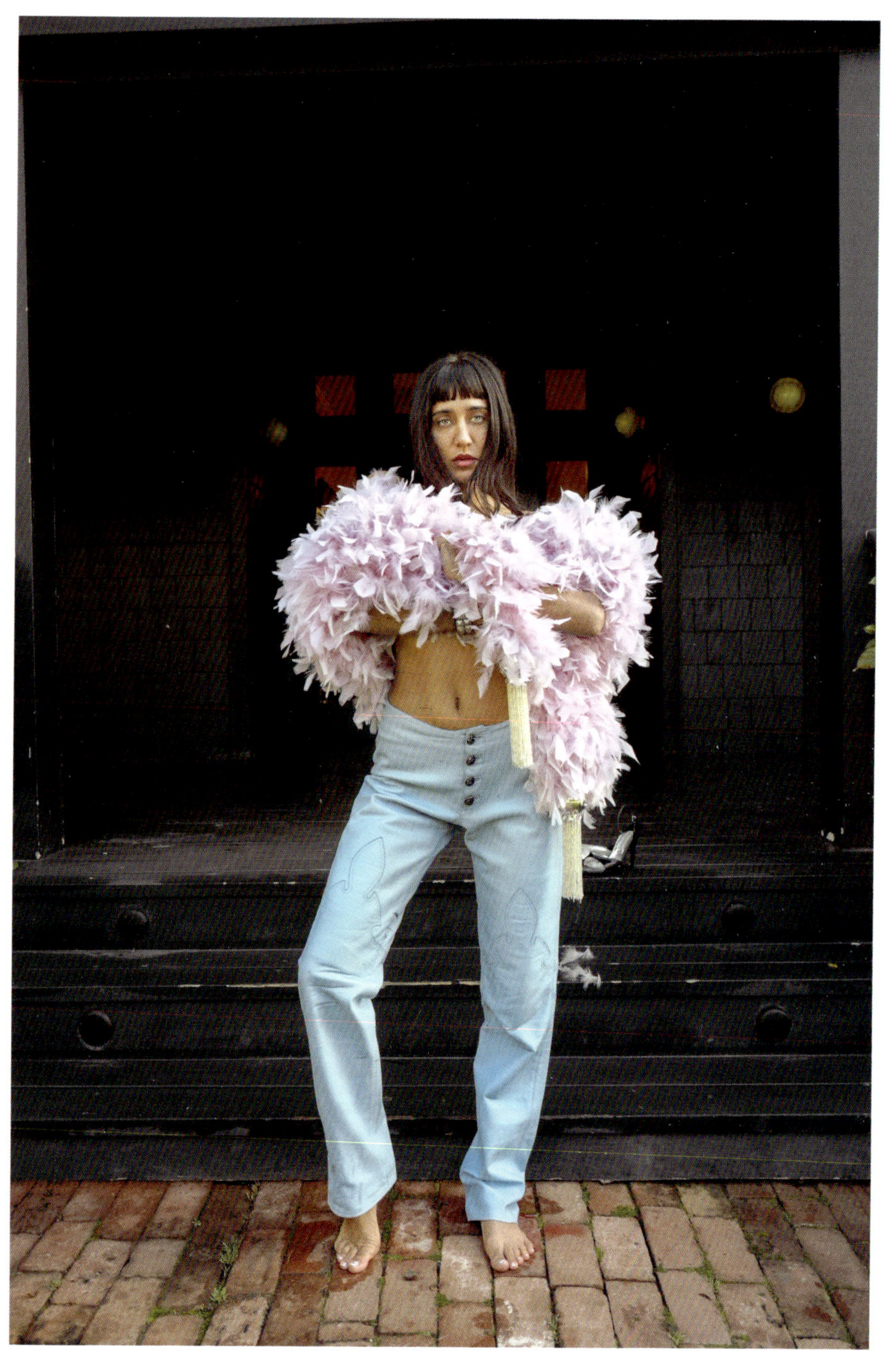

JESSE JO STARK

Name

Jesse Jo Stark

Where in Los Angeles are you from?

Malibu

What do you love most about LA?

I love being able to drive. The food. The Sun.

What would you tell someone who has never been to LA before?

Don't get lost.

What about LA inspires your personal style?

At heart I truly am a beach girl. As much as I love black leather, somehow I end up naked or in blue denim.

First childhood memory of LA style?

Lots of silver. Lots of leather. Lots of black. Bright colored hair. Chrome Hearts teddy bears. Those bears were better dressed than people at the time.

Create your soundtrack for LA in 1-3 songs

Purple Sun -Canons
Story of my Life -Social Distortion
Real Love Baby -Father John Misty

Sugar High by me. (Wink wink).

Malibu

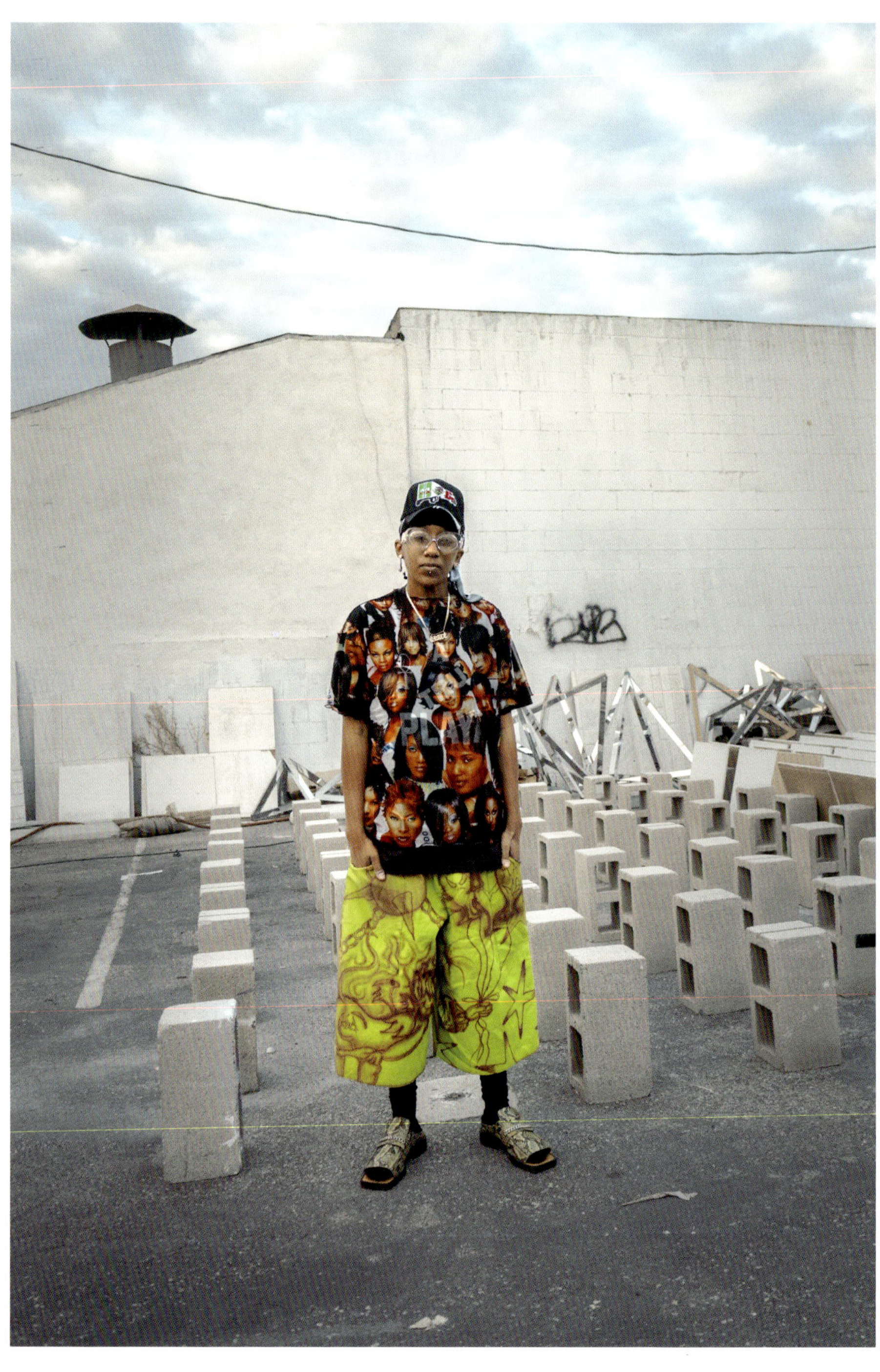

LAUREN HALSEY

Name

Lauren Halsey

Where in Los Angeles are you from?

South Central.

Where do you like to hang?

Dockweiler Beach. Backyard parties.

What do you love most about LA?

My Family, the ocean, the heat.

What about LA inspires your personal style?

South Central and the colors of the buildings, just like the variety of hues there. You will see lavender and yellow buildings. Women's hair styles growing up + the colors of the candy paint of the lowriders and all the cars.

First childhood memory of LA style?

Early '90s my father cut my hair on the side. I remember my cousin and friends getting these beautiful haircuts and the outfits when I was 16/15 years old in the '90s.

What is the one thing people get wrong about LA?

They conflate it with Hollywood, and they miss out how dense and lush Los Angeles truly is culturally.

Create your soundtrack for LA in 1-3 songs

Try to Make a Fool of Me -The Delfonics
You Know How We Do It -Ice Cube
To Each His Own -Patrice Rushen

South Central

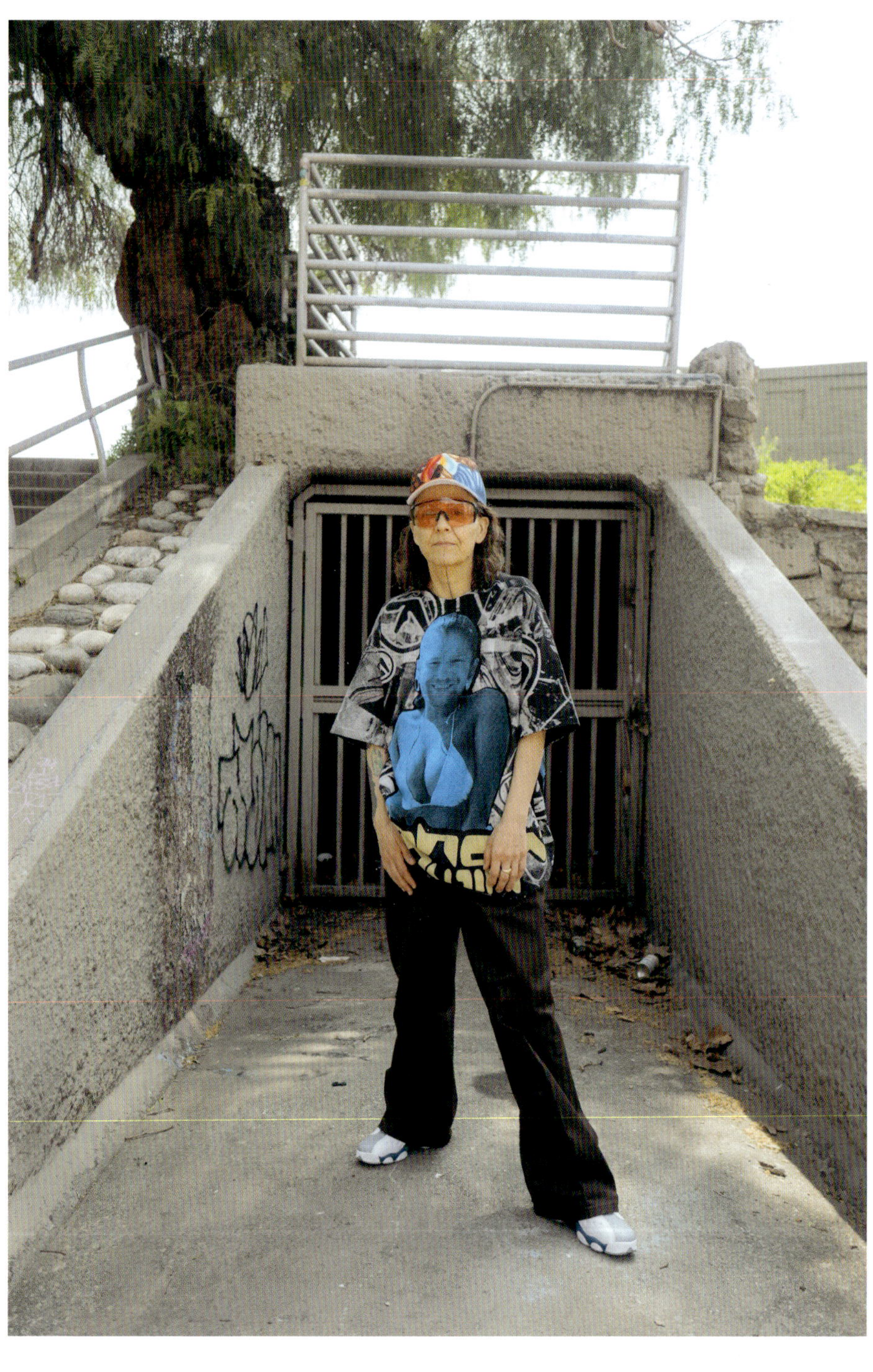

GUADALUPE ROSALES

Name

Guadalupe Rosales

Where in Los Angeles are you from?

East LA

What do you love most about LA?

The community, family, food, the hidden corners that only true LA people know about. I like the landmark's that we create.

What would you tell someone who has never been to LA before?

You need a car and show respect.

What about LA inspires your personal style?

My friends.

First childhood memory of LA style?

Pro-Wings from Payless. IYKYK (if you know you know)

What is the one thing people get wrong about LA?

Everything. LA is not what you see on mainstream media or tv.

Create your soundtrack for LA in 1-3 songs

Any song -Chalino Sanchez
Hey Love -Delfonics
How Many Latinas Are in the House -DJ Irene

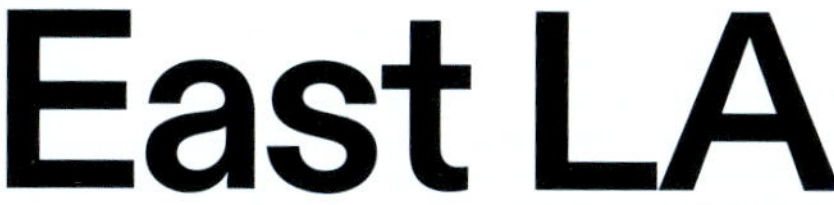

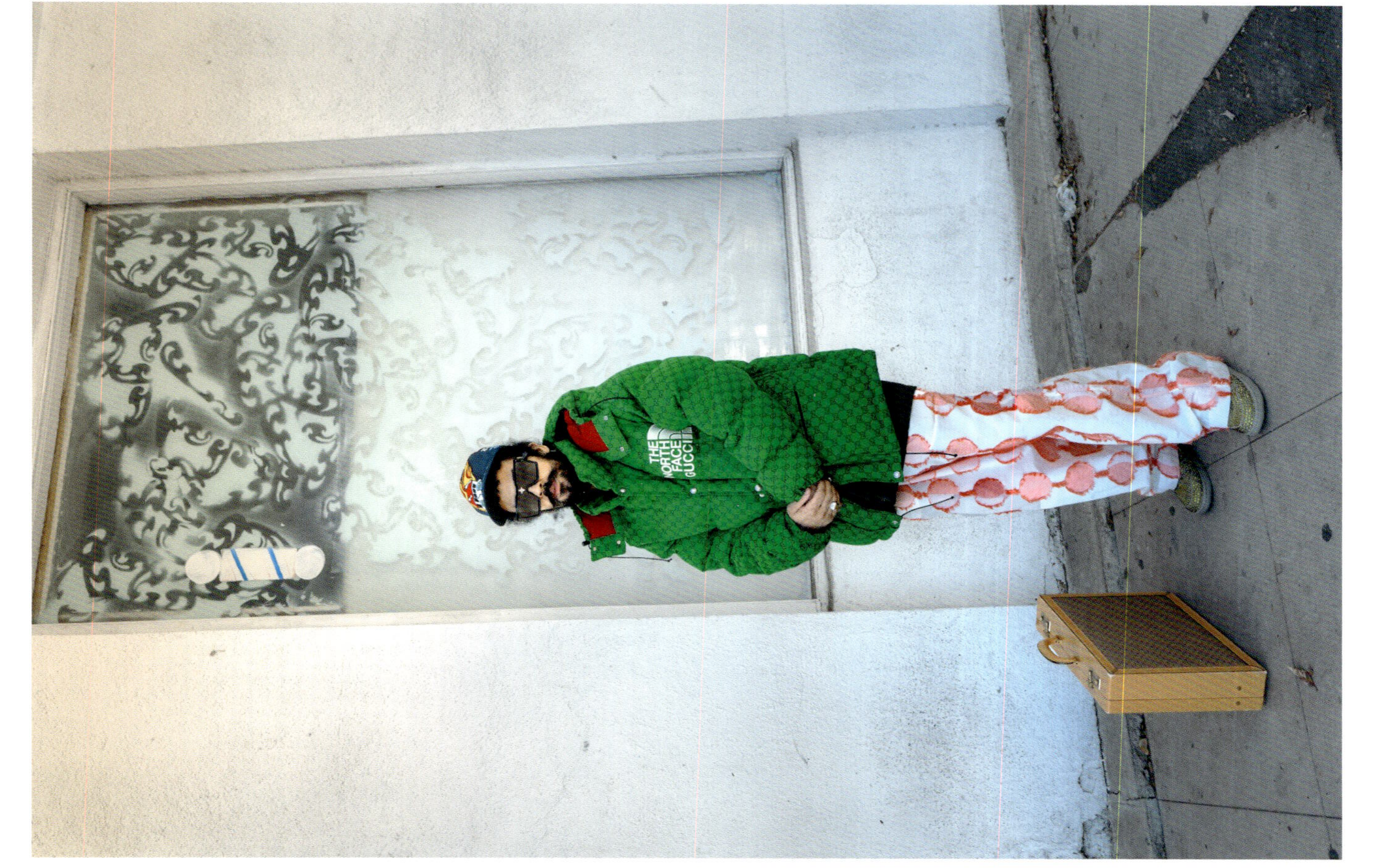

TAZ ARNOLD

Name

Taz Arnold

Where are in Los Angeles you from?

South Central/ Inglewood

What do you love most about LA?

The culture, it's a terrestrial paradise, it's an ancient place.

What about LA inspires your personal style?

The struggle between not having money and the quest for having money.

Describe your personal style?

Jazz music.

What is something people get wrong about LA?

That people are Hollywood and fake. It's a farce. I'm 4th generation LA. My parents are down to earth and beautiful people.

Occupation?

Musician. Fashion designer.

First childhood memory of LA style?

Being at my parents in Inglewood and 111th place, my parents in the '70s were black hippies. They grew vegetables and weed. I was a kid who had an Afro. My parents were outside in the garden on a sunny day, and I wanted to put some clothes on and I went outside and said look at my outfit. I was 4 years old and this was the first time I dressed myself. I kept changing my outfit and showing them my looks and then my parents were cheering and encouraging me. It gave me confidence. And the rest of my life it influenced me to come outside and get a reaction.

A lot of cats would bag on me, I'm dressing gay or looking crazy. It was my self expression. The first time I went to Paris I was 18. I had a girlfriend who was an exchange student. I saw photos of Miles Davis and Thelonious Monk. Black people in jazz blew my mind. It was inspiring to see the street style. I was lo-life, I was a skater around the age of 6 or 8. I was in South Central and I was surfing and going to health food stores.

My mother would go to the beach and run barefoot. She would run from imperial to Marina del Rey and she would have me on her back. She was the most eclectic.

My mother gave me half a tab of LSD at McArthur Park as a child. It was a good experience and it allowed me to connect with adult artists at a young age. It touched my soul.

Create your soundtrack for LA in 1-3 songs

Hotel California -The Eagles

Inglewood

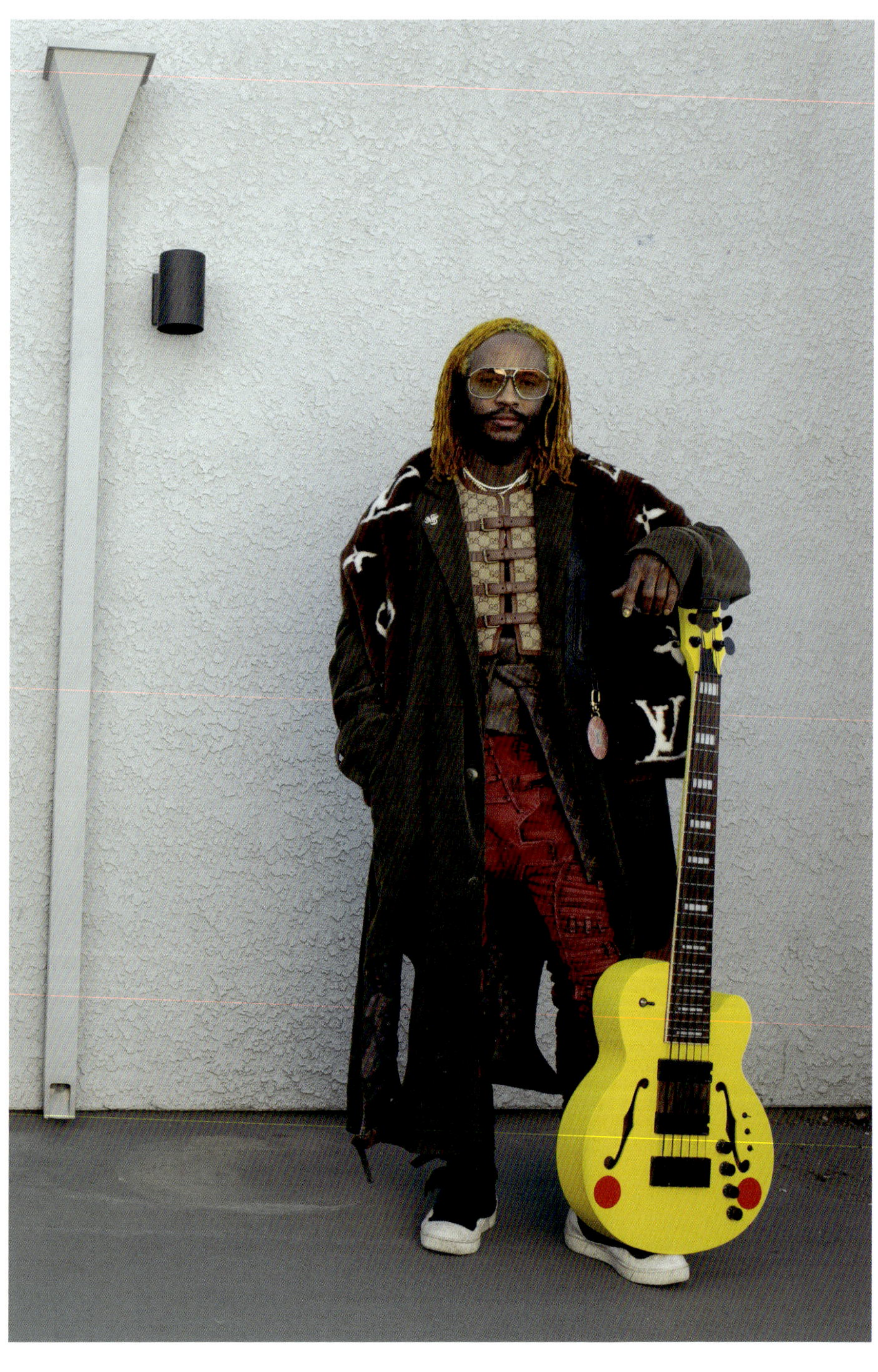

THUNDERCAT

Name

Thundercat

Where in Los Angeles are you from?

Compton

What do you love most about LA?

The Dodgers

Where do you like to hang?

At Yo Momma's house, on the couch with your Momma.

What would you tell someone who has never been to LA before?

Stay out of LA.

What about LA inspires your personal style?

I inspire my city.

First childhood memory of LA style?

The Thundercats and Crippin.

What is the one thing people get wrong about LA?

People forget to tuck their chain in.

Create your soundtrack for LA in 1-3 songs

Never Going to Give You Up -Rick Astley
Sweat Of My Balls -CB4
Come With Me -Godzilla soundtrack

Compton

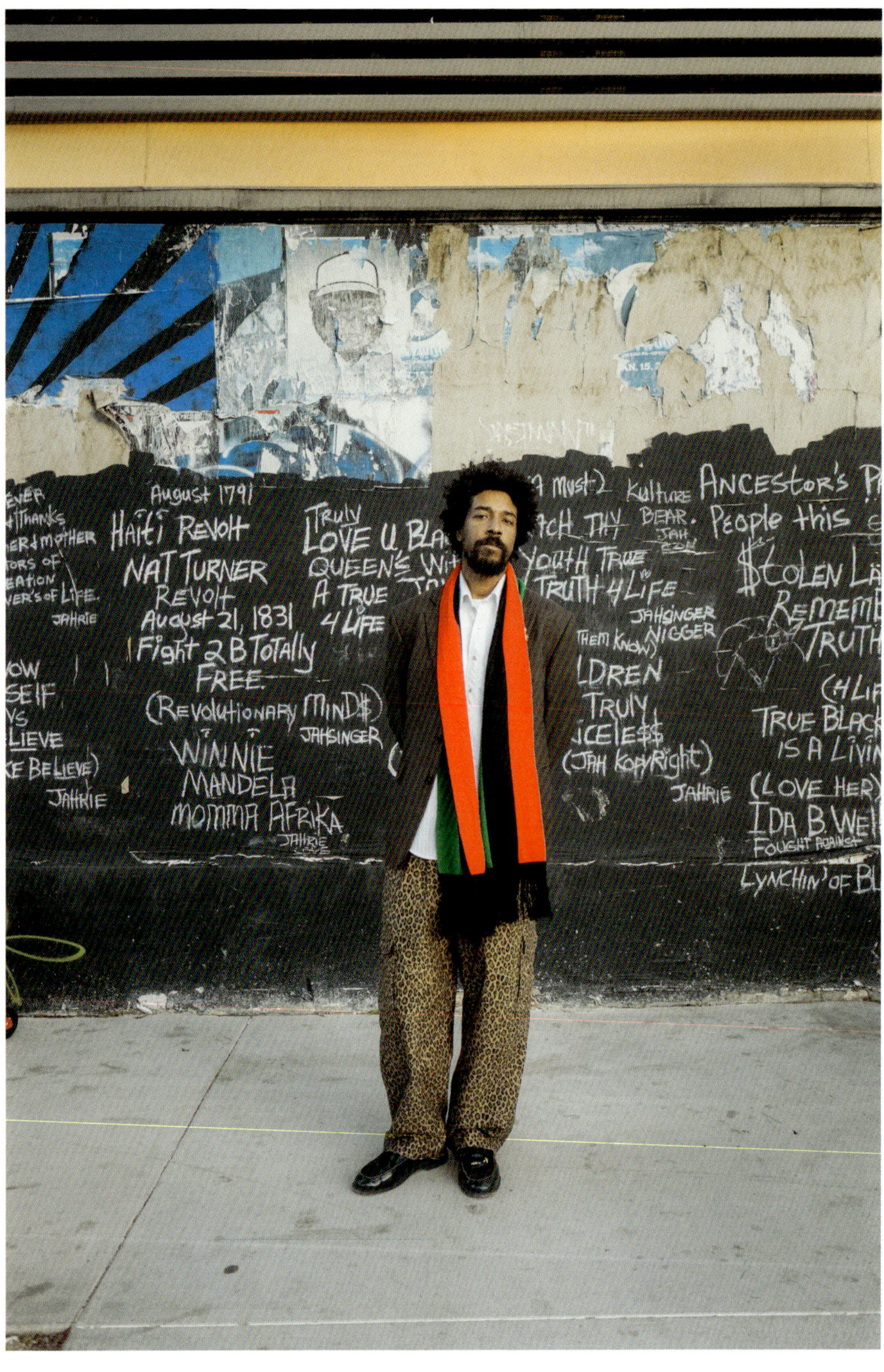

TRÉ

Name

Trè

Where in Los Angeles are you from?

Leimert Park

Where do you like to hang?

I like to hang out at my shop and Harun Coffee.

What do you love most about LA?

I like everything about LA culture. The music, the lowriders, the weather, and the people. Everything is amazing to me about this city.

What about LA inspires your personal style?

Los Angeles is super laid back but has a lot of history and a signature. Rather, whether it's the music, or the way we wear an outfit, or the skate community, the city has definitely helped shape my eye and the pieces that make up my uniform.

Describe your personal style?

It's a mixture of where I've been, where I'm at, and where I'm going. I came from a streetwear background, now I'm a business owner so I'm trying to make my style feel more like a boss, but then I also remember that I can do whatever I want.

What would you tell someone who has never been to LA before?

I would say it's beautiful and it's got a little bit of everything for everyone. I would also tell them...Don't come to LA and not tap in with somebody from LA.

First childhood memory of LA style?

Hmmm… it honestly starts with my older cousin . He would wear jerseys with different LA teams across them and it's something about that memorabilia and repping your city that I just respected. It was gangster with the Raiders Starter jackets and then the Lakers jackets with the snapback. I think seeing his style and then witnessing the style of mechanics inspired me. They'd wear the work shirts with the dickies pants which was dope to me so I would say that those are my first childhood memories of streetwear and just style in general.

What is the one thing people get wrong about LA?

Everybody thinks it's all Hollywood glitz and glamor and palm trees until they come out here and see there's homeless people on every corner and a lot of spaces being gentrified.

Create your soundtrack for LA in 1-3 songs

How to Survive in South Central -Ice Cube
California Über Alles -Dead Kennedys
Leimert Park -Billy Childs

Leimert Park

Musician

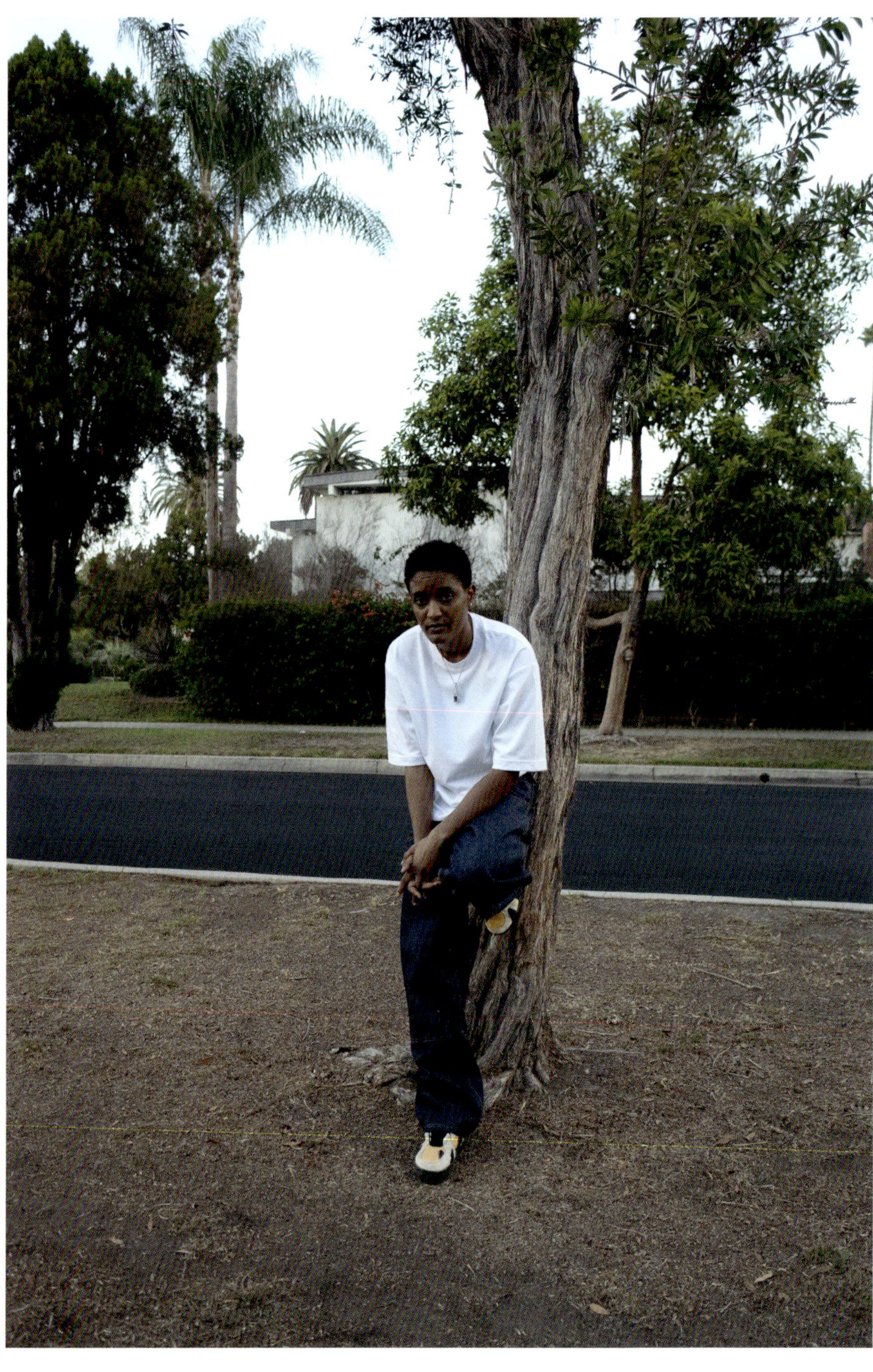

SYD

Name

Sydney Bennett

Where in Los Angeles are you from?

Mid City

Where do you like to hang?

At home. Creating diff vibes.

What do you love most about LA?

Weather. Easiest weather.

What about LA inspires your personal style?

Something about LA feels casual, it's a casual place. It's not like Wall Street. Every economic class dresses in casual clothes. Successful people dress like they want to dress. Regardless of context.

Describe your personal style.

A little bit of skater, a lot of tomboy and usually pretty comfy. Baggy is a must.

What would you tell someone who has never been to LA before?

Venture outside of Hollywood and the Sunset Strip. Visit Silver Lake. Drive down Hyperion. Drive through Leimert Park. Drive down Crenshaw between Obama and Colosseum Bvld. Go eat at My Two Cents.

First childhood memory of LA style?

Watching Snoop as a kid. He was the biggest inspiration who embodied LA style. Snapback with green under the brim. Flannel button all the way up to the top. Creased khakis.

Create your soundtrack for LA in 1-3 songs

Love song-1 -Meshell Ndegeocello
And If -Sa-Ra
Lil Big Heads -J*Davey

Mid City

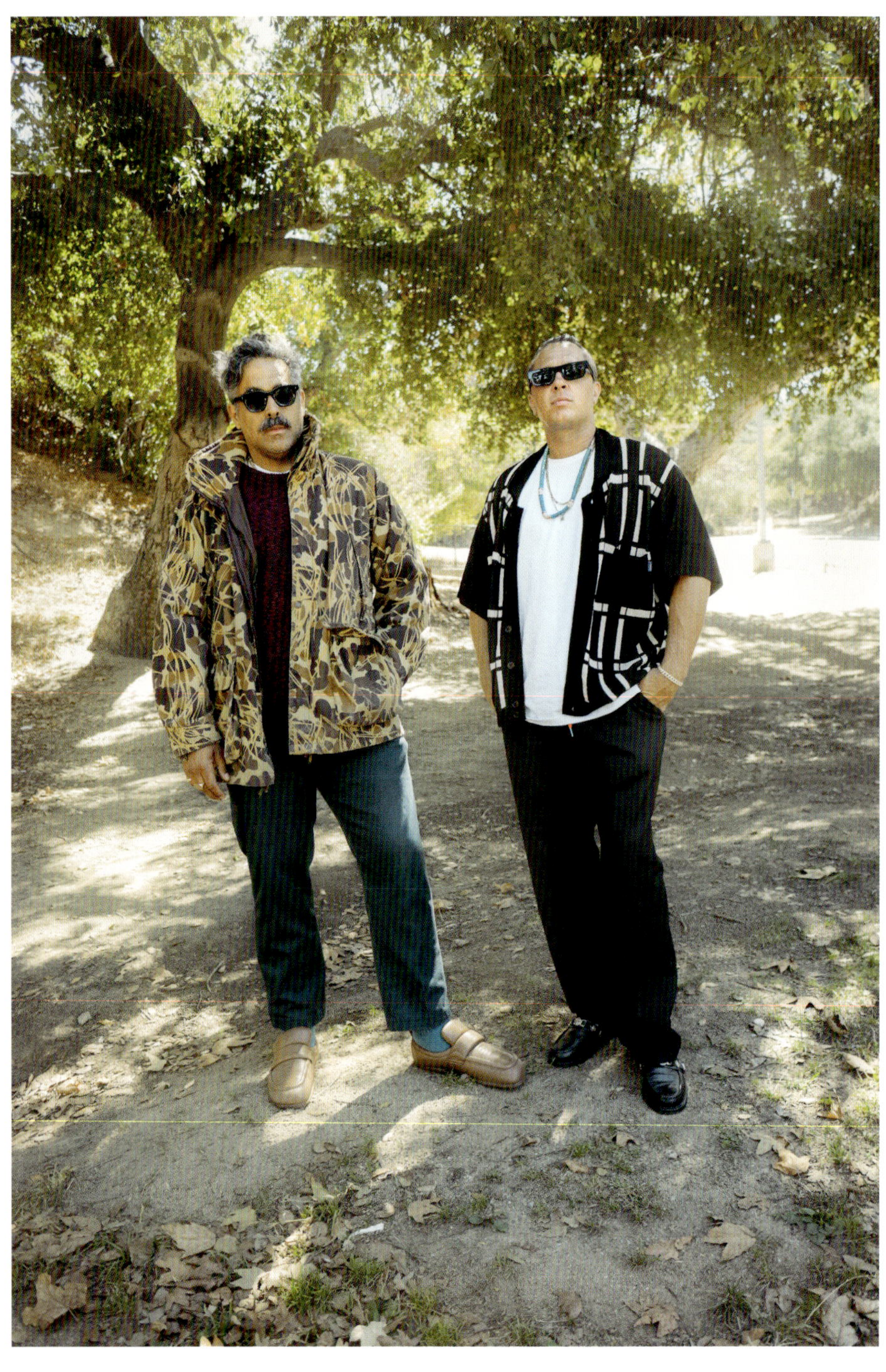

Born x Raised Founders

Venice

SPANTO & 2TONE

Born x Raised

Born X Raised was founded in 2013 by Chris "Spanto" Printup and Alex "2Tone" Erdmann, two native Angelenos who set out to make a statement against the deterioration and homogenization of their hometown in Venice and beyond.

Since its inception, Born X Raised has garnered a cult following of like-minded individuals, hungry for a brand POV built on more than just hype. This brand was built on storytelling, and Born X Raised is a time capsule.

Interview by 2tone

Occupation?

Creative Director, Film Director, Artist, Designer, Podcast Host, and co-founder of the brand Born X Raised.

Where in Los Angeles are you from?

I'm from Venice.

Where do you like to hang?

The mountains of Griffith Park.

What would you tell someone who has never been to LA before?

Good luck.

What about LA inspires your personal style?

It's a very casual city where the millionaires wear flip flops. I just want to be comfortable/functional above all else. But I don't wear flip-flops.

First childhood memory of LA style?

Girls in high school wearing Nike Cortez & pom pom socks.

What is the one thing people get wrong about LA?

People's assumptions about LA are probably based off of people who aren't from LA.

Create your soundtrack for LA in 1-3 songs

Talk Down -Dijon
I Love L.A. -Randy Newman
Nights -Frank Ocean

Venice

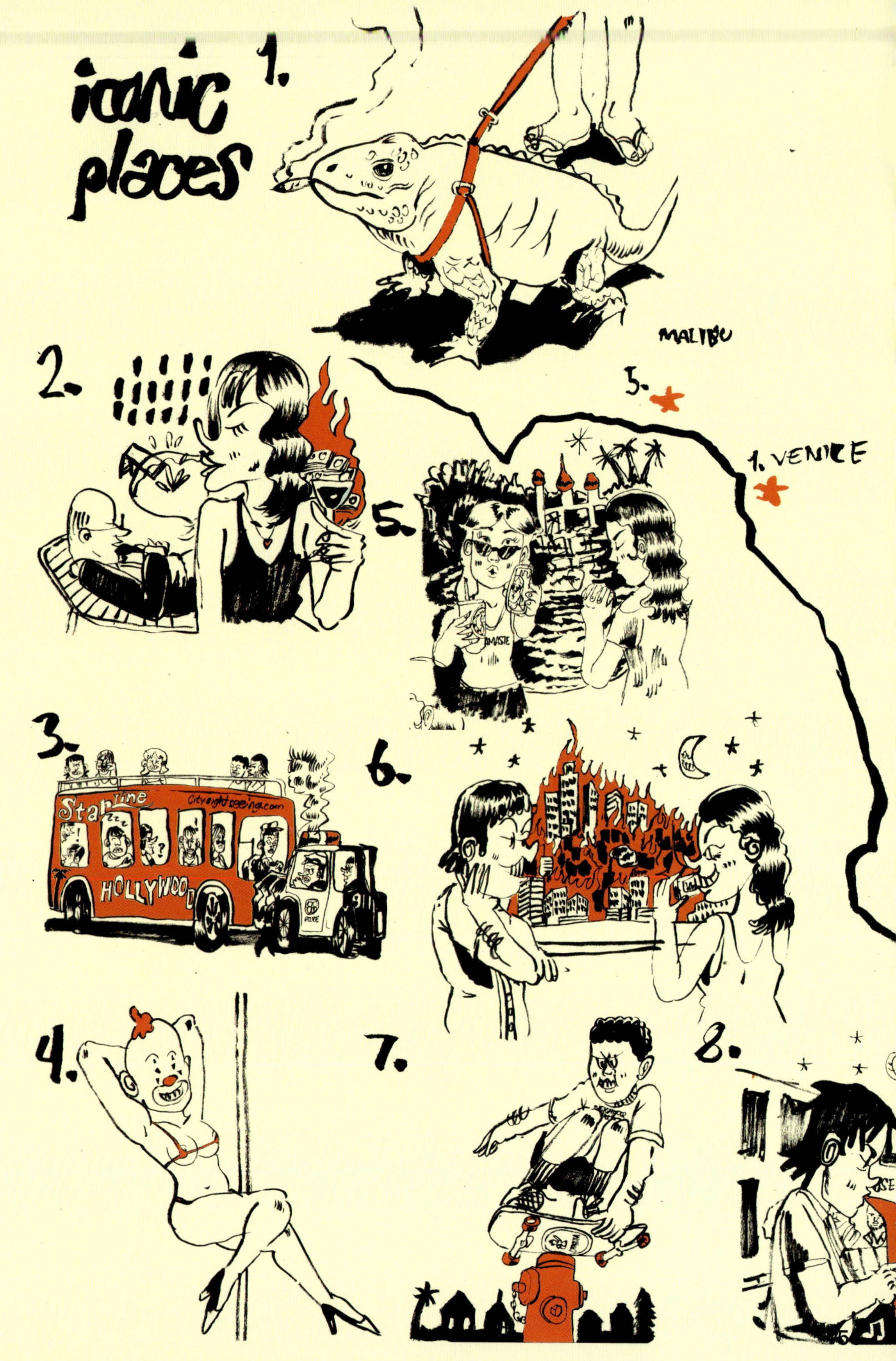
iconic
places
1.
2.
3.
4.
5.
5.
6.
7.
8.
MALIBU
1. VENICE
Starline
Citysightseeing.com
HOLLYWOOD
POLICE
NAMASTE

Guide to the City of Angels

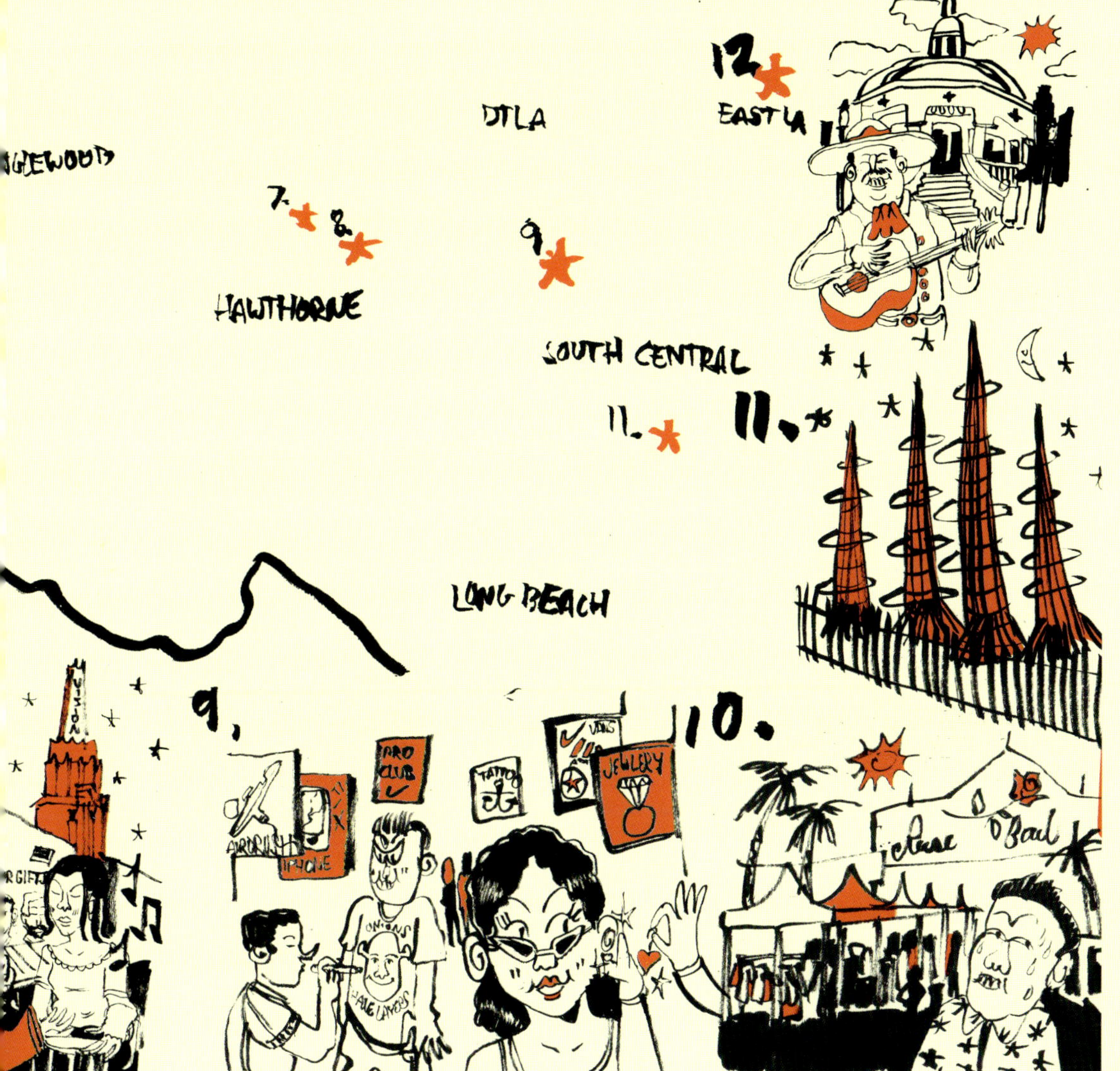

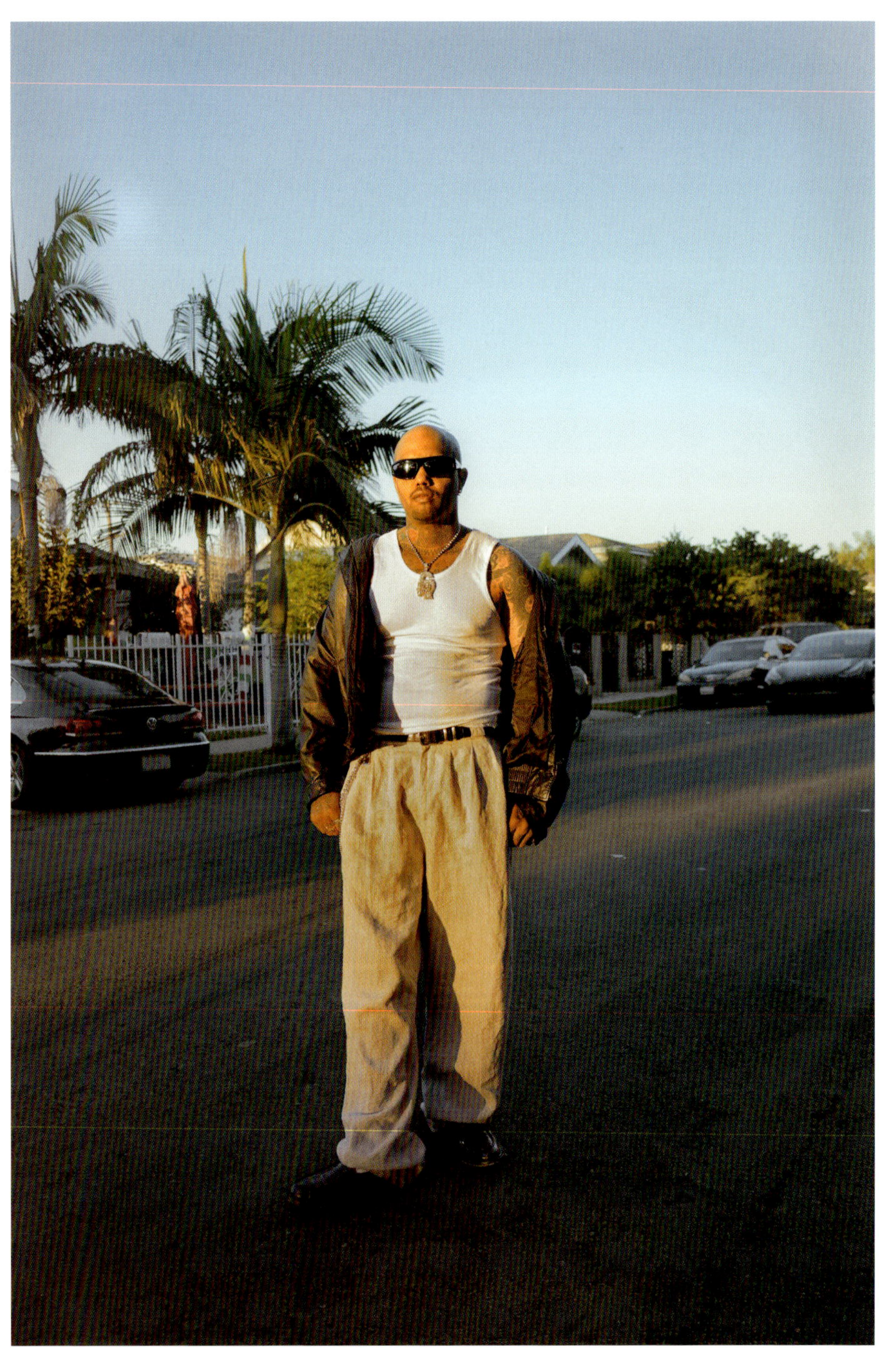

CEO Of Creative Soundz

South Central

BODY
PRIVATE
PROPERTY
NO TRESPASSING

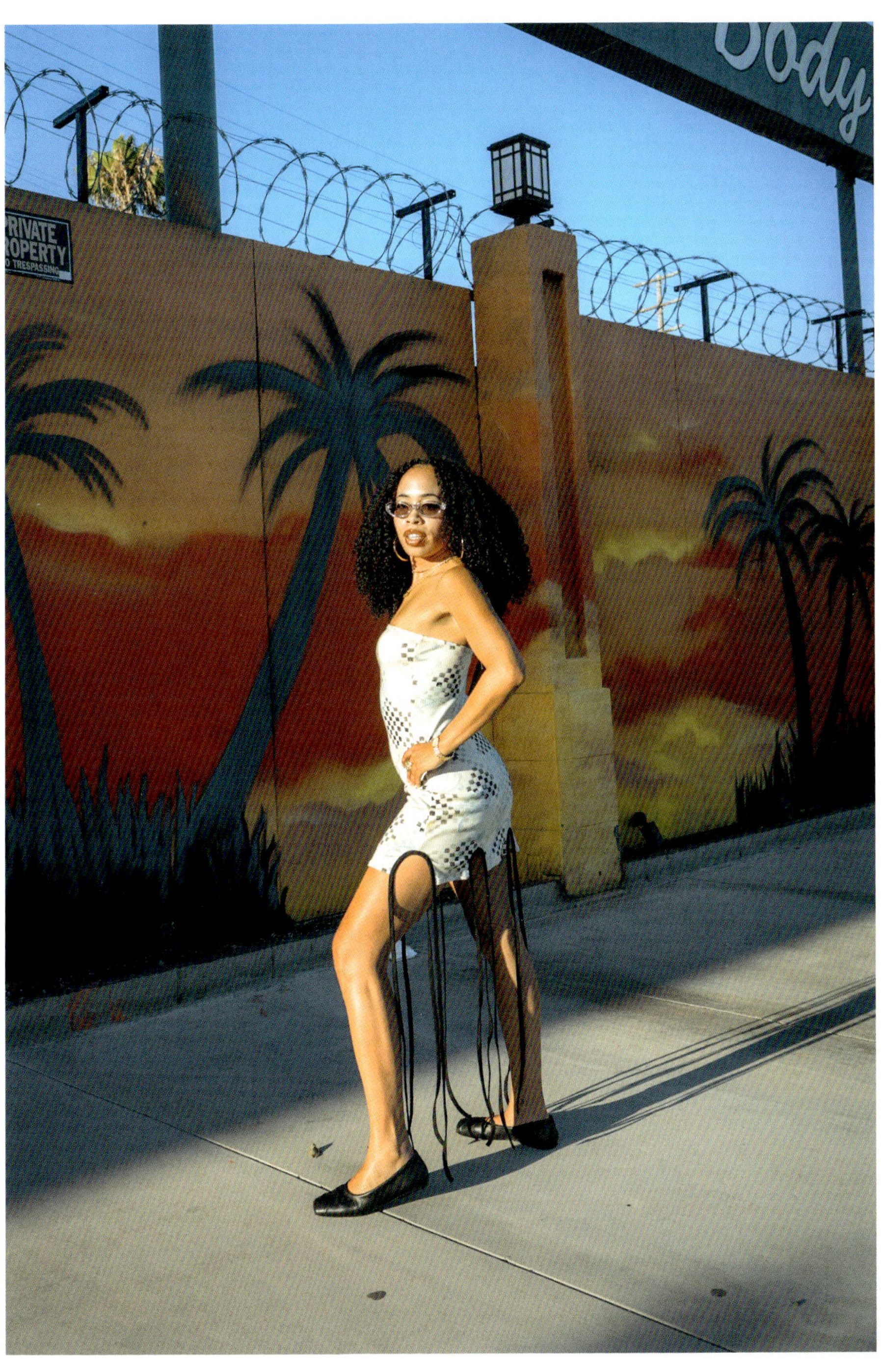

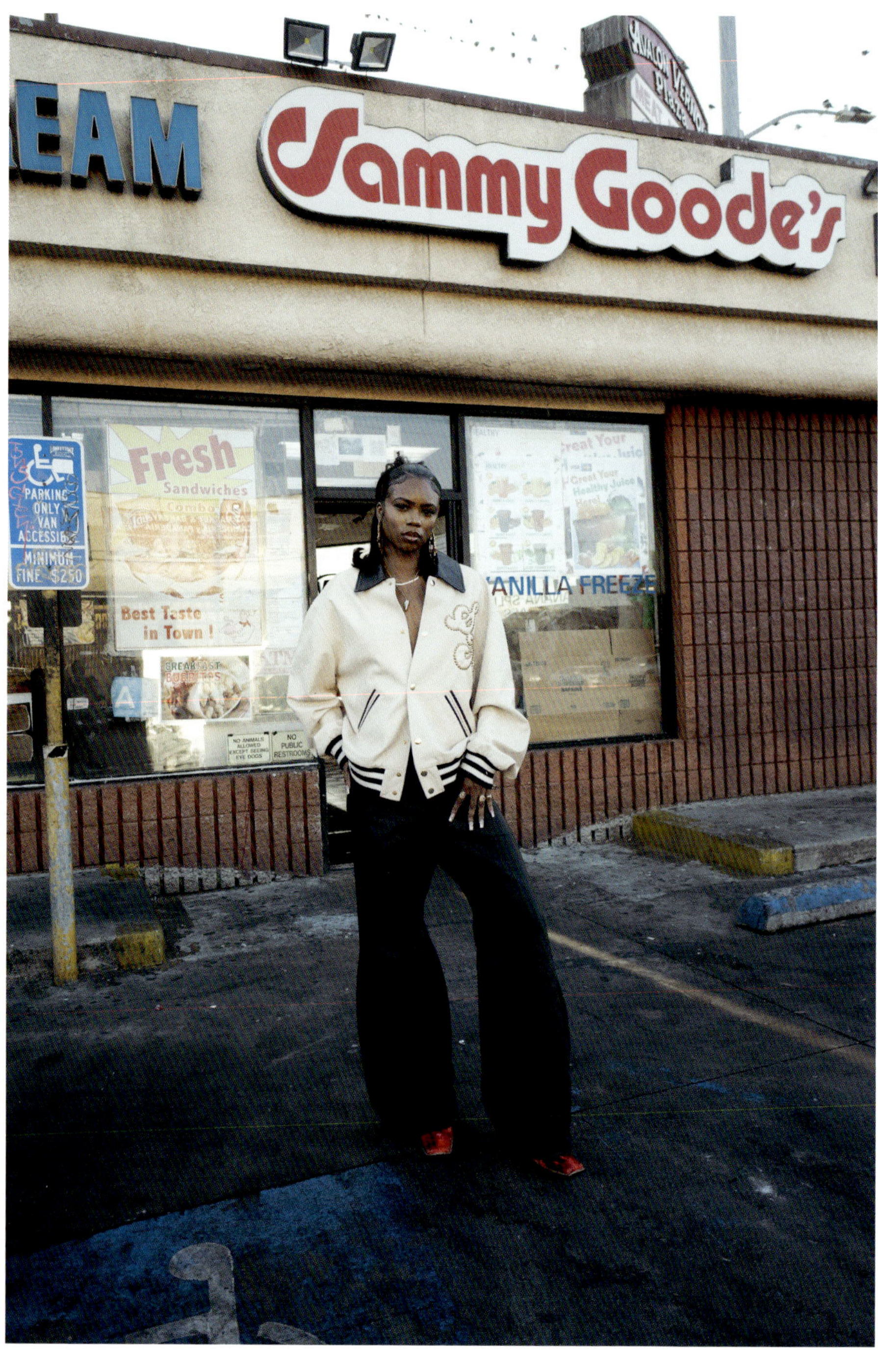

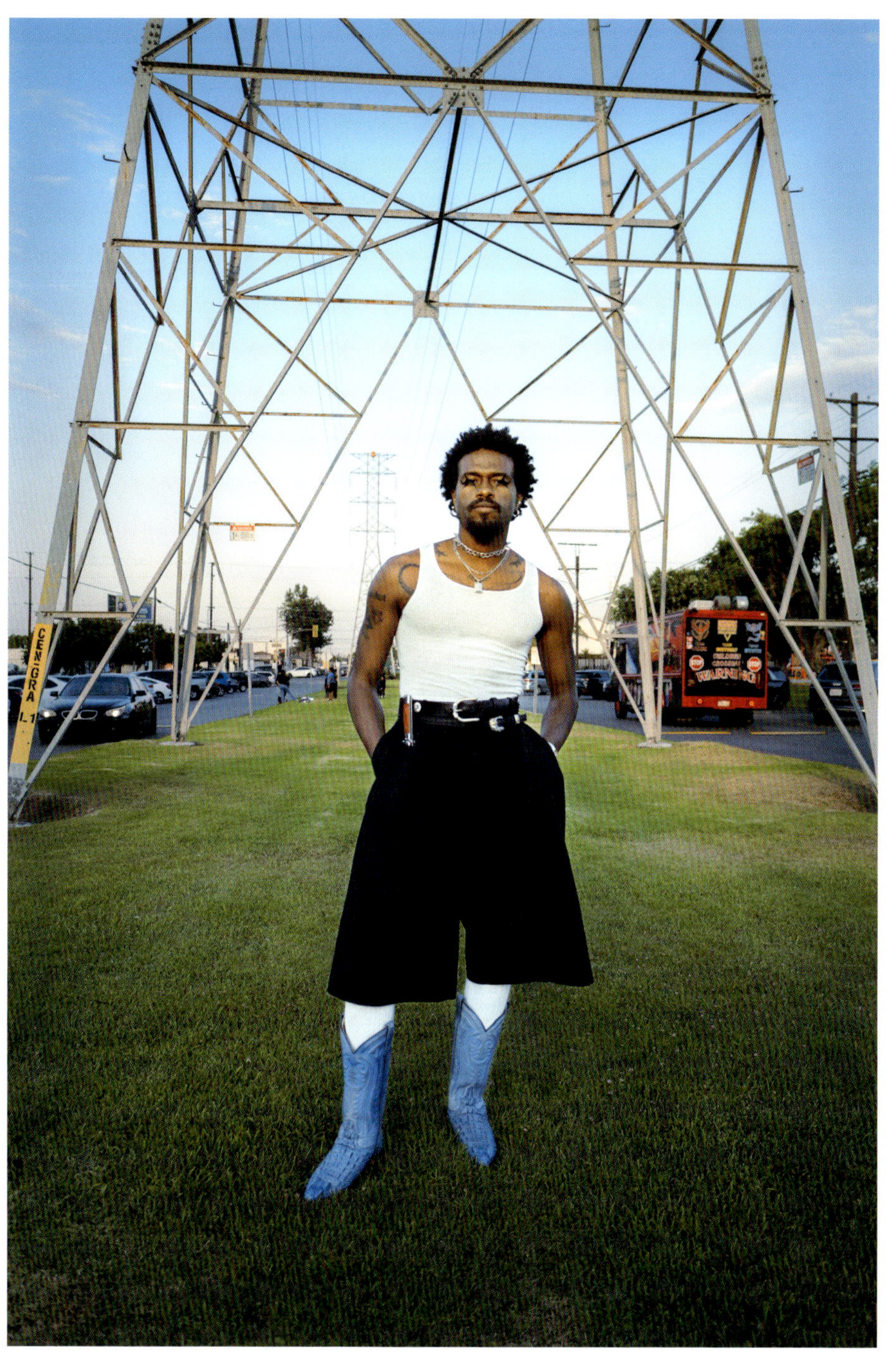

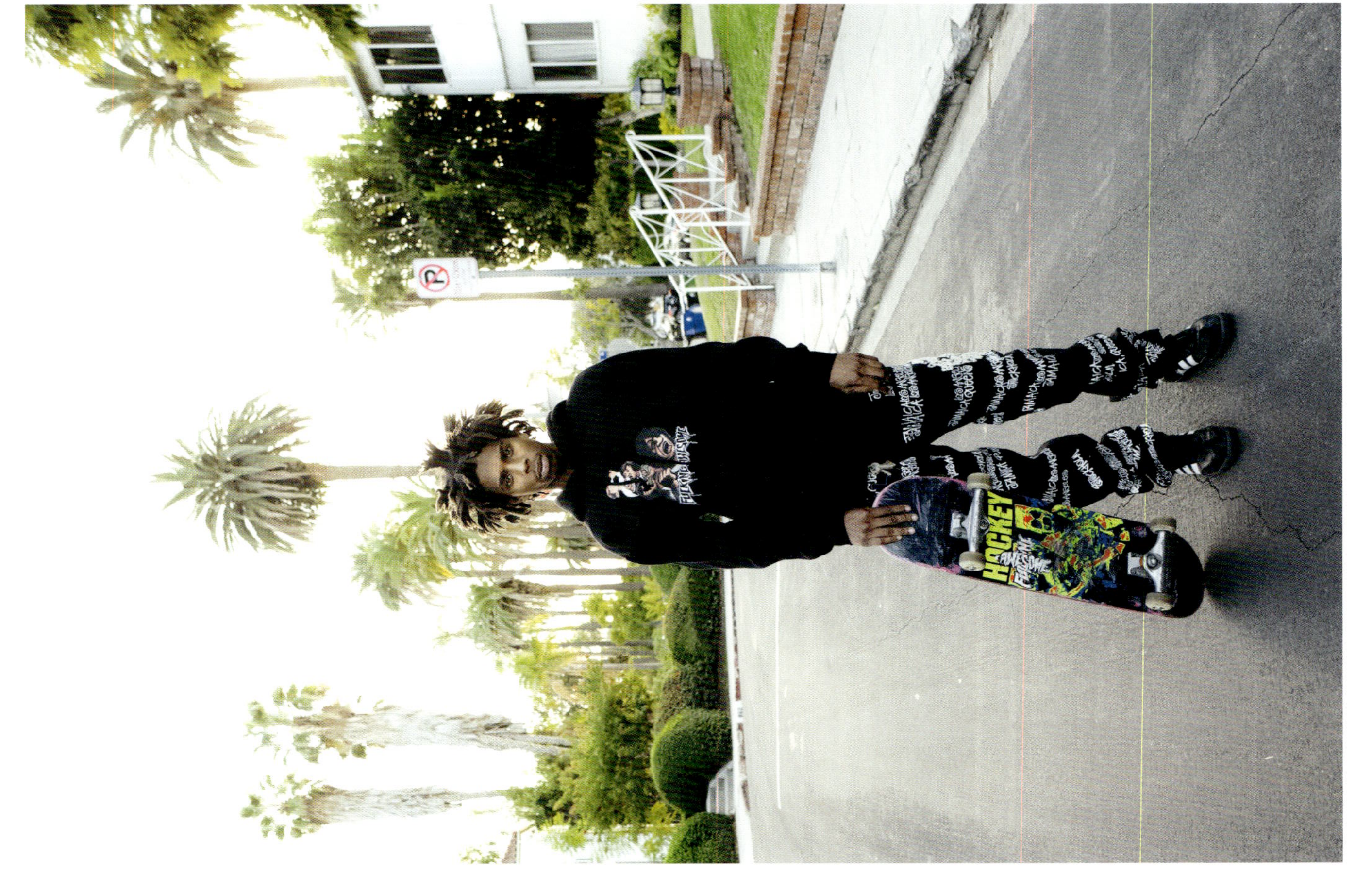

Artist

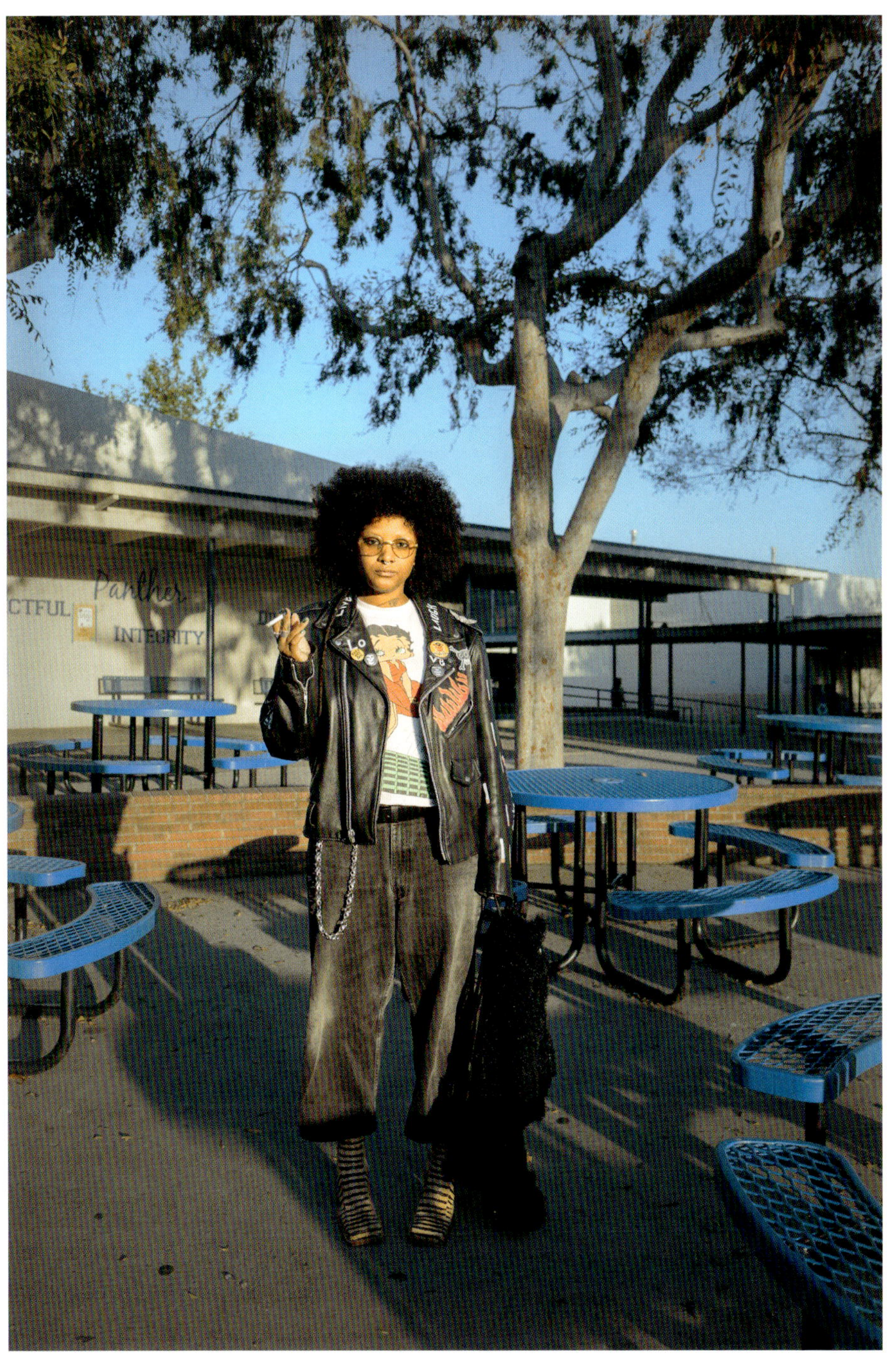

Leimert Park

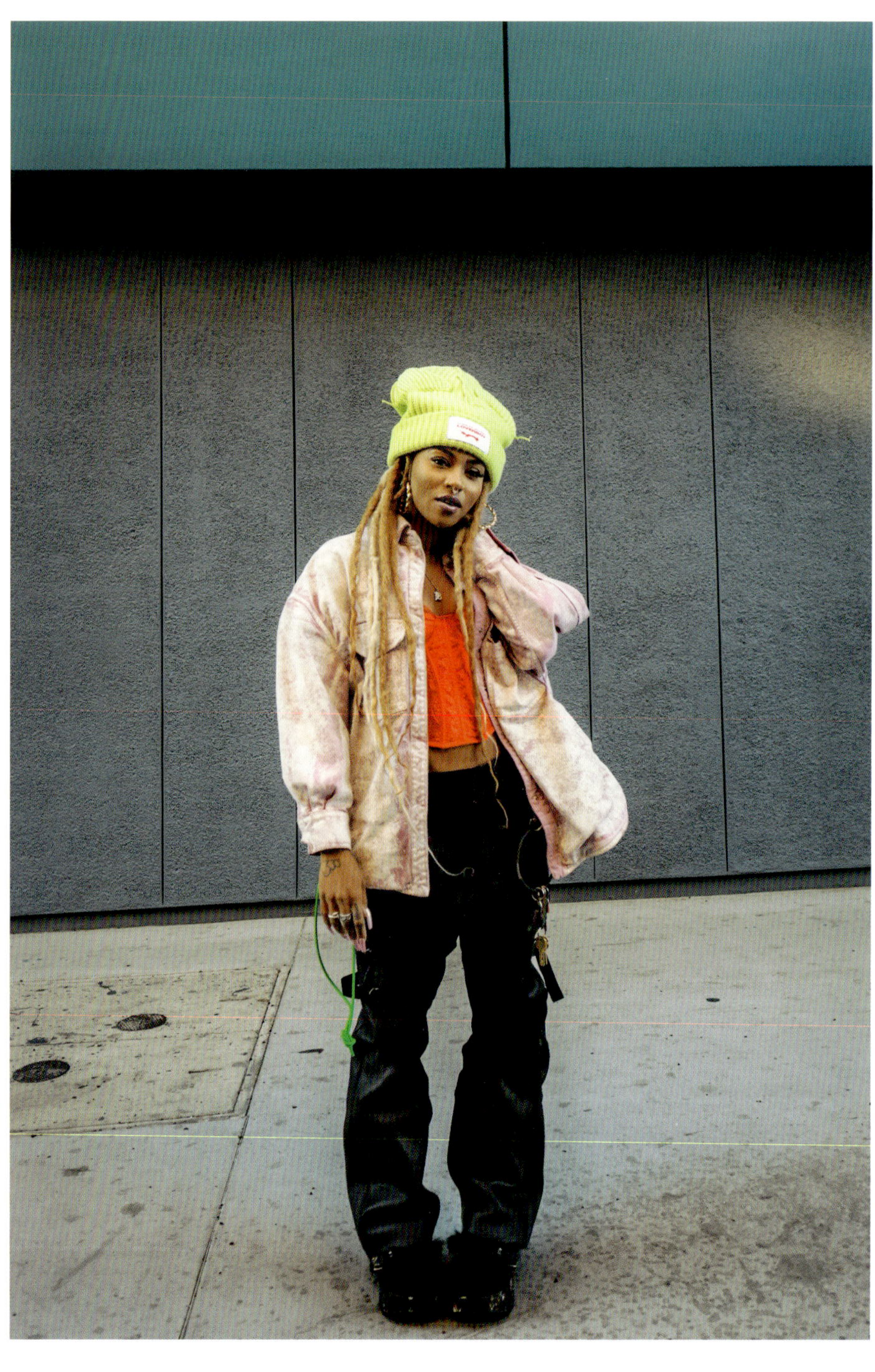

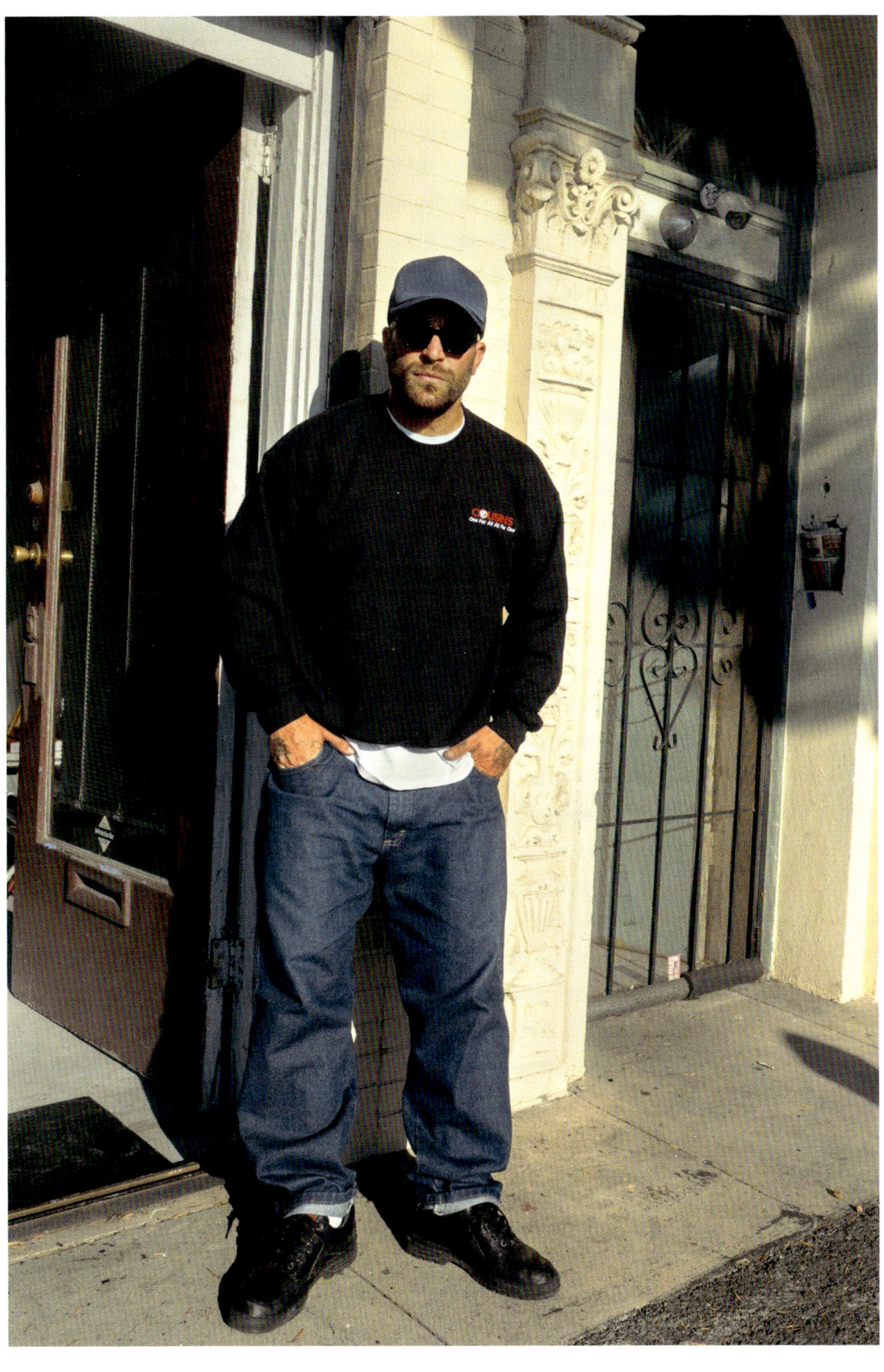

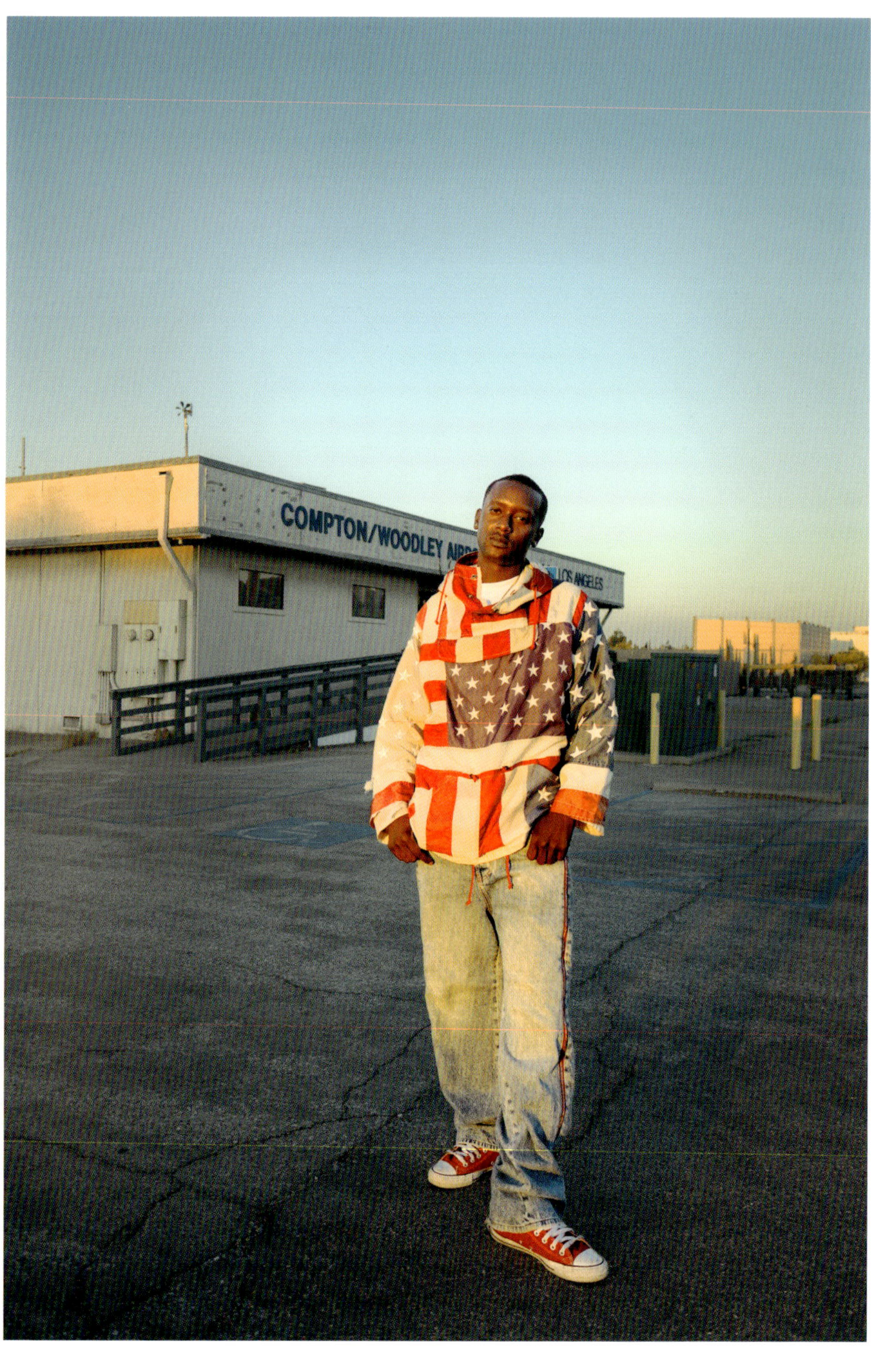

Musican

Compton

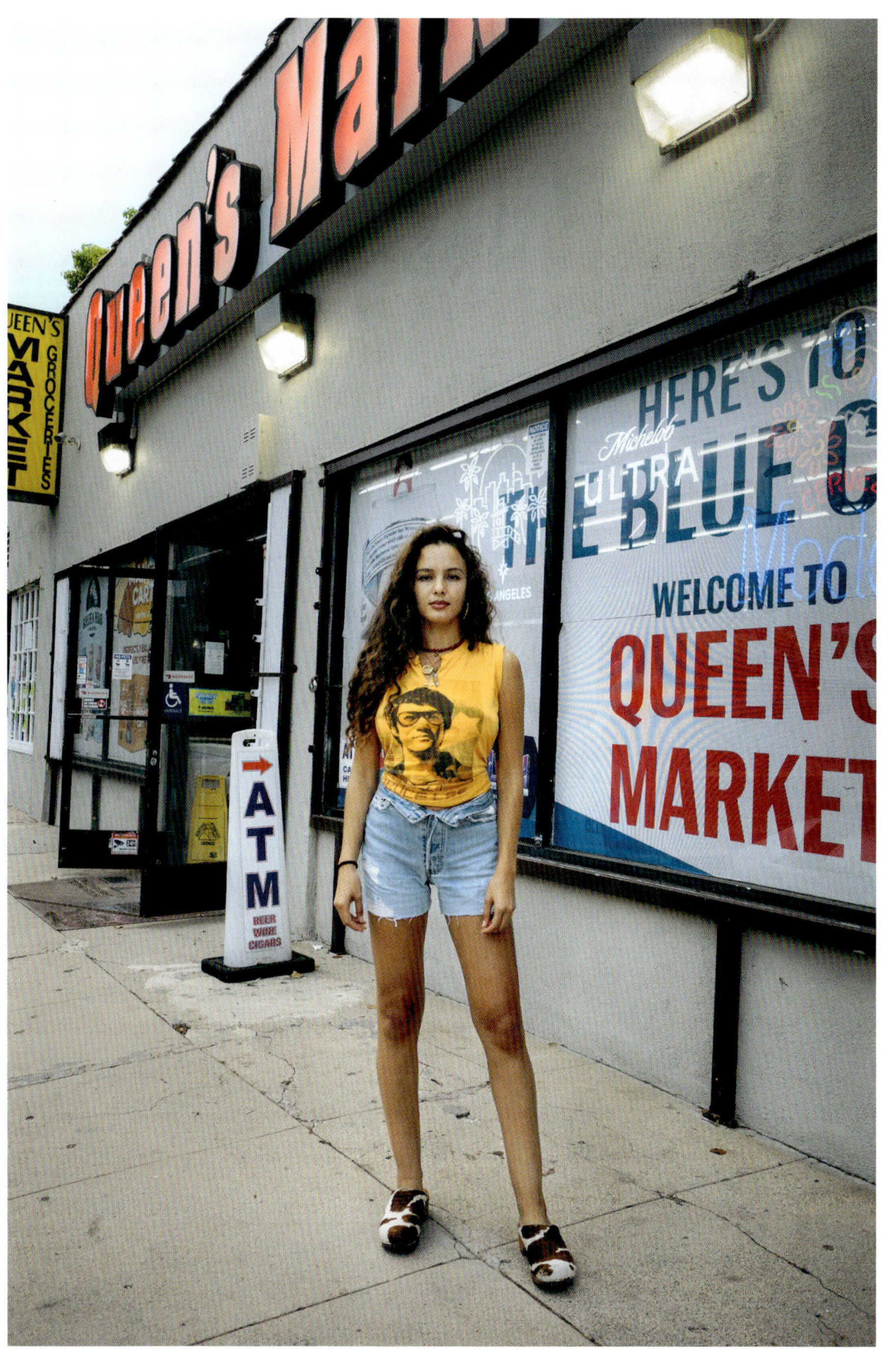

Model / Musician

Venice

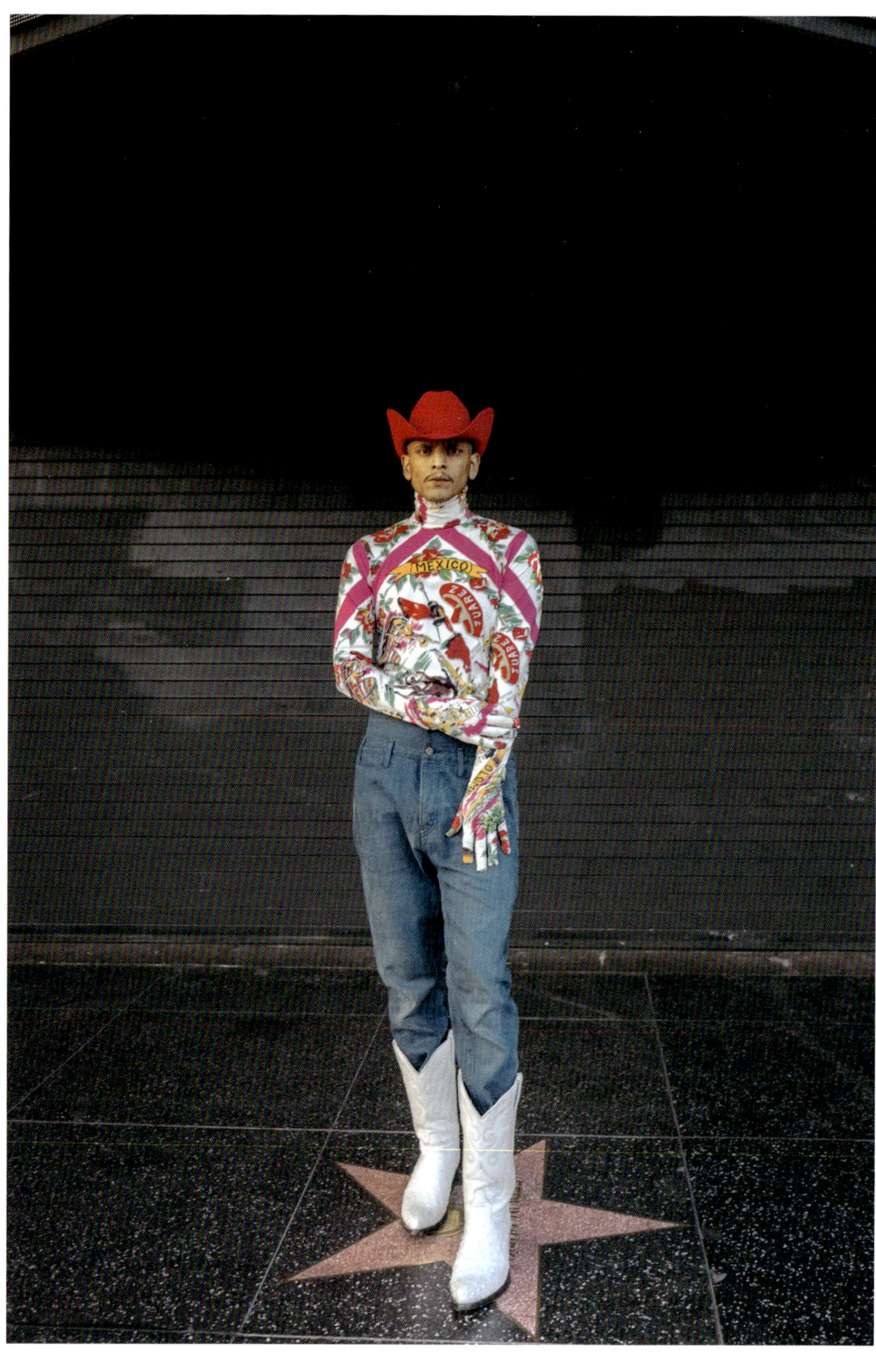

Union Costumer

Hollywood

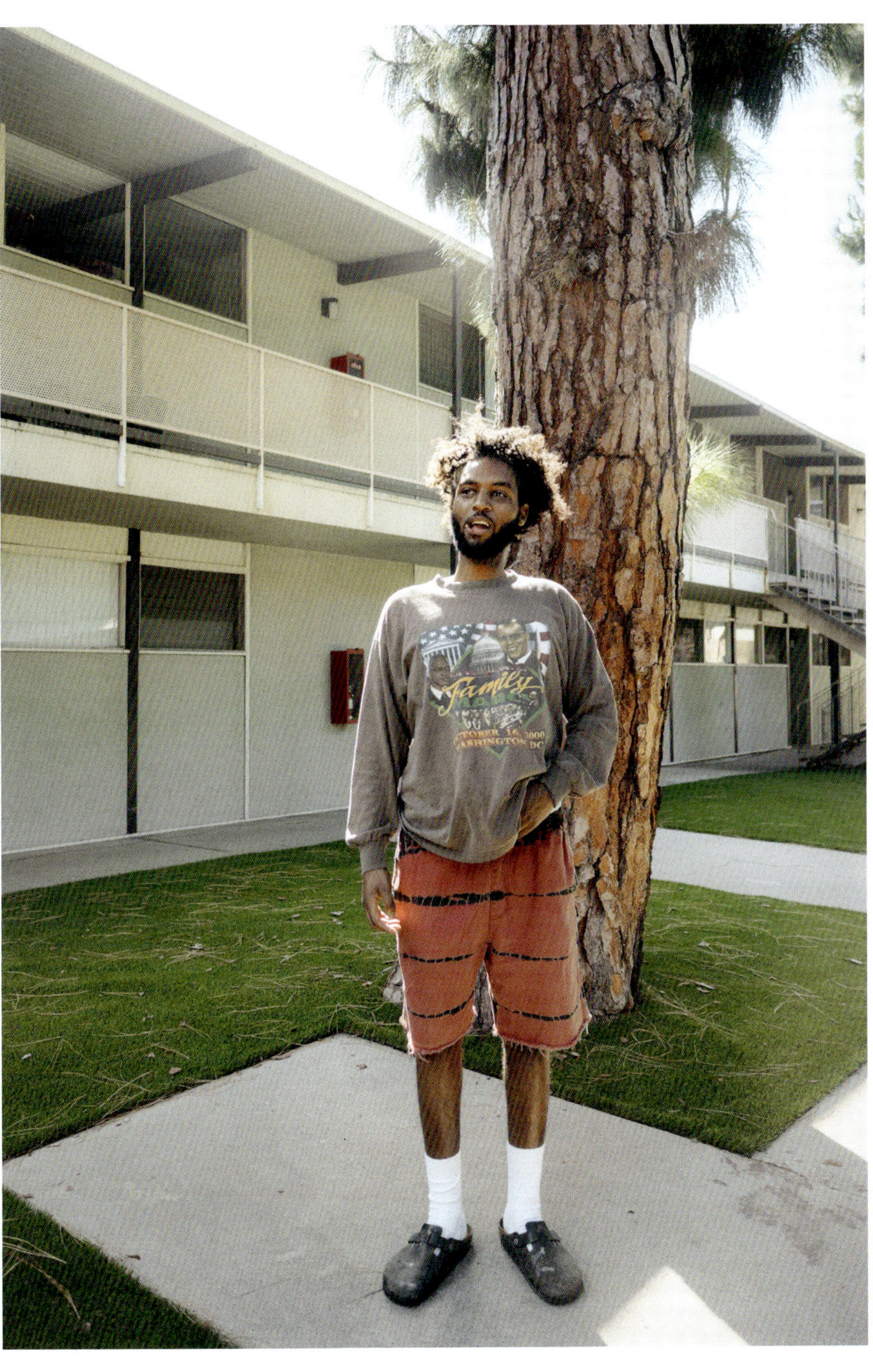

Actor

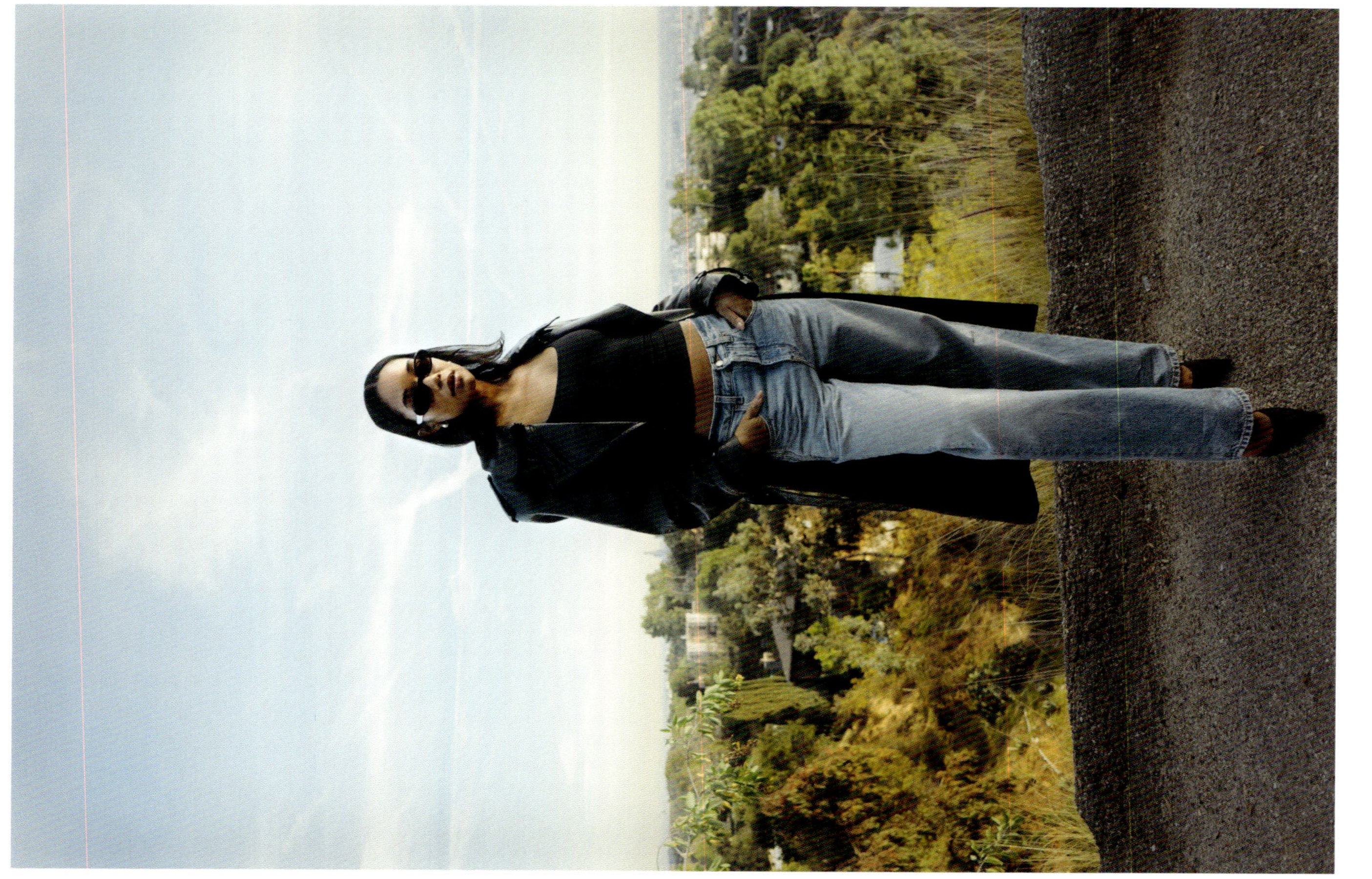

Clothing Designer Lumières

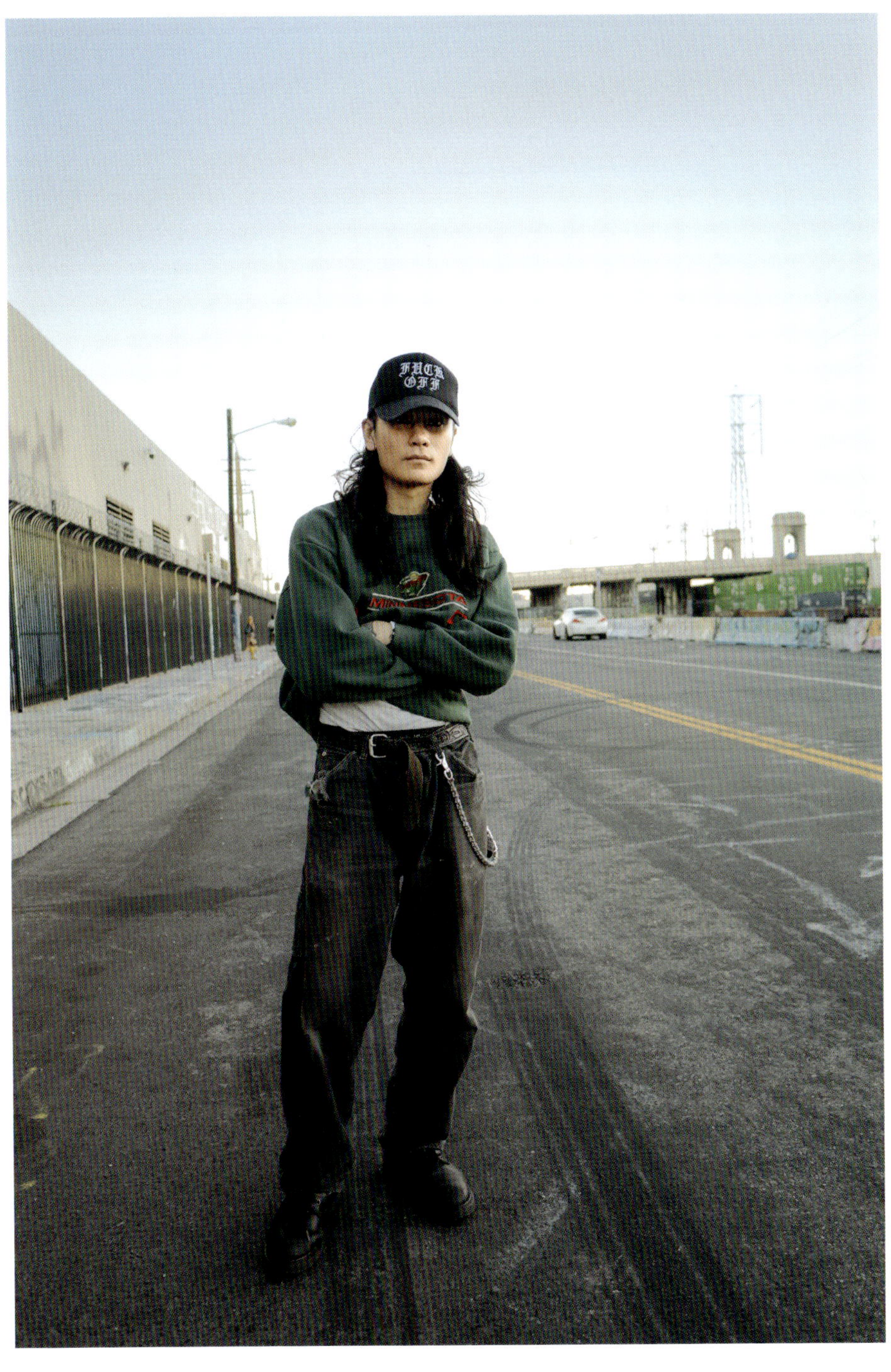

Crenshaw

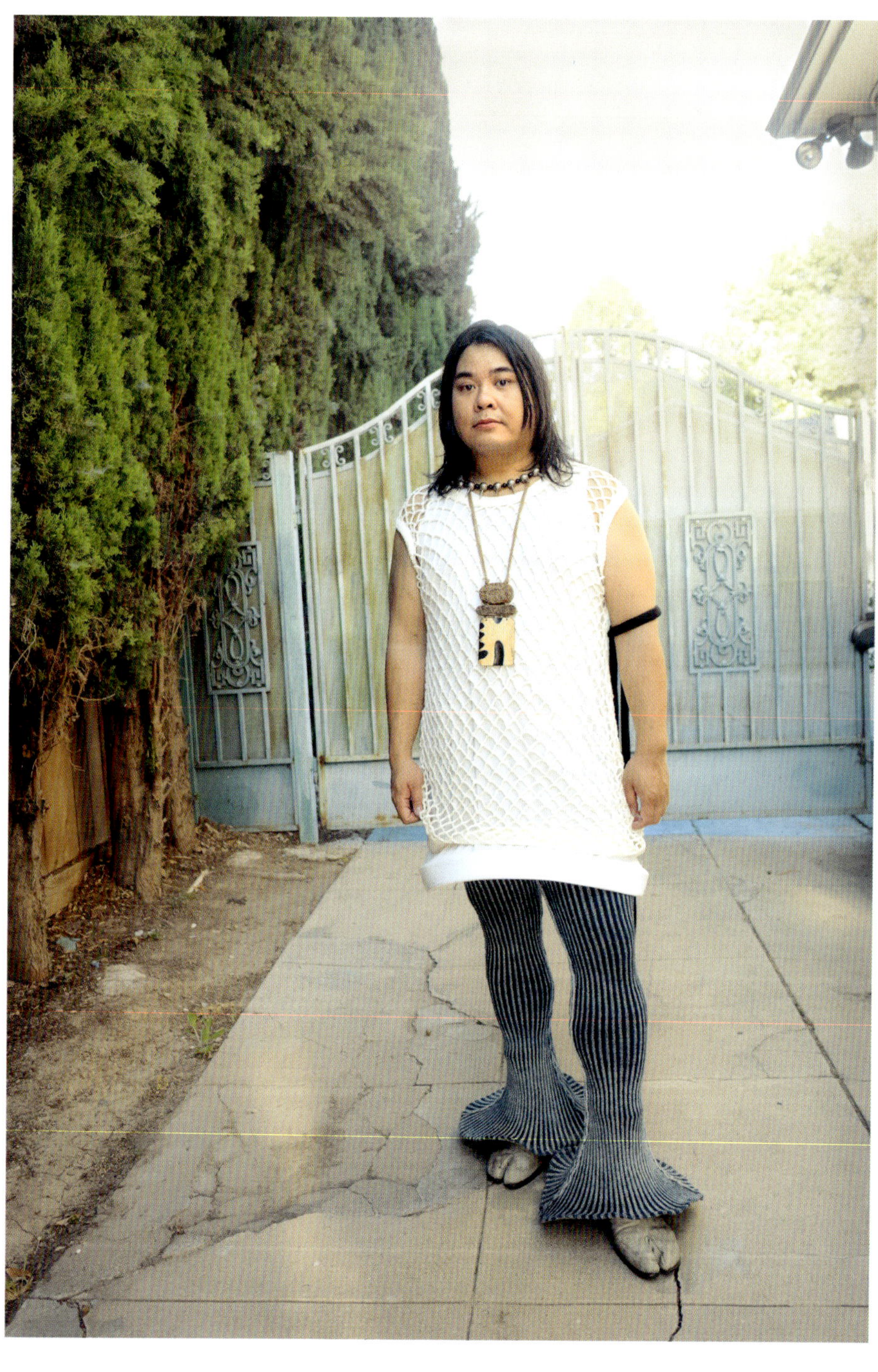

DJ / Fashion Editor / Cultural Consultant

Beverly Hills

I YUEN CO.
ARTS·GIFTS
利源公司
IN SUN
COMPANY
Jade & Jewelry
榮生
玉器

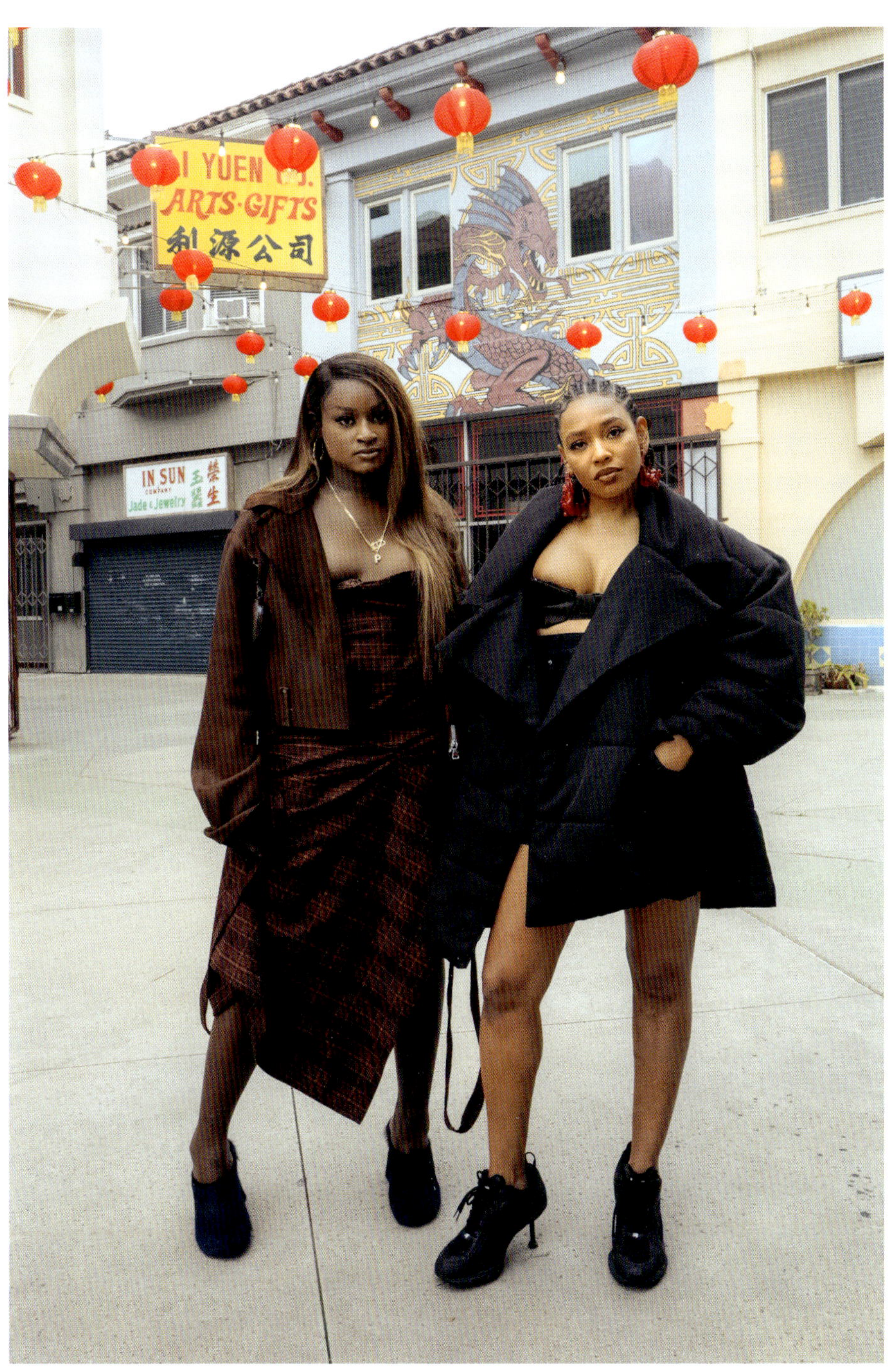

Pia Davis & Autumn Randolph

Founders of Nosesso

Monetcito Heights and West Adams

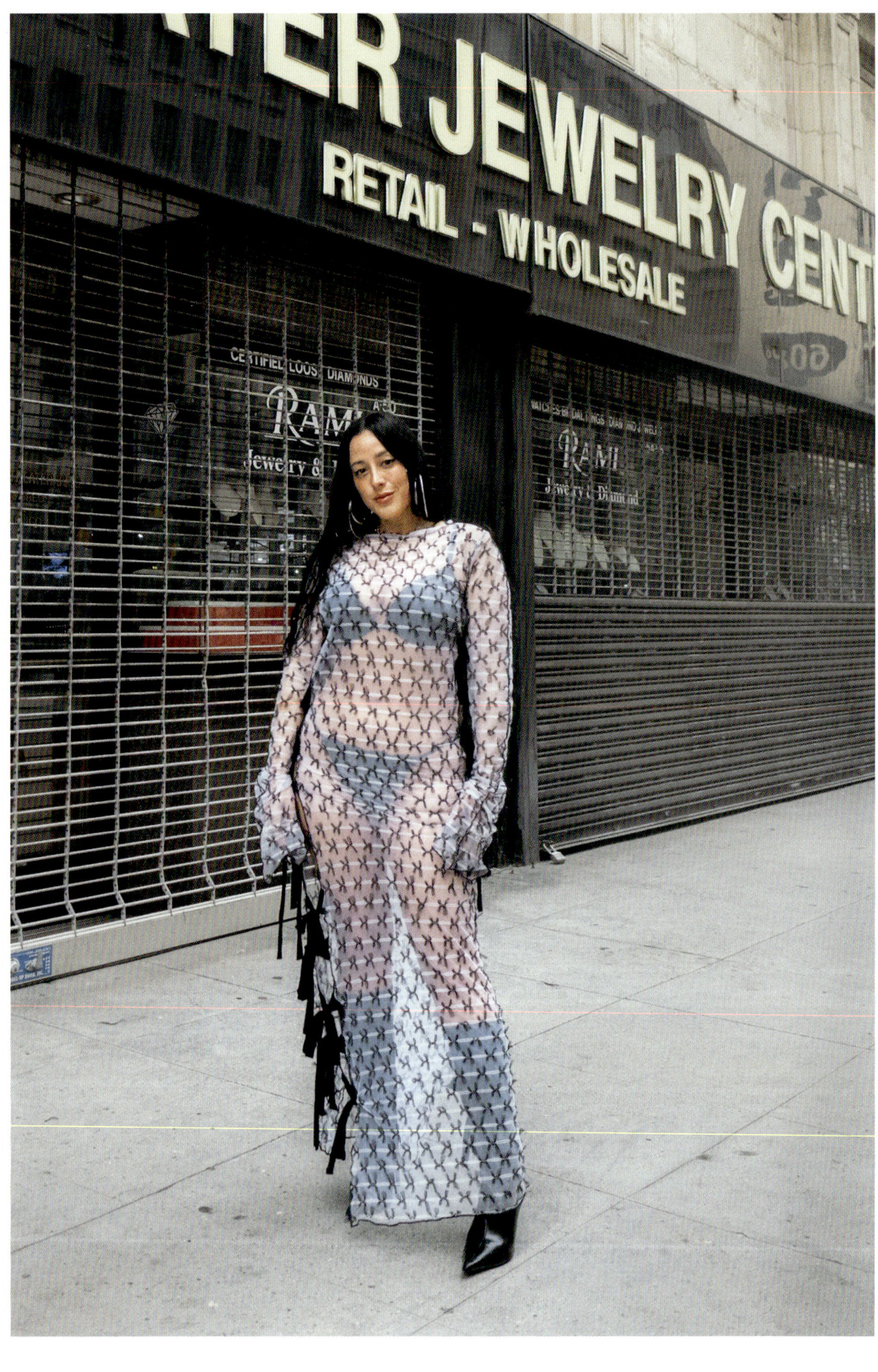

JEWELRY CENT
RETAIL - WHOLESALE
CERTIFIED LOOSE DIAMONDS
RAMI
Jewelry &
RAMI
Jewelry & Diamond

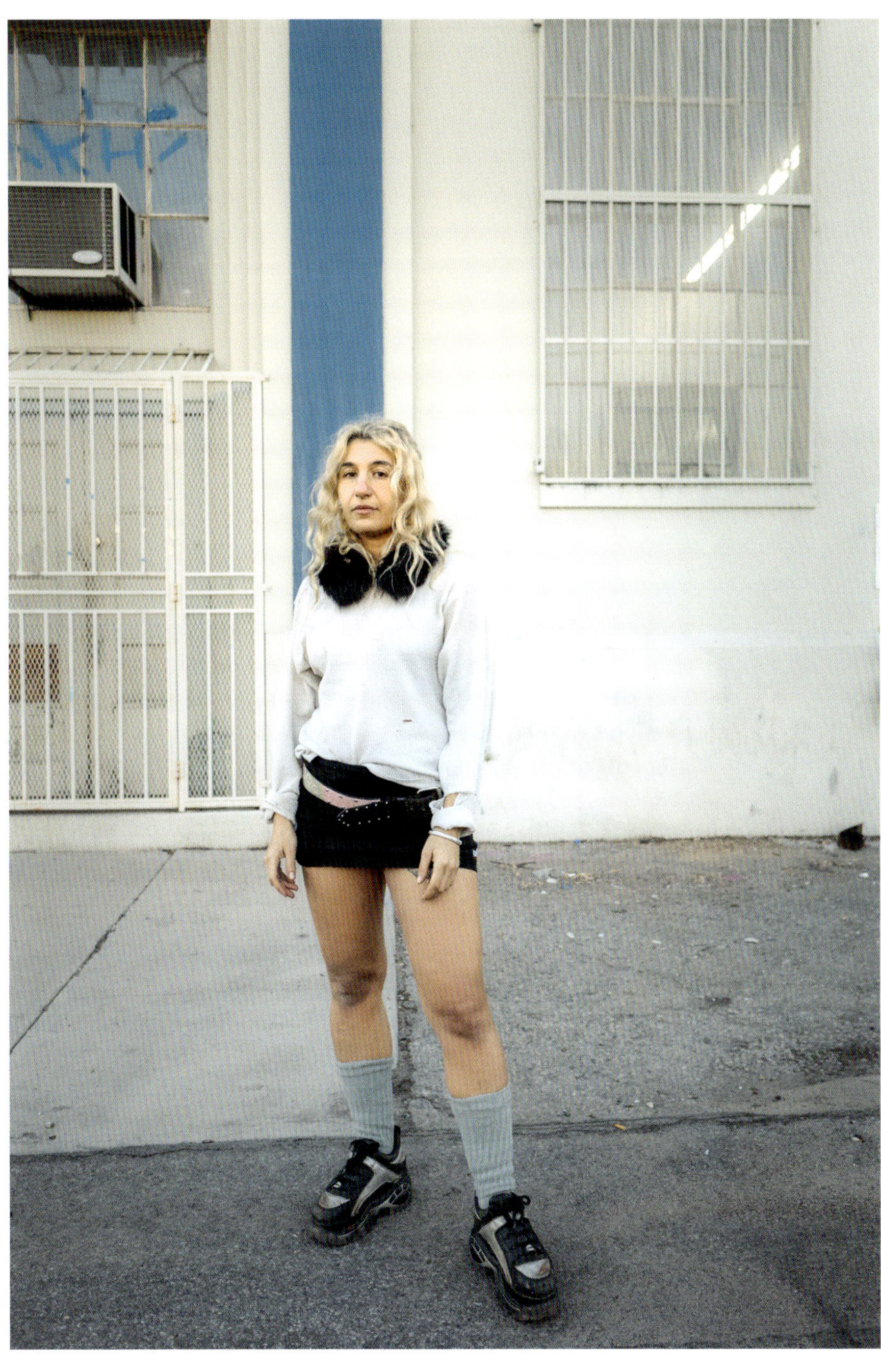

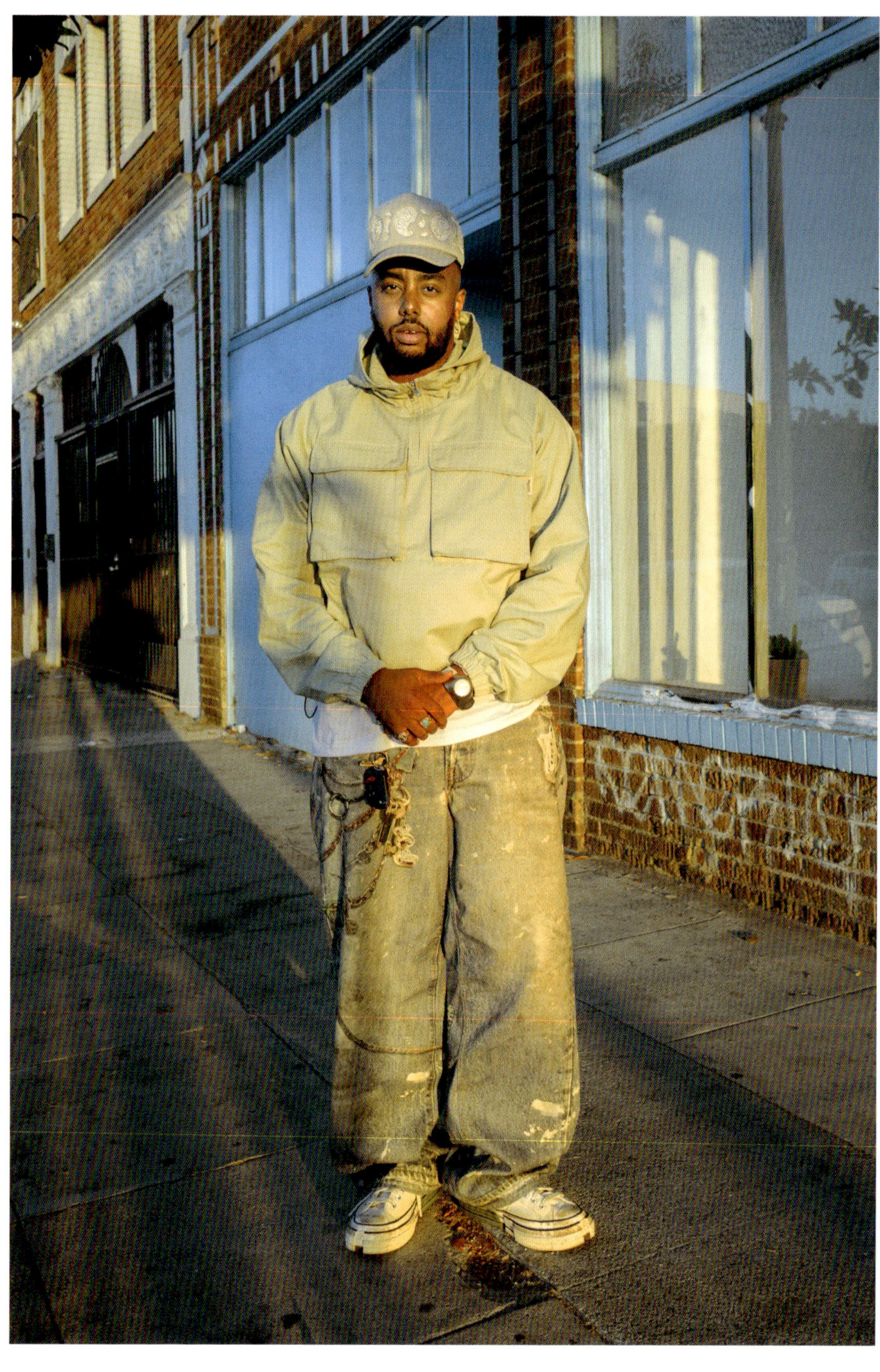

Owner of Bricks & Wood

South Central

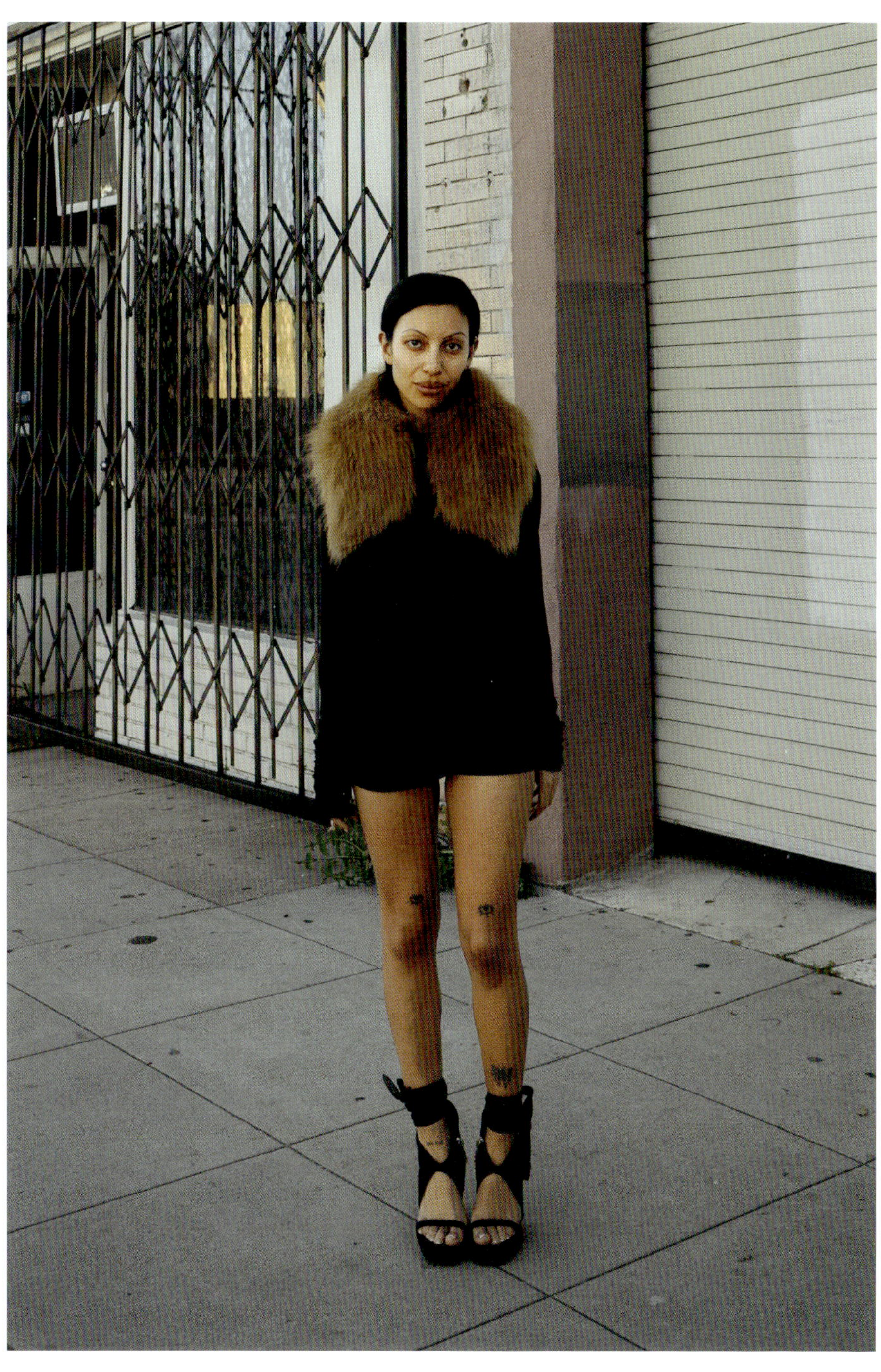

Artist

Altadena

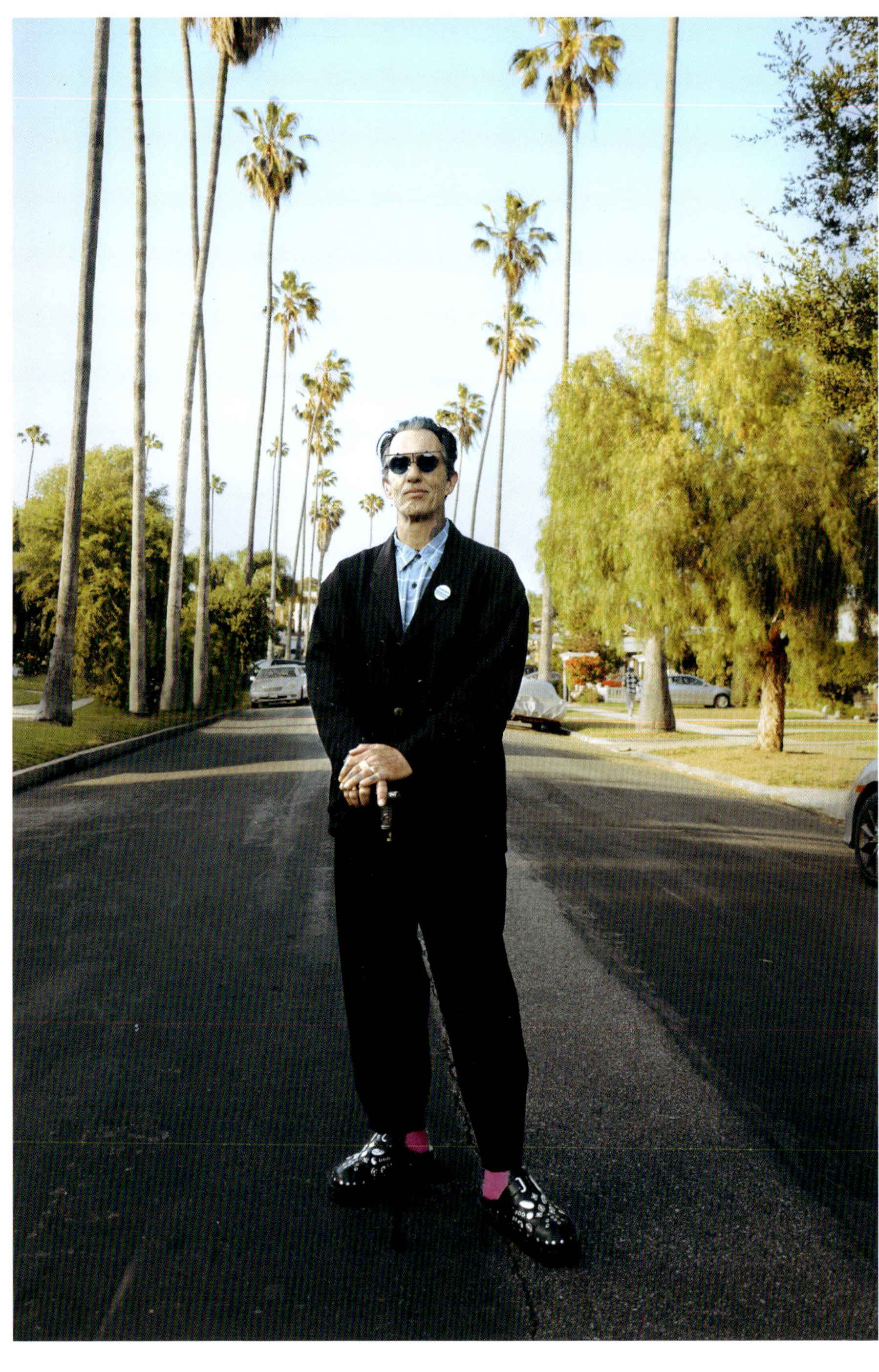

Artist

Los Feliz

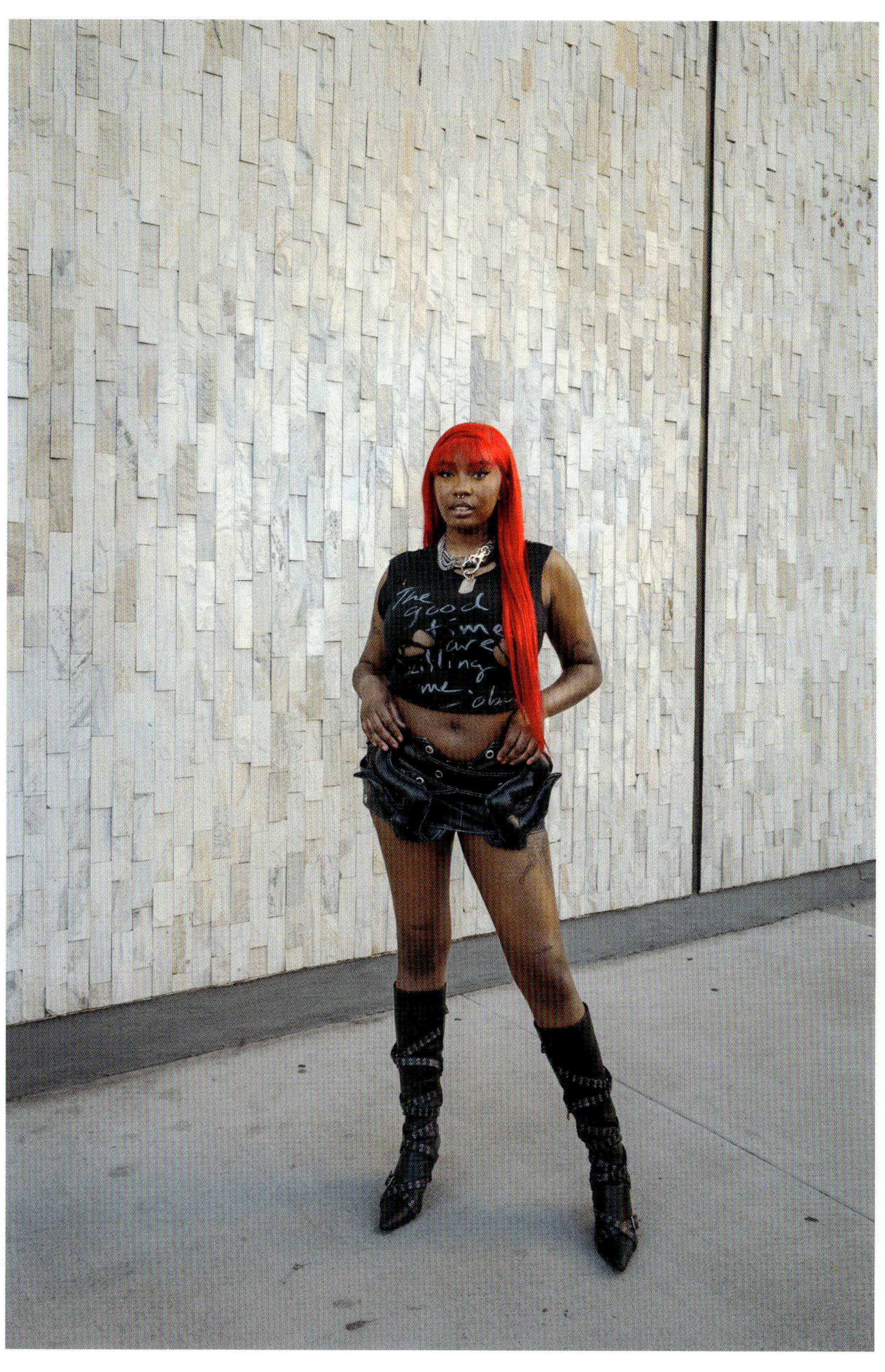
The good
time are
killing
me. obs

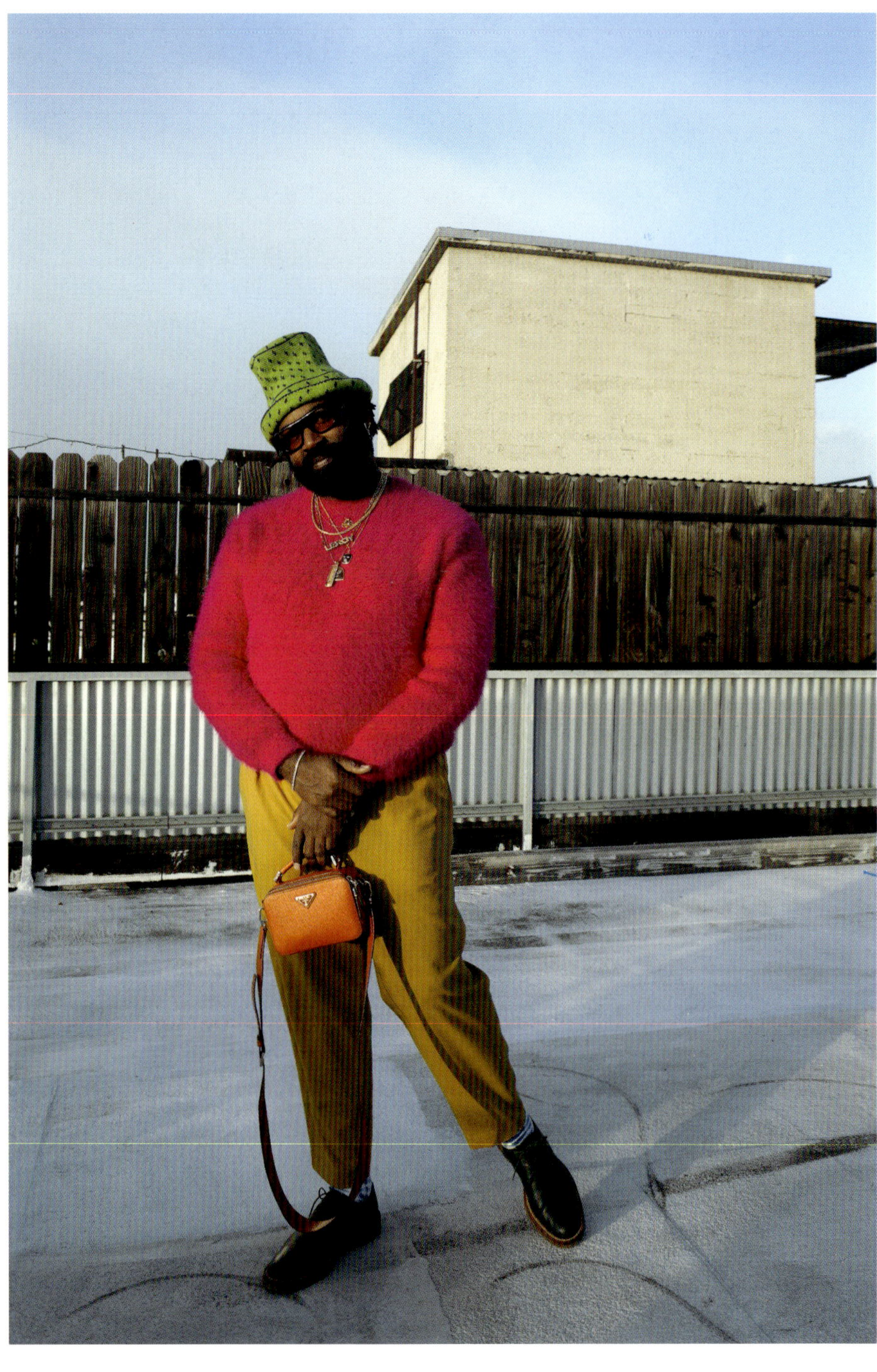

Serena Morris

Founder of She's Underrated

Pasadena

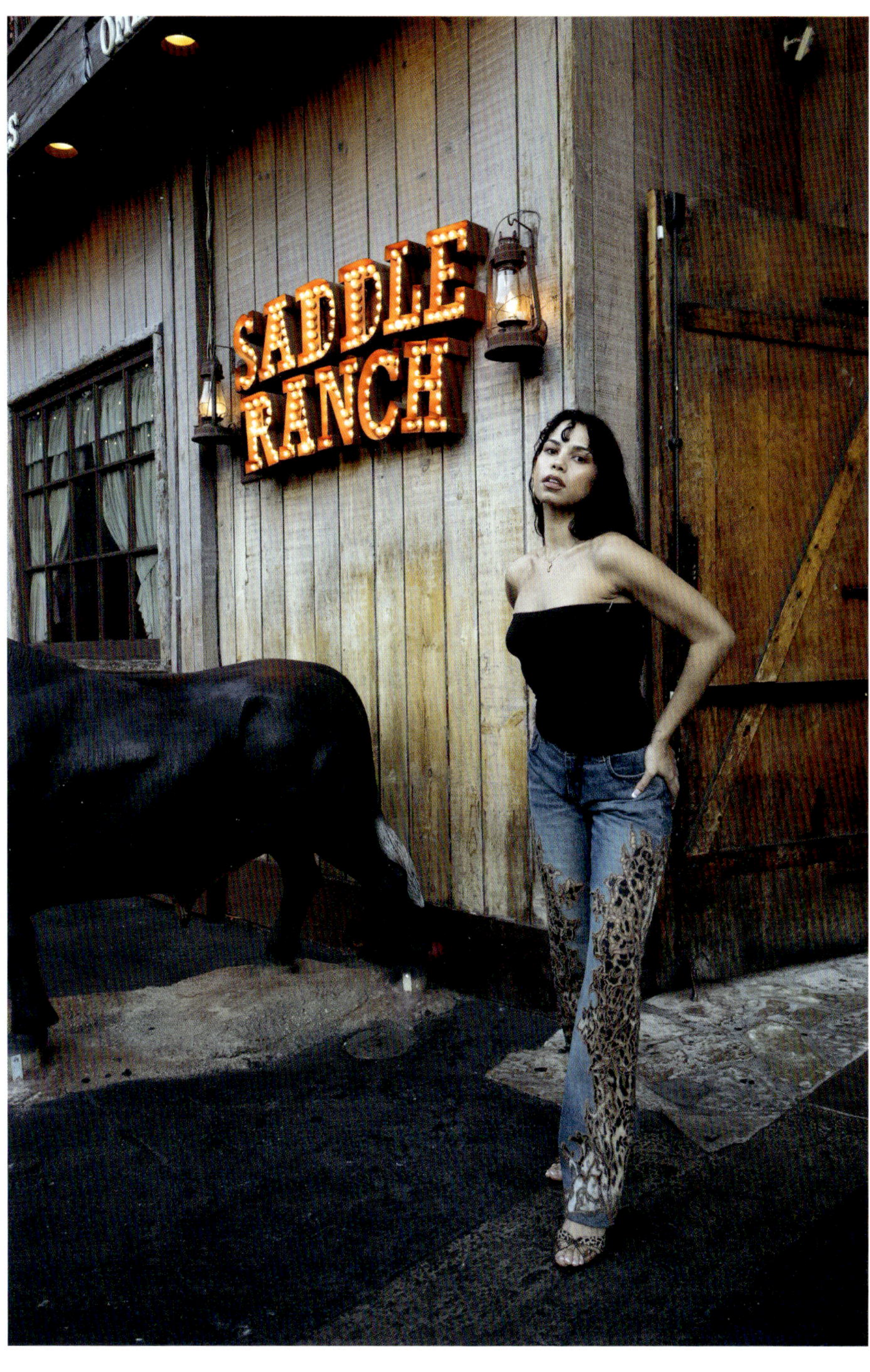
SADDLE
RANCH

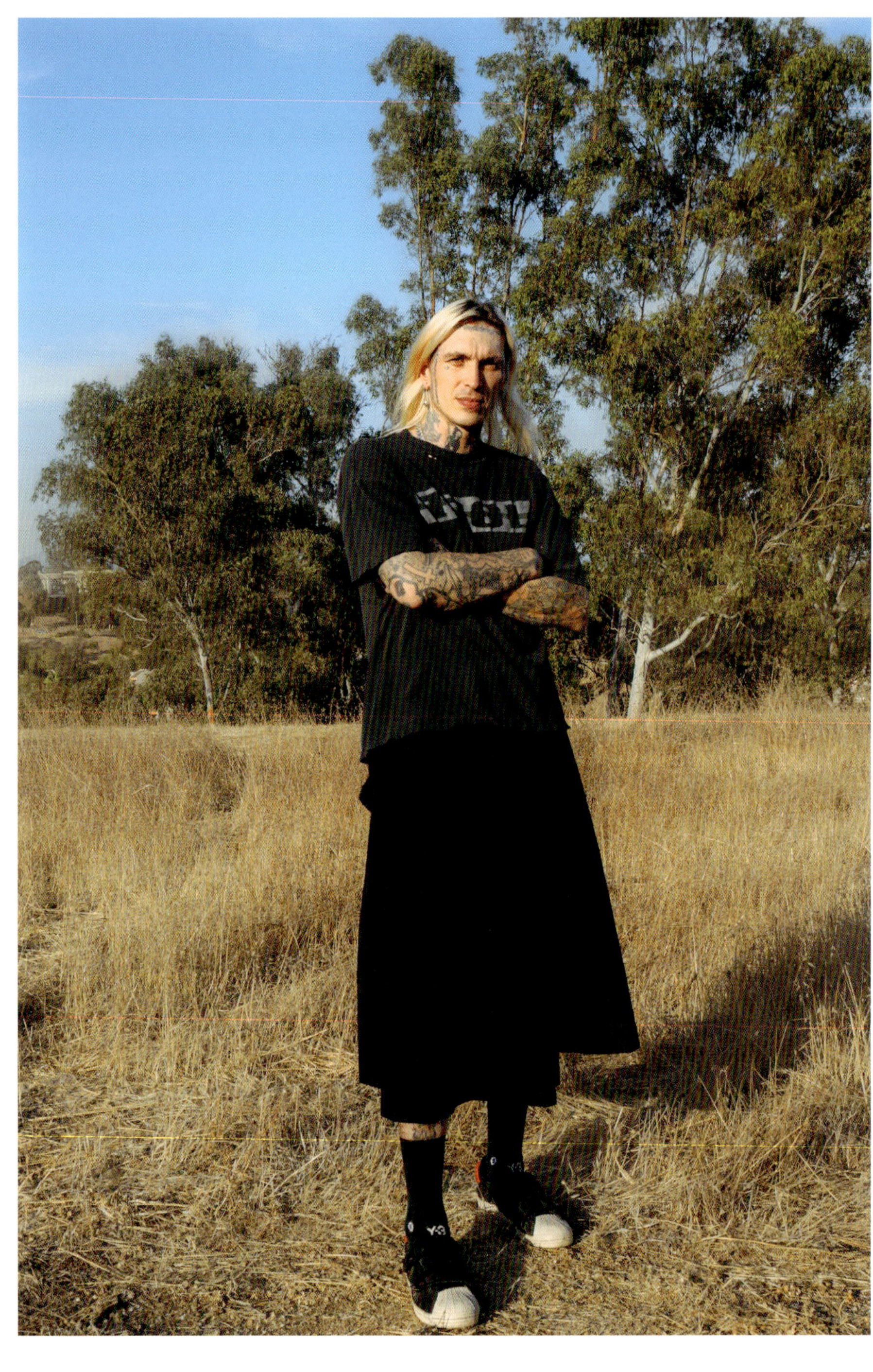

Musician / Designer

Mount Washington

Musician

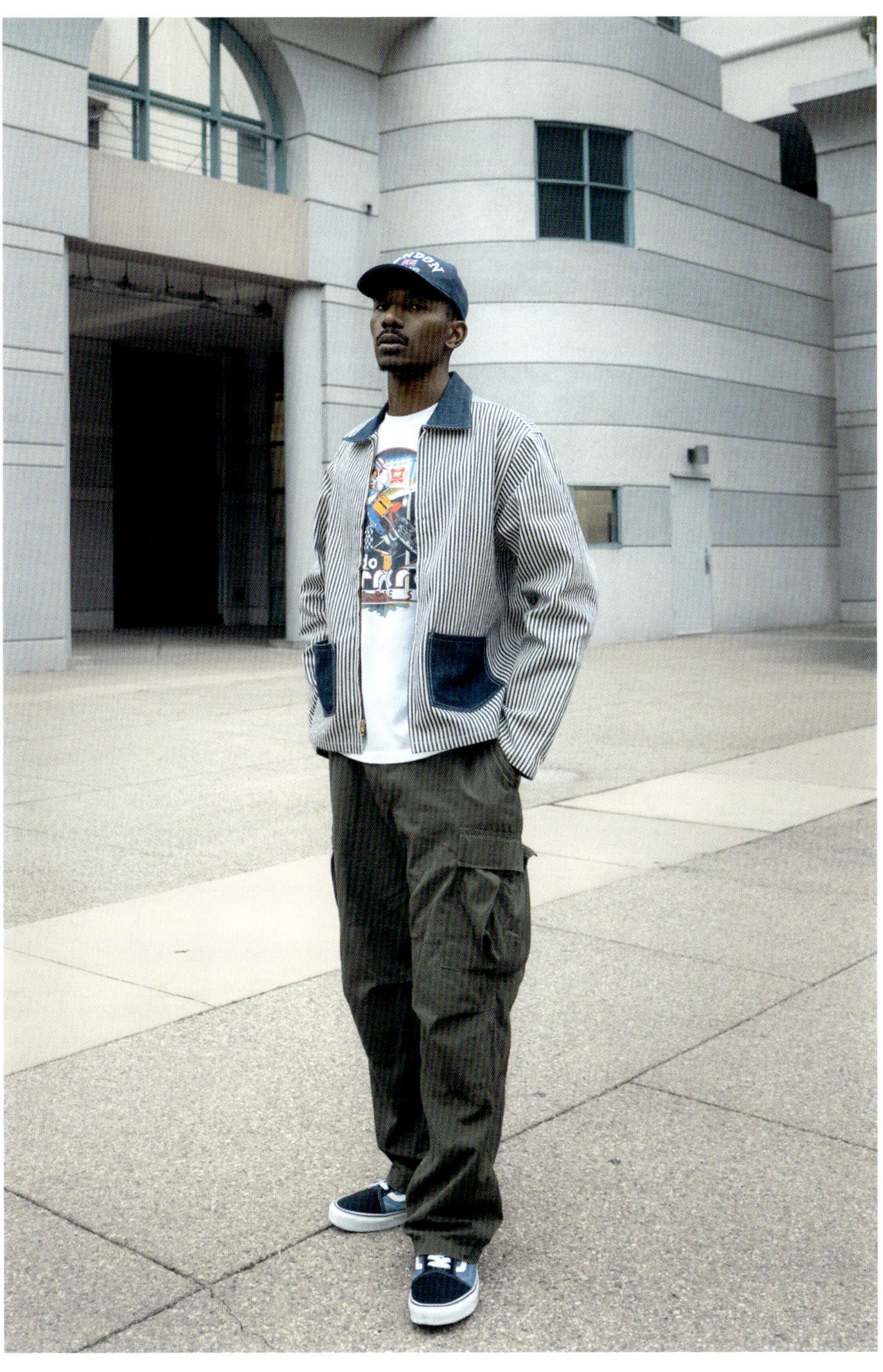

Downtown

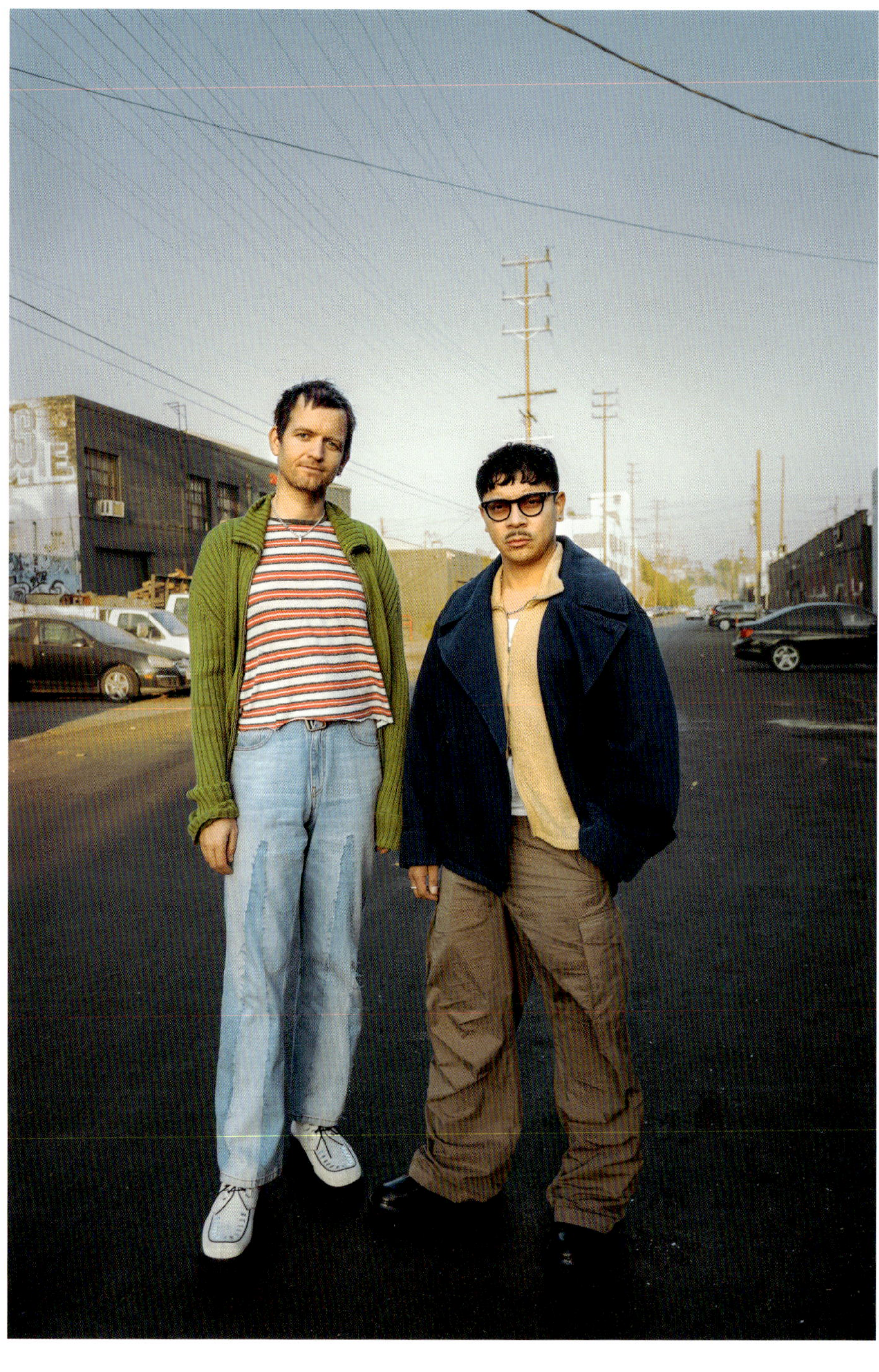

Zion Estrada
Co-founder of Black Discourse
San Bernardino

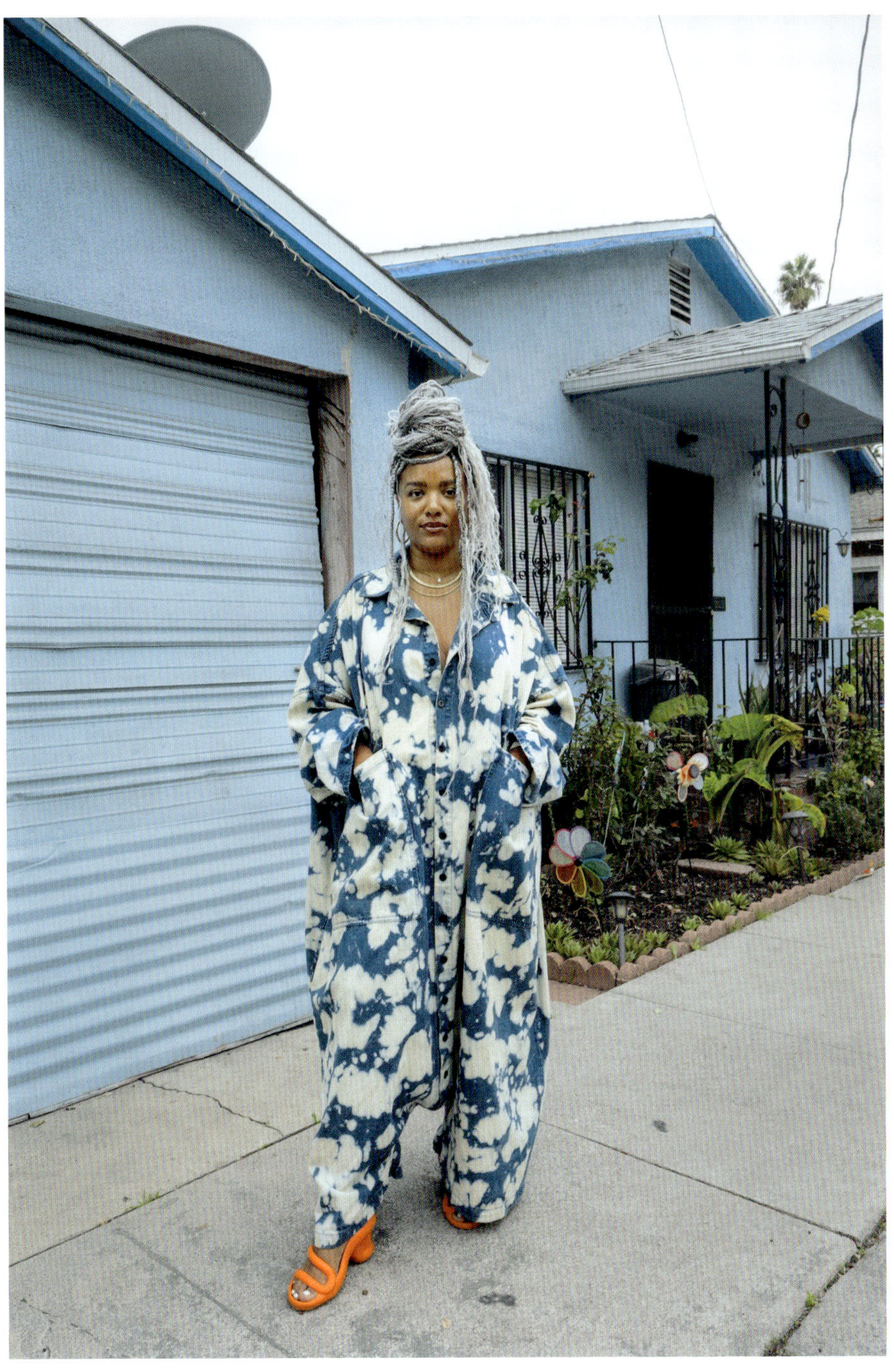

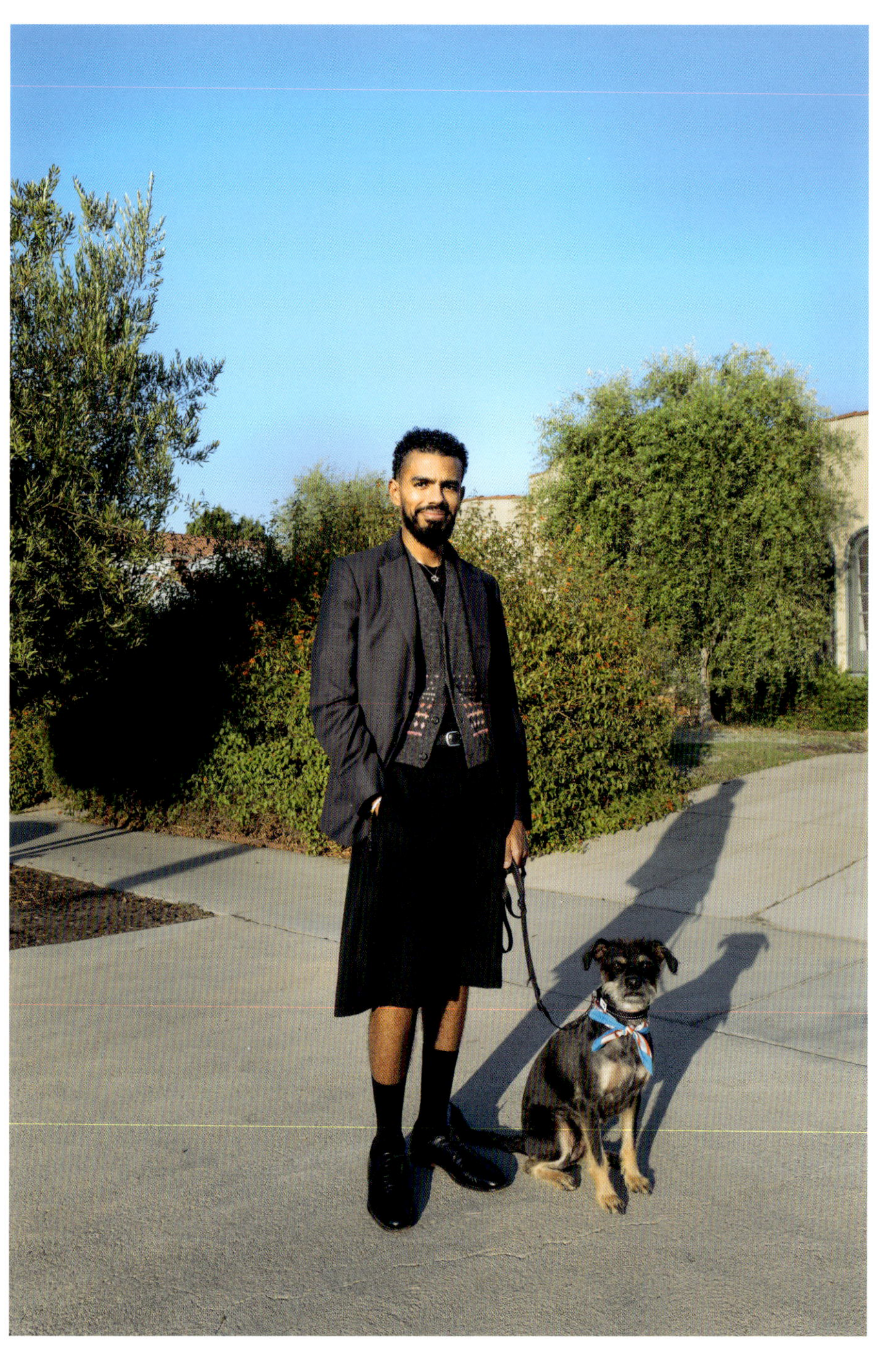

Artist

South Central

Shop Girl

San Fernando Valley

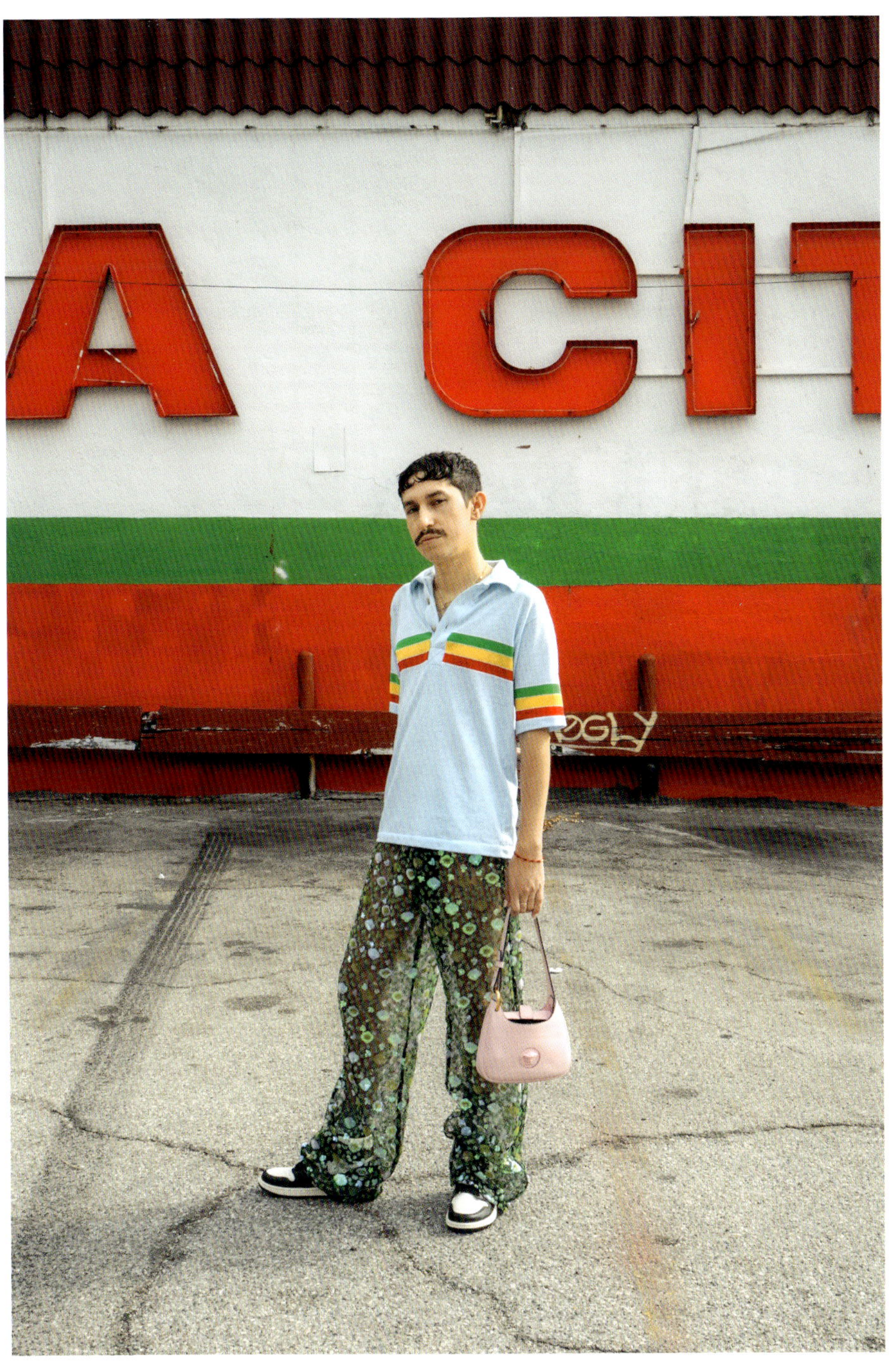

Artist / Curator

South Central

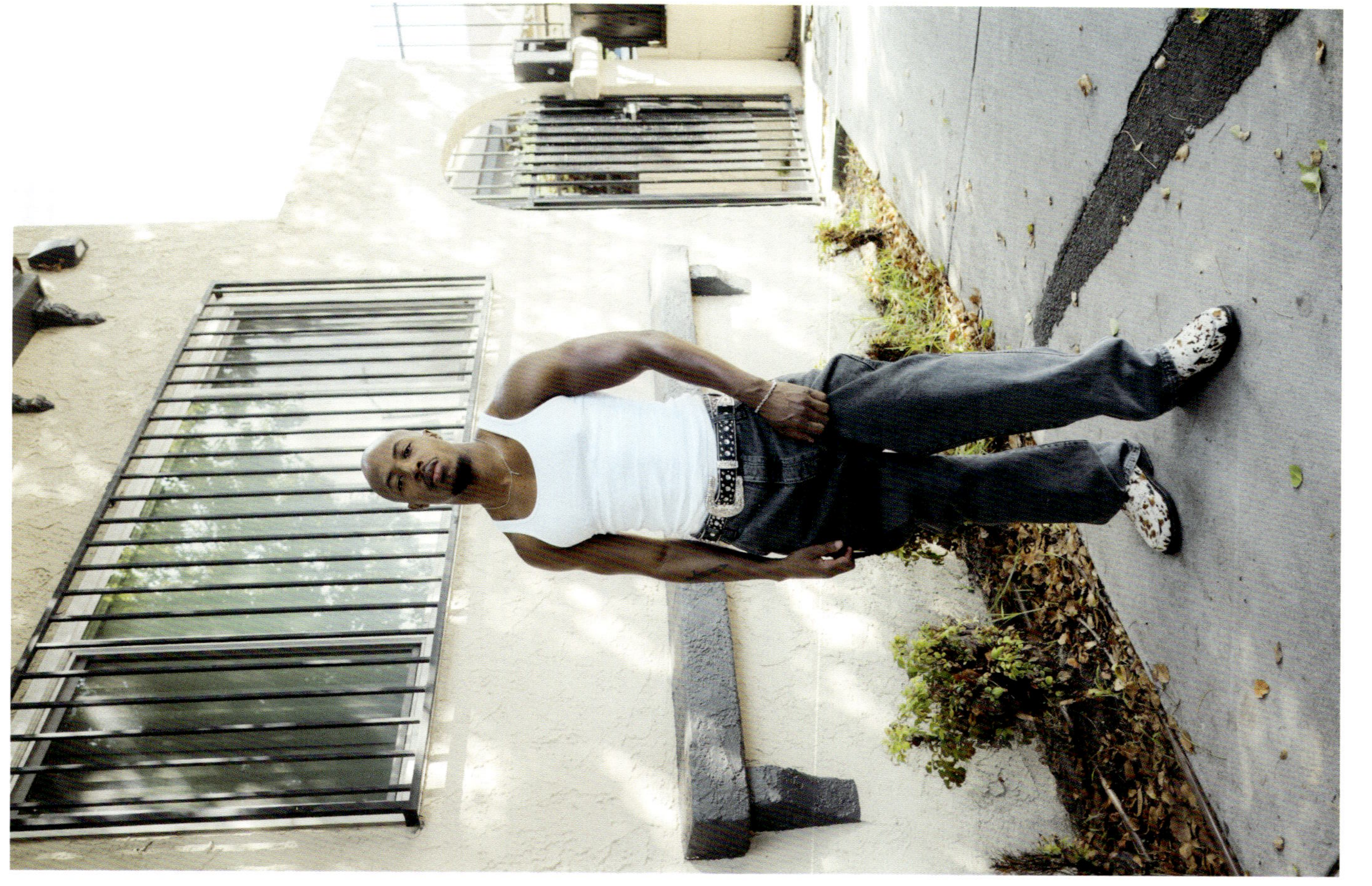

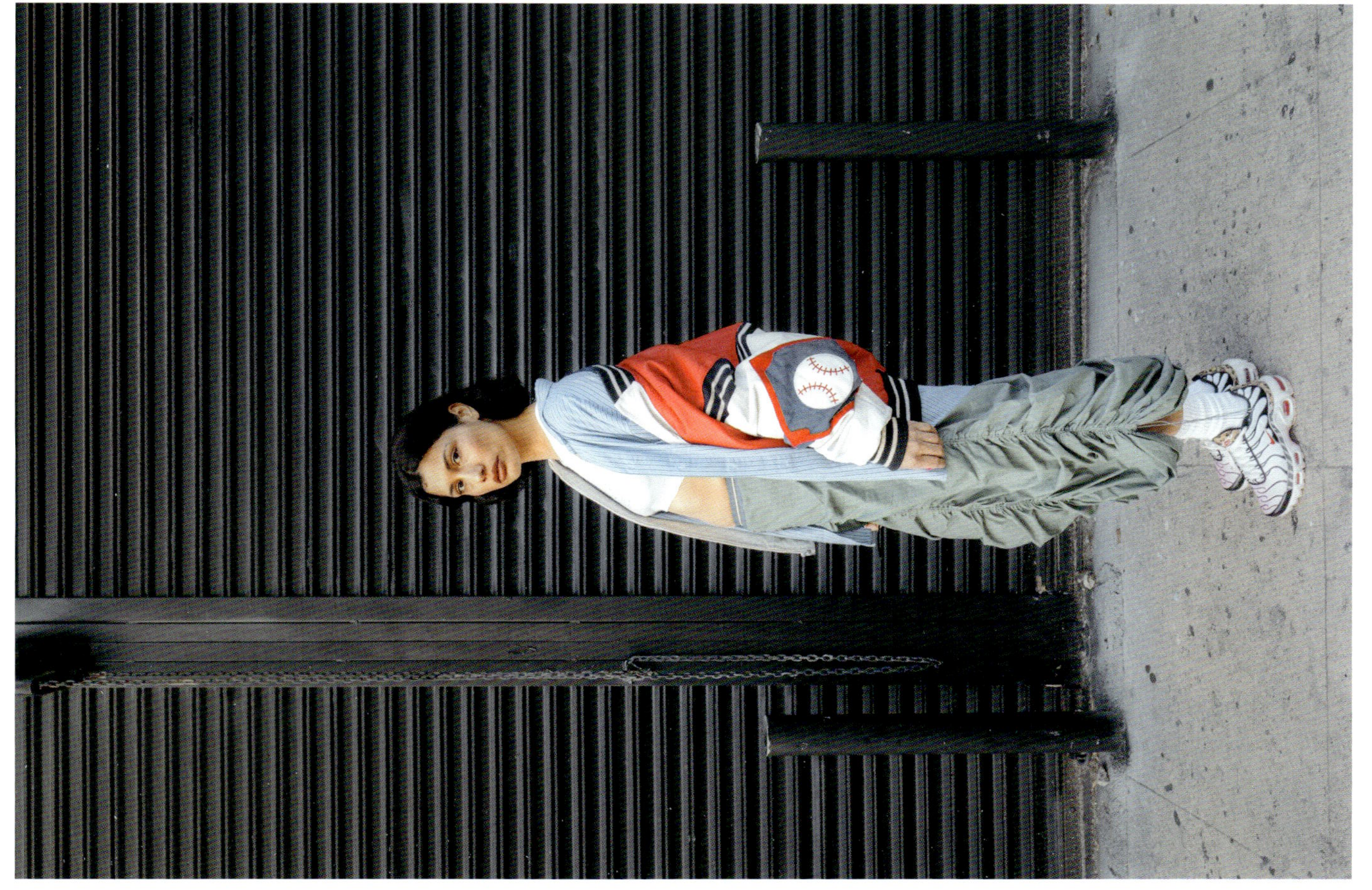

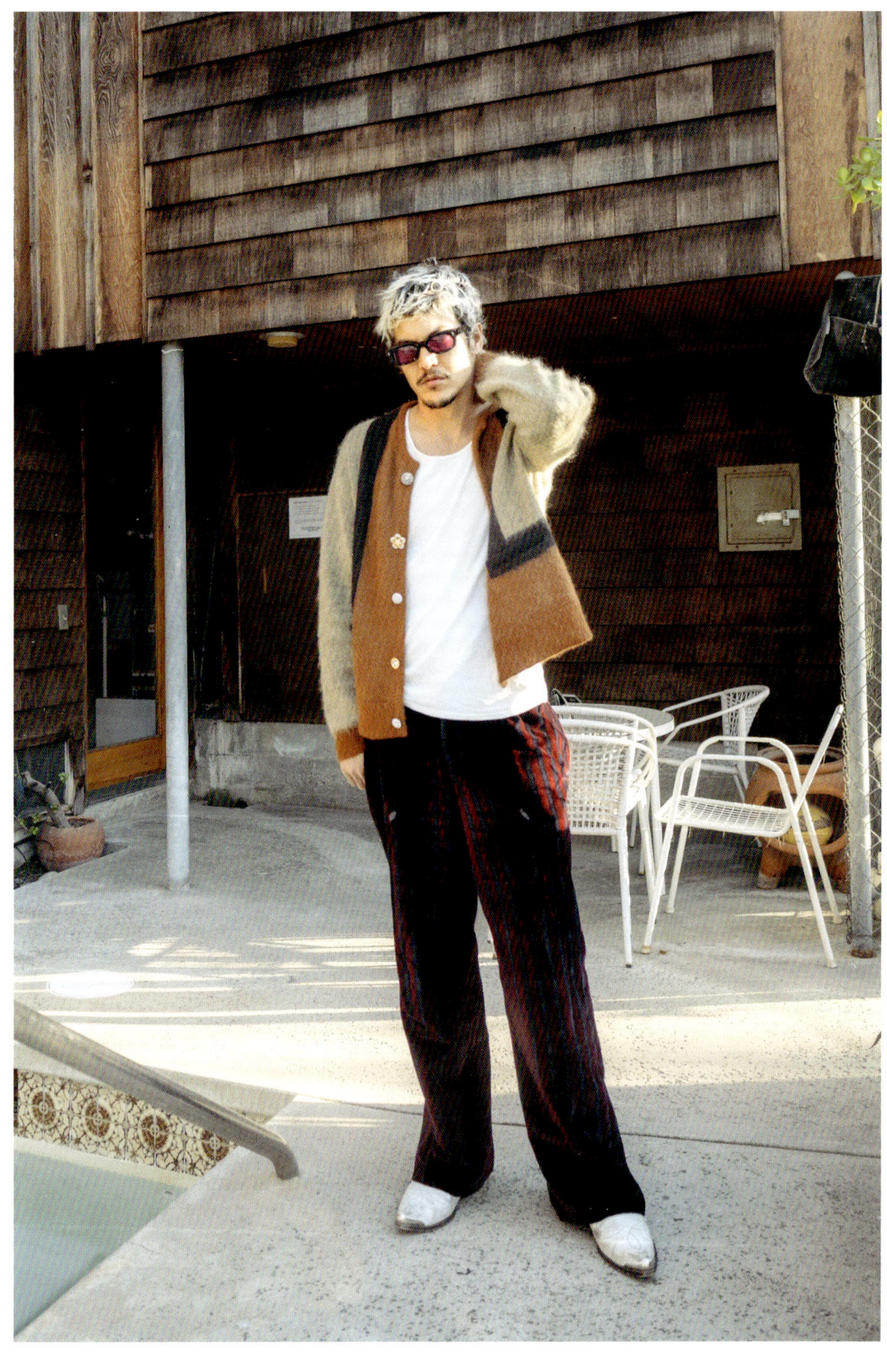

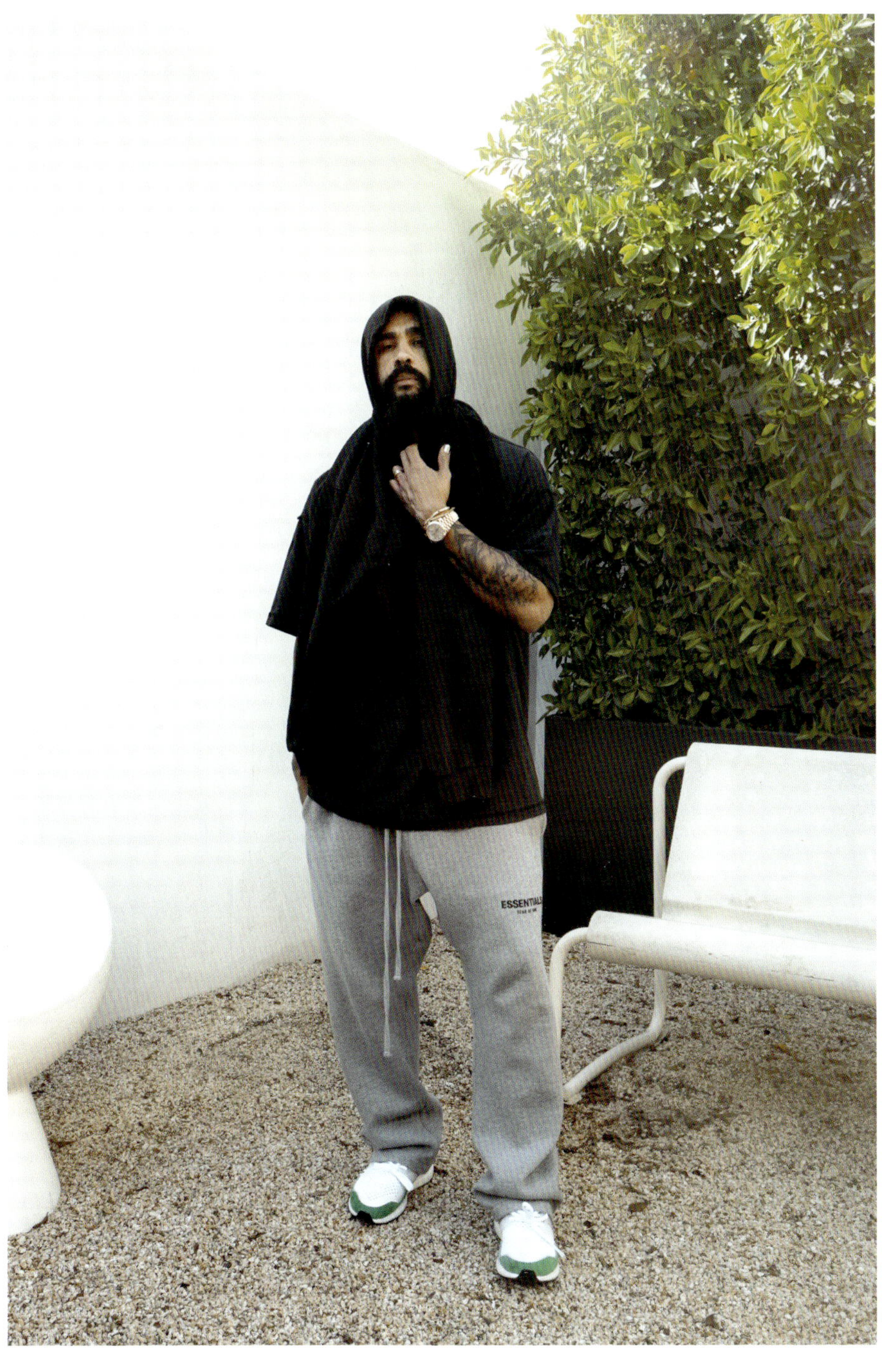

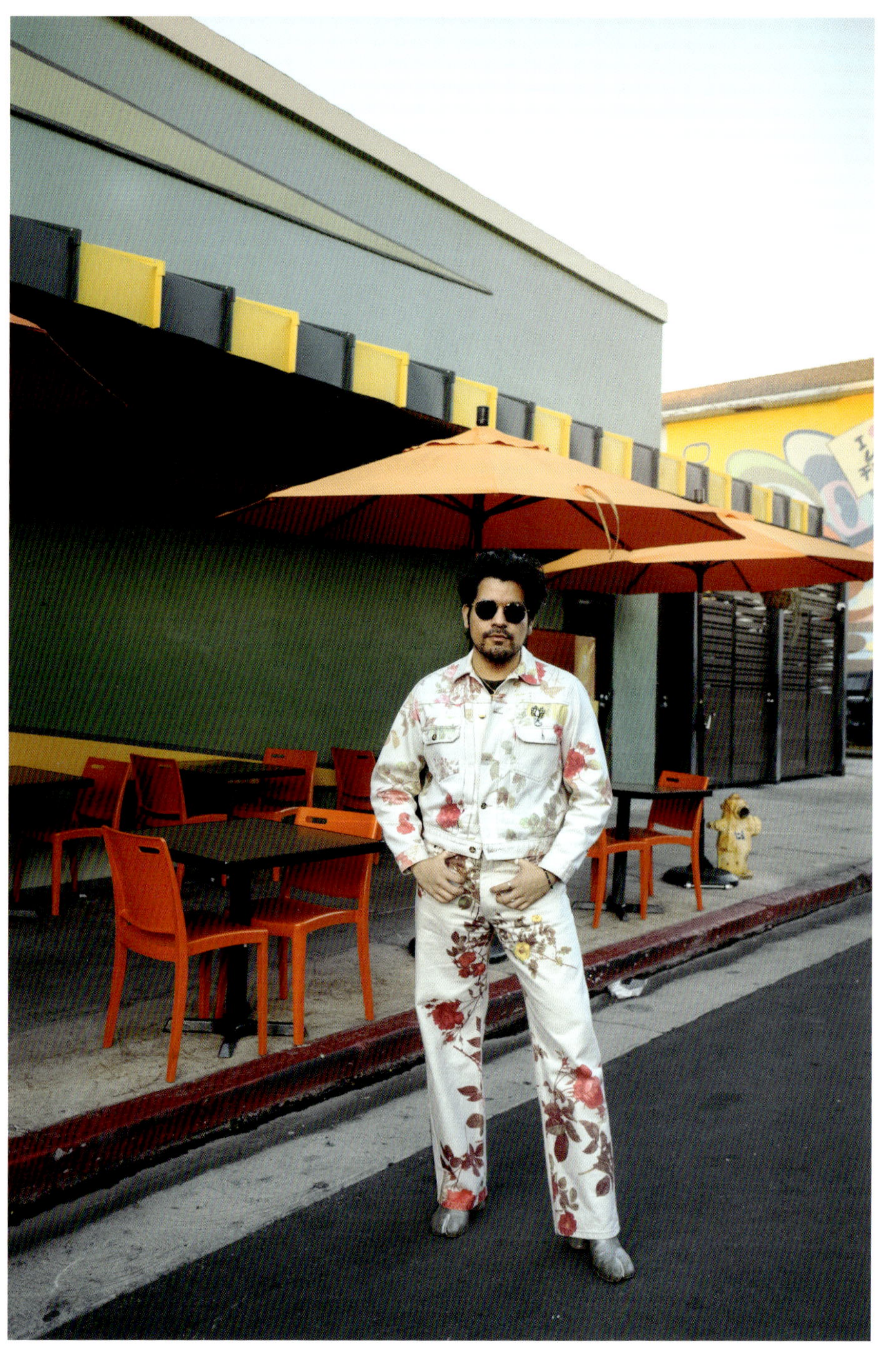

Owner of Pechunga Vintage

Natalia Leckey
Model
Highland Park

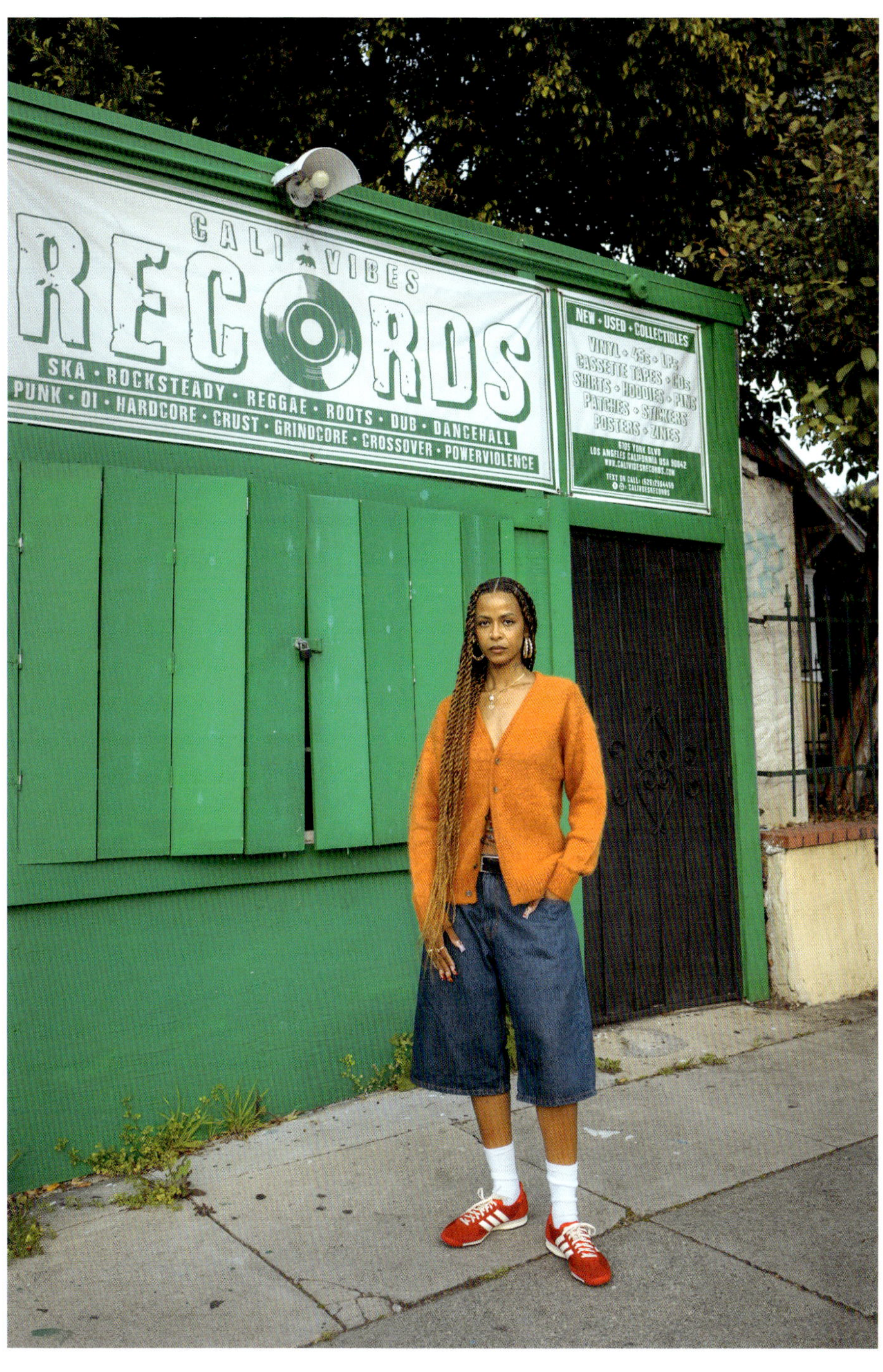

CALI VIBES
RECORDS
SKA · ROCKSTEADY · REGGAE · ROOTS · DUB · DANCEHALL
PUNK · OI · HARDCORE · CRUST · GRINDCORE · CROSSOVER · POWERVIOLENCE
NEW · USED · COLLECTIBLES
VINYL · 45s · LPs
CASSETTE TAPES · CDs
SHIRTS · HOODIES · PINS
PATCHES · STICKERS
POSTERS · ZINES
6705 YORK BLVD
LOS ANGELES CALIFORNIA USA 90042
WWW.CALIVIBESRECORDS.COM
TEXT OR CALL: (626) 296-4459
@ CALIVIBESRECORDS

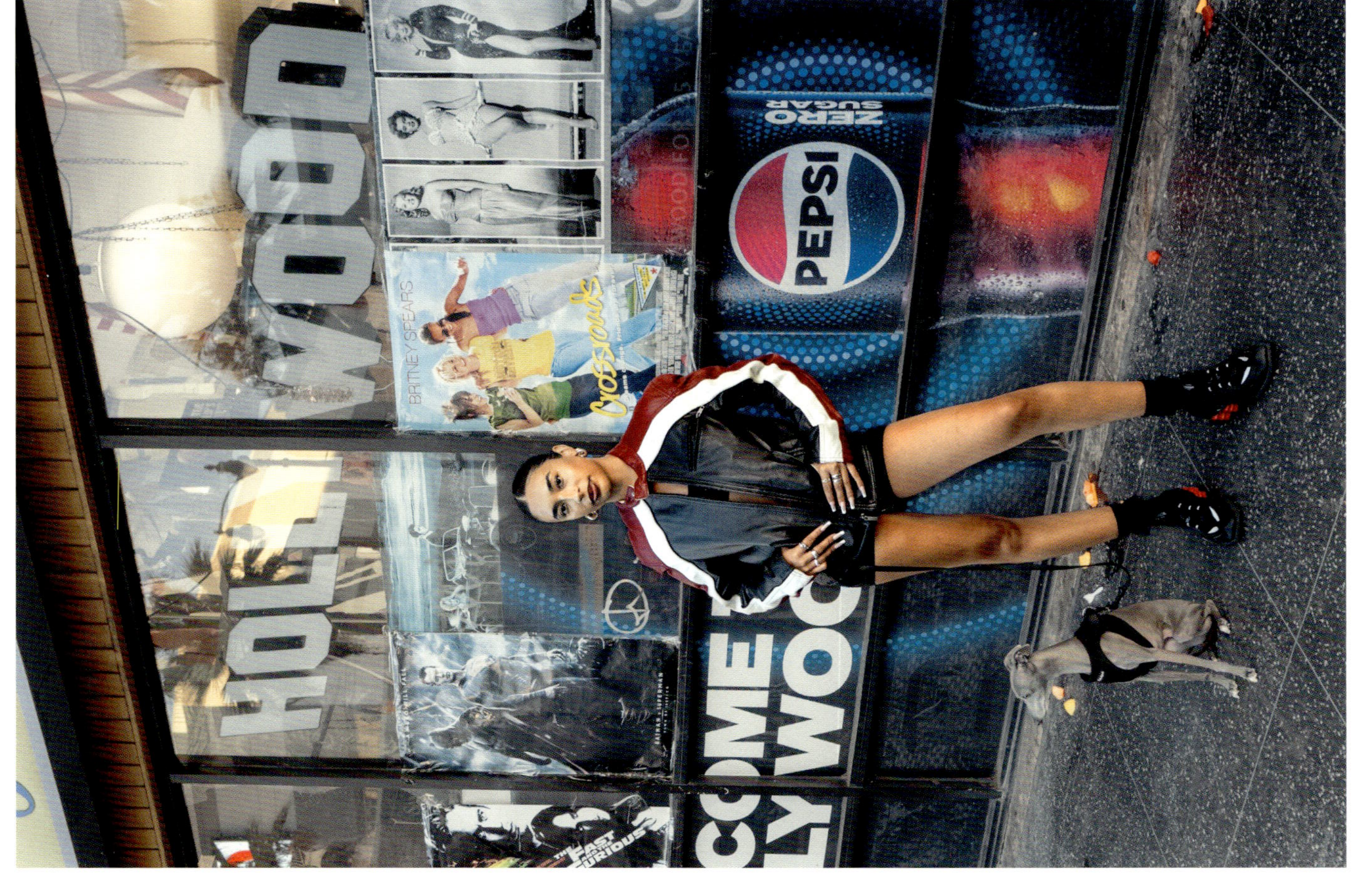
HOLL WOOD
BRITNEY SPEARS
Crossroads
COME
LY WOOD
PEPSI
ZERO SUGAR

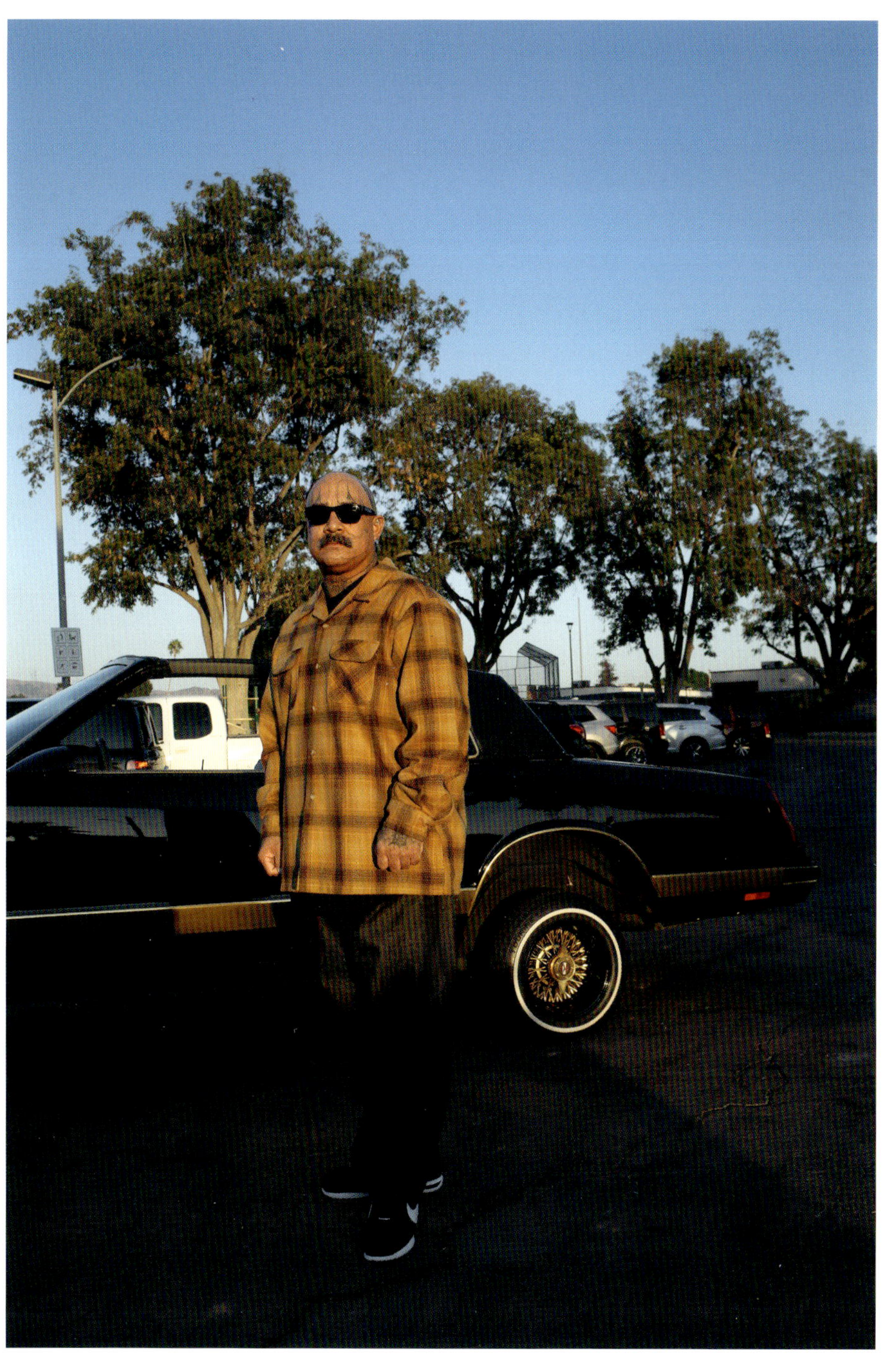

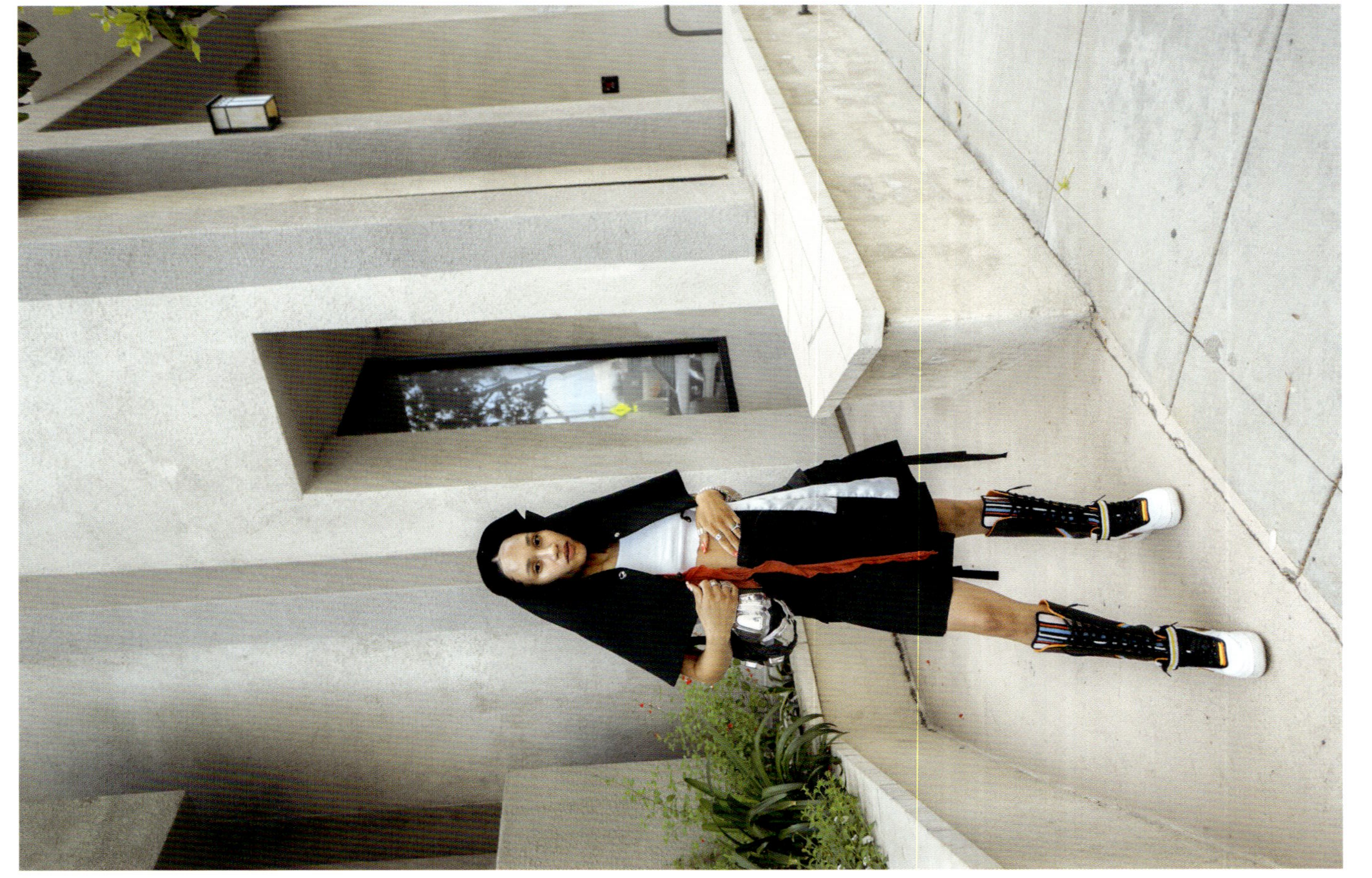

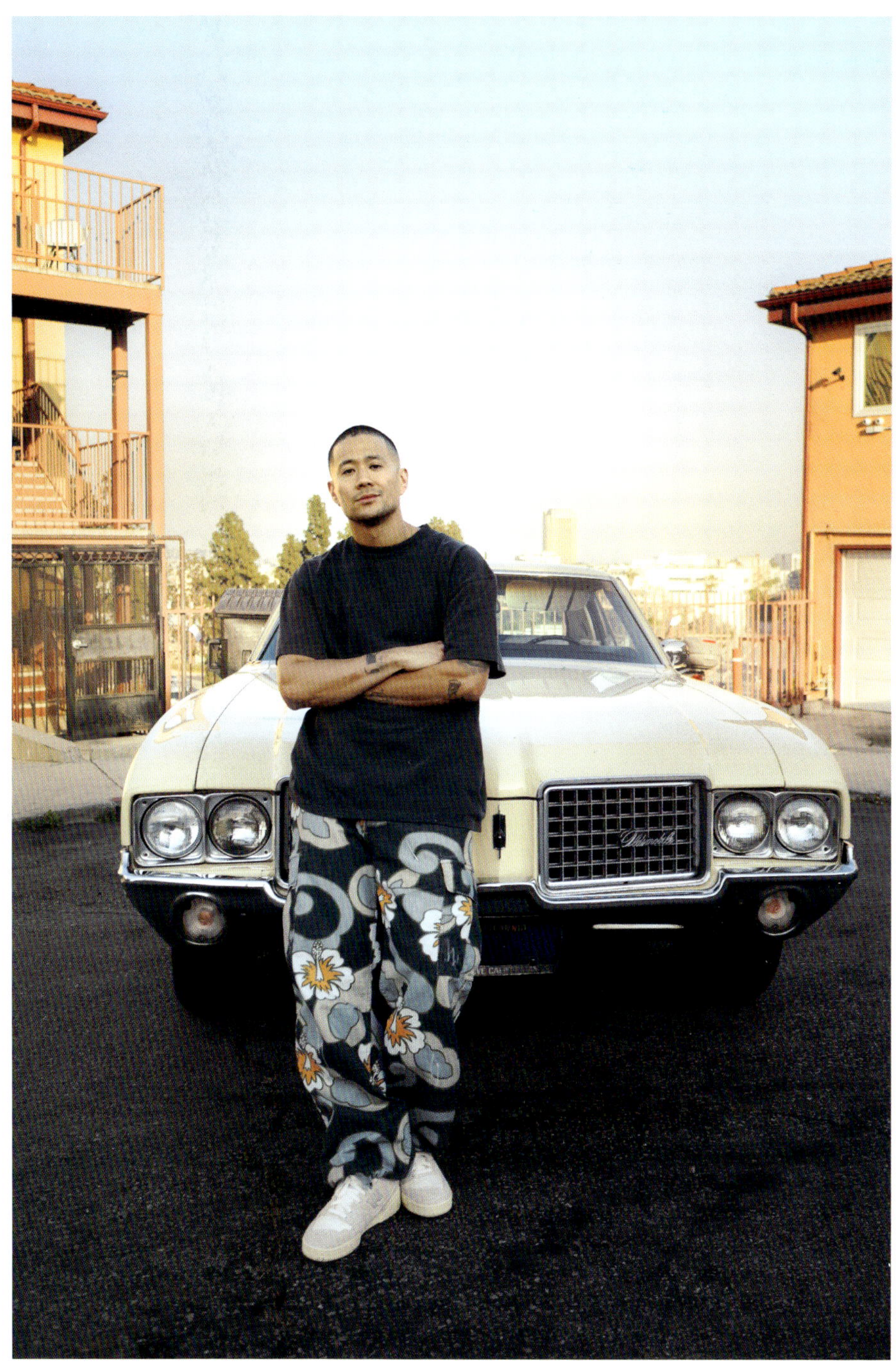

DJ / Producer Donavan's Yard

Echo Park

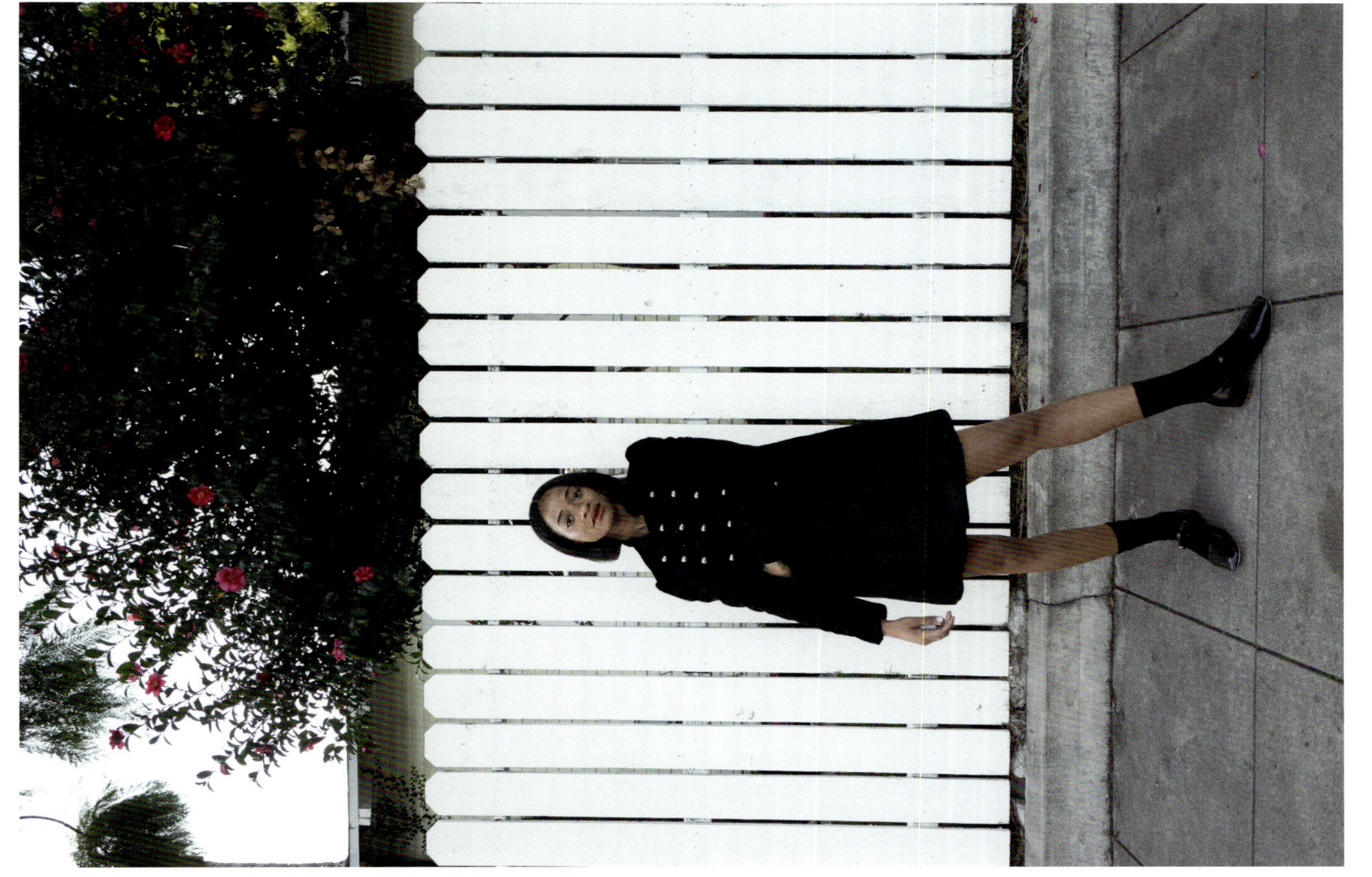

Creative

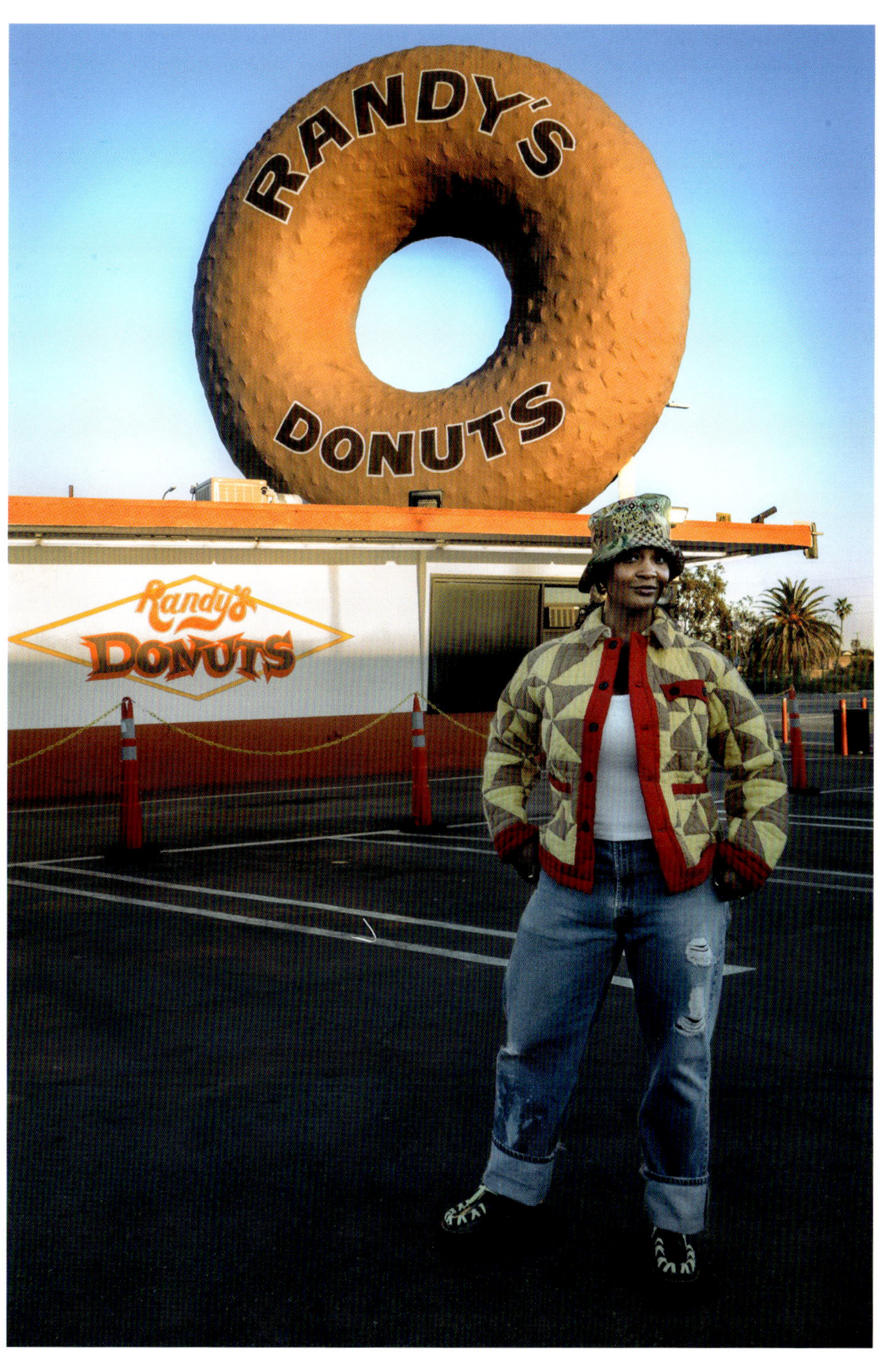

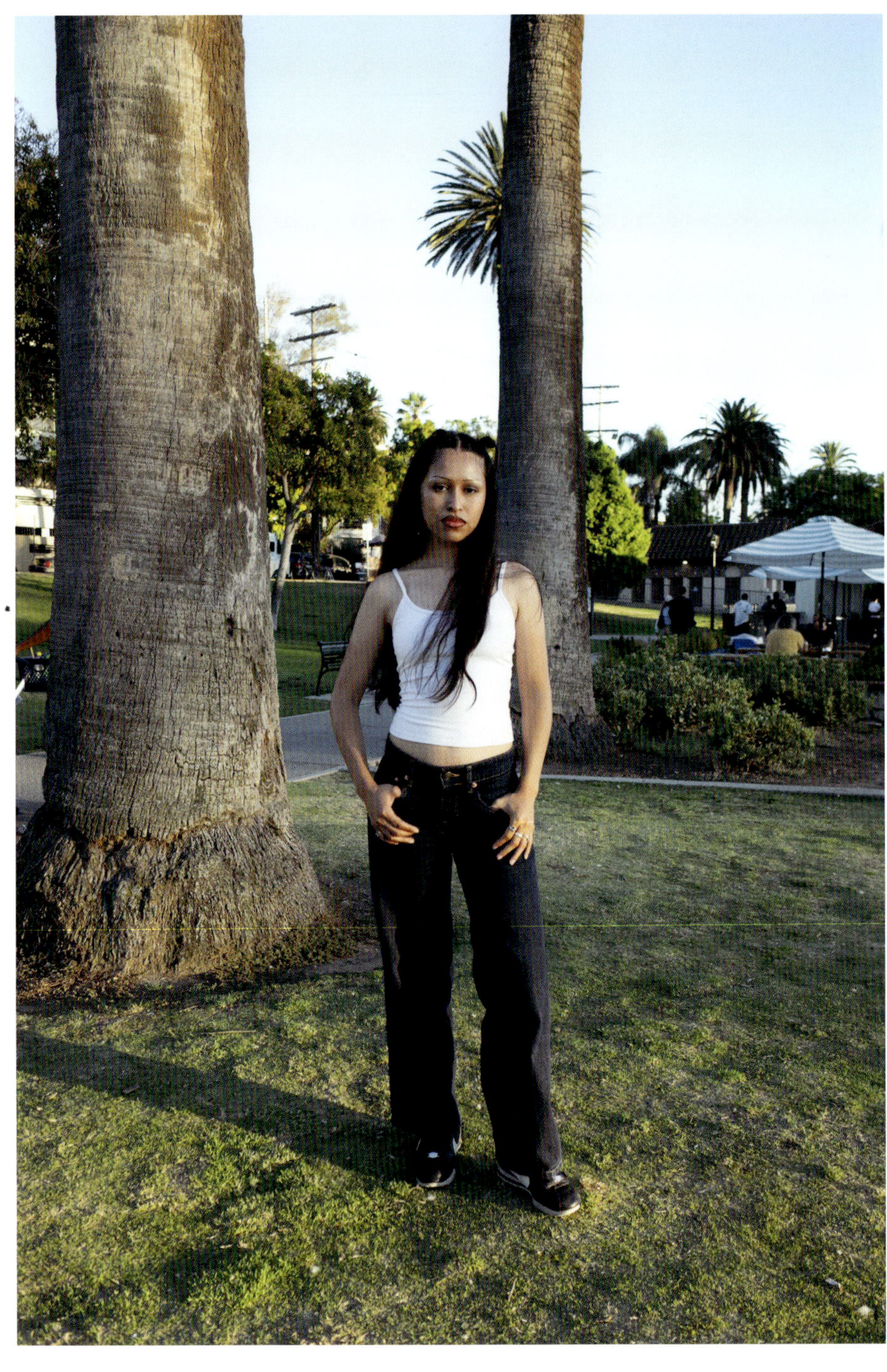

Artist / Curator / Owner Tlaloc Studios

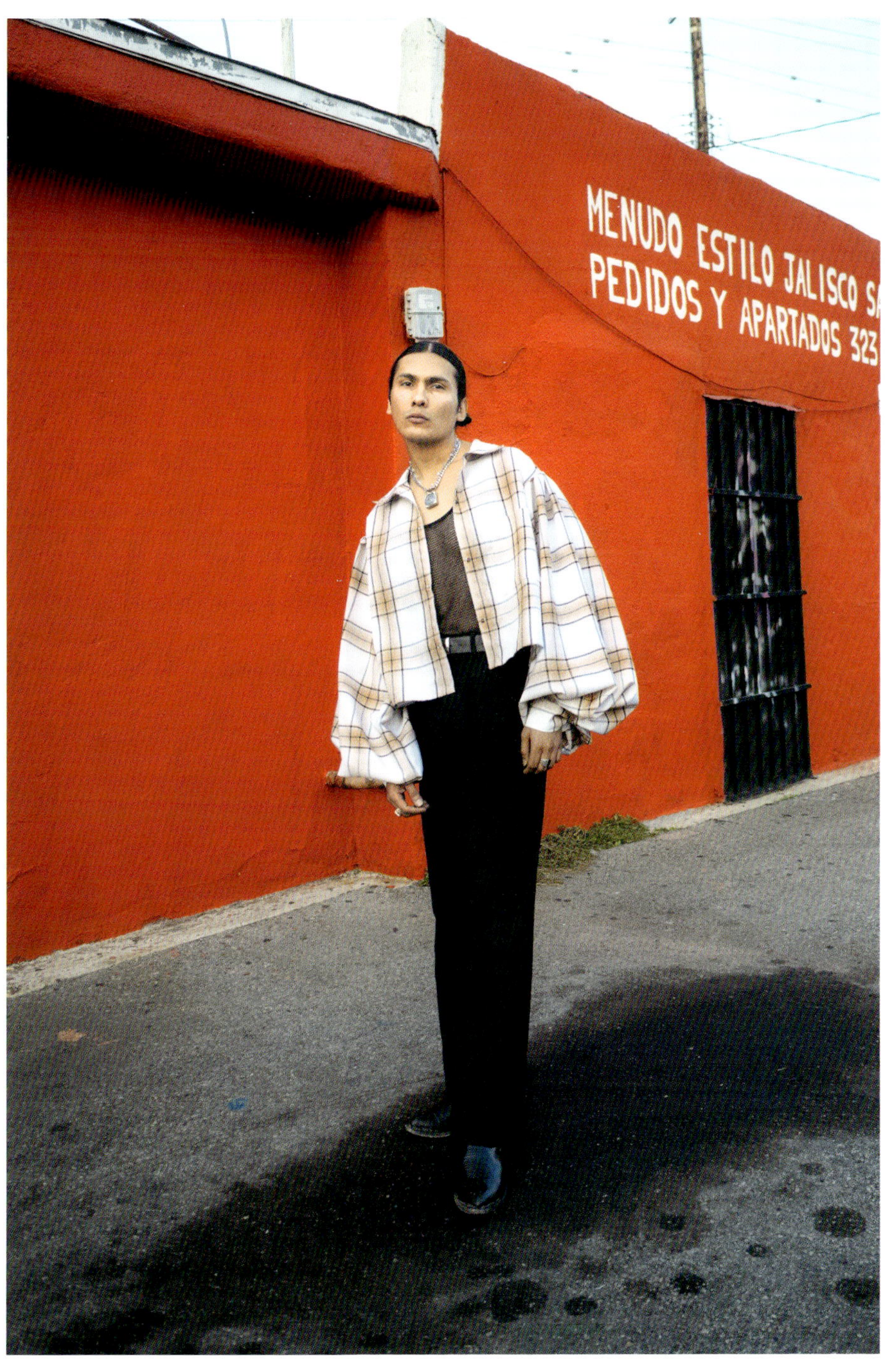

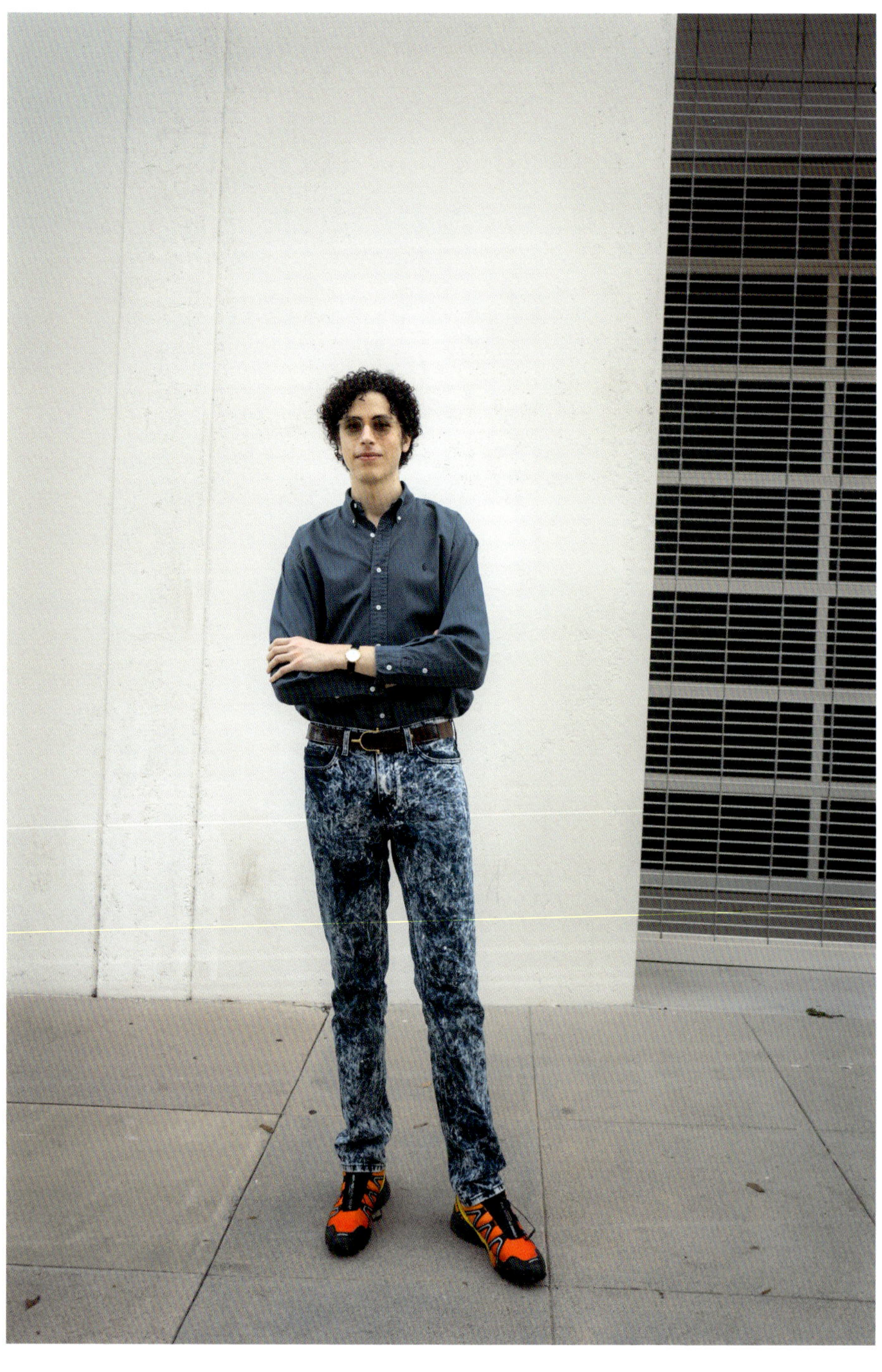

Gallery Associate Jeffrey Deitch

West LA

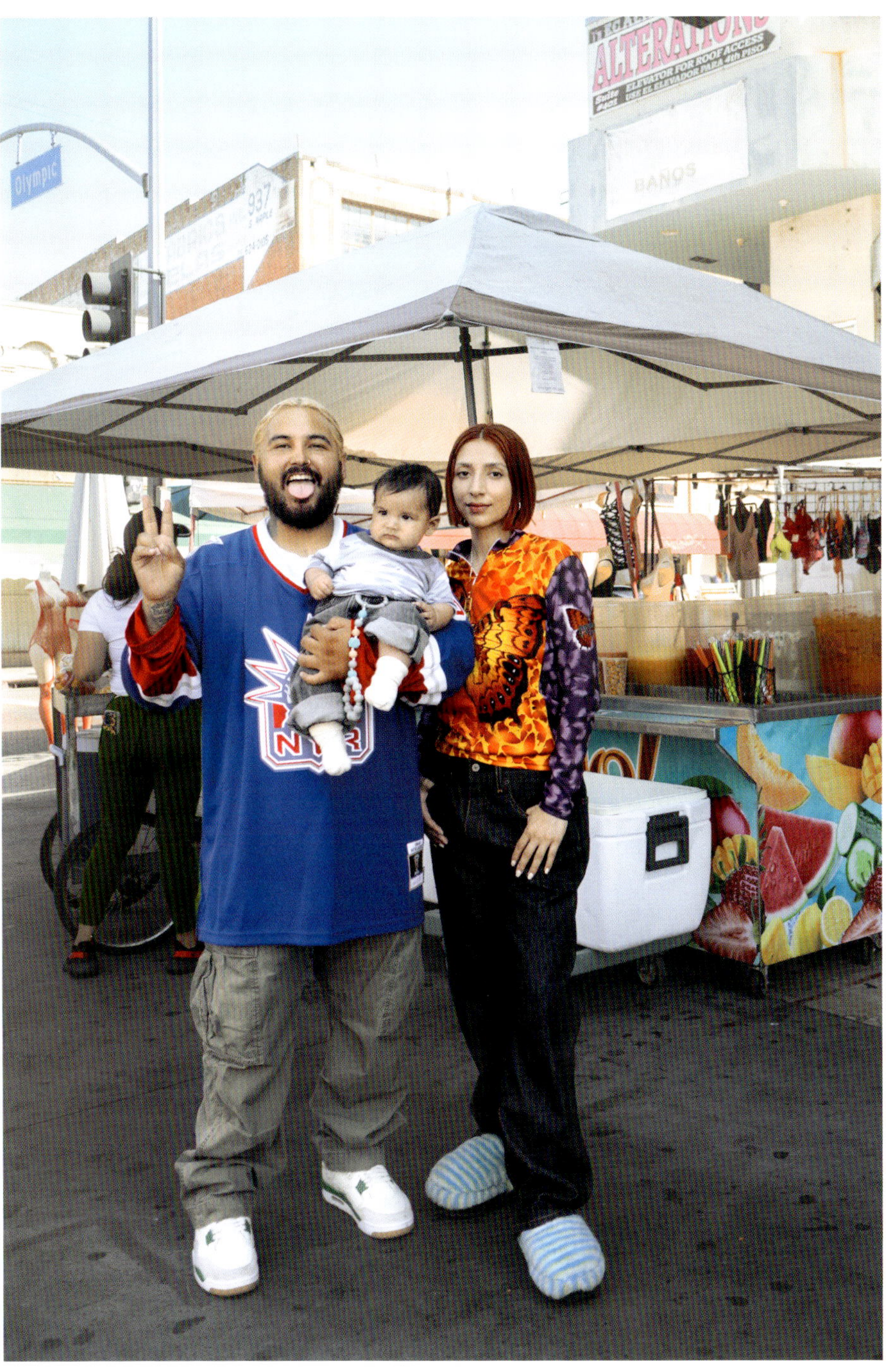
Olympic
ALTERATIONS
BAÑOS

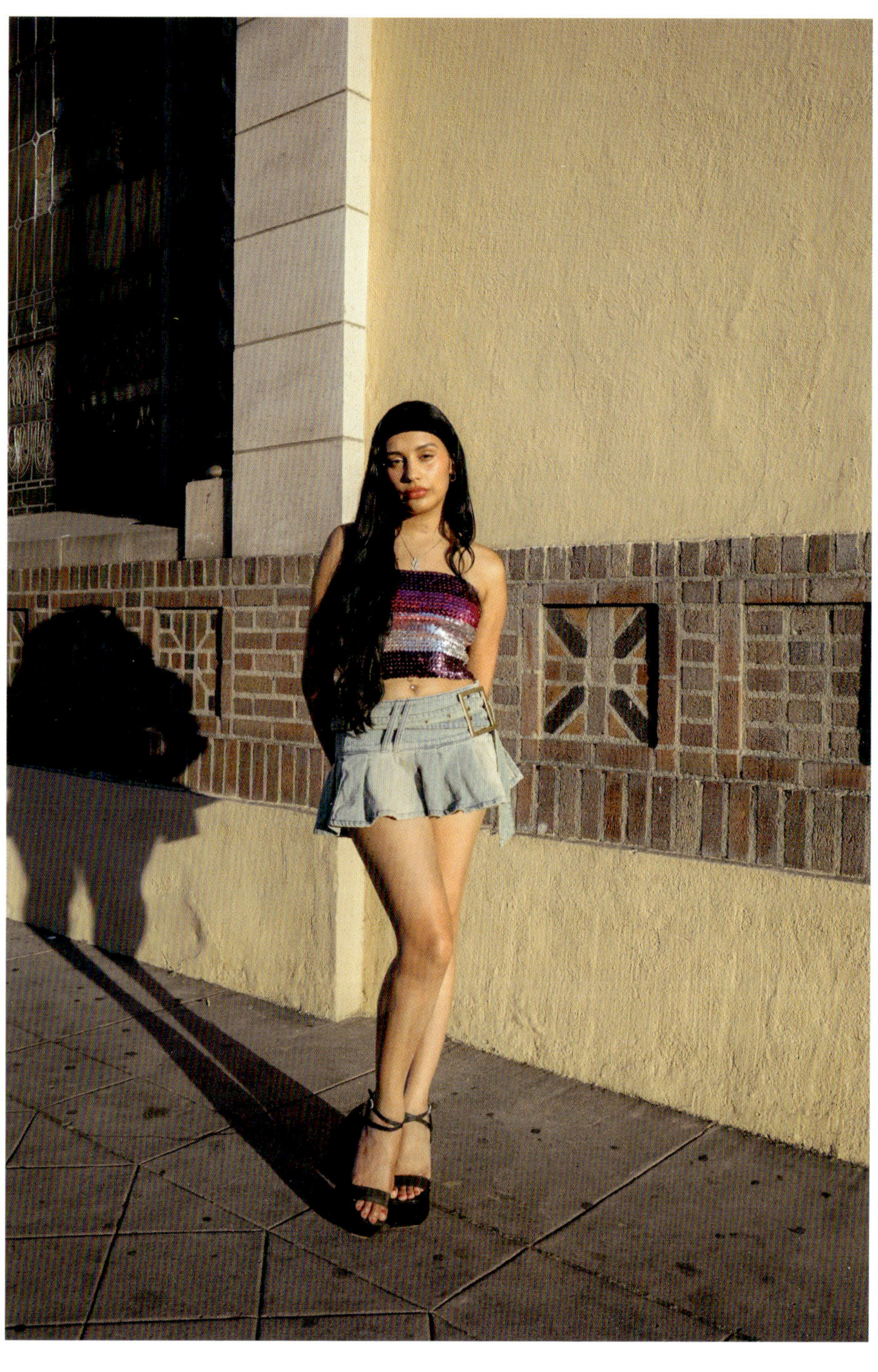

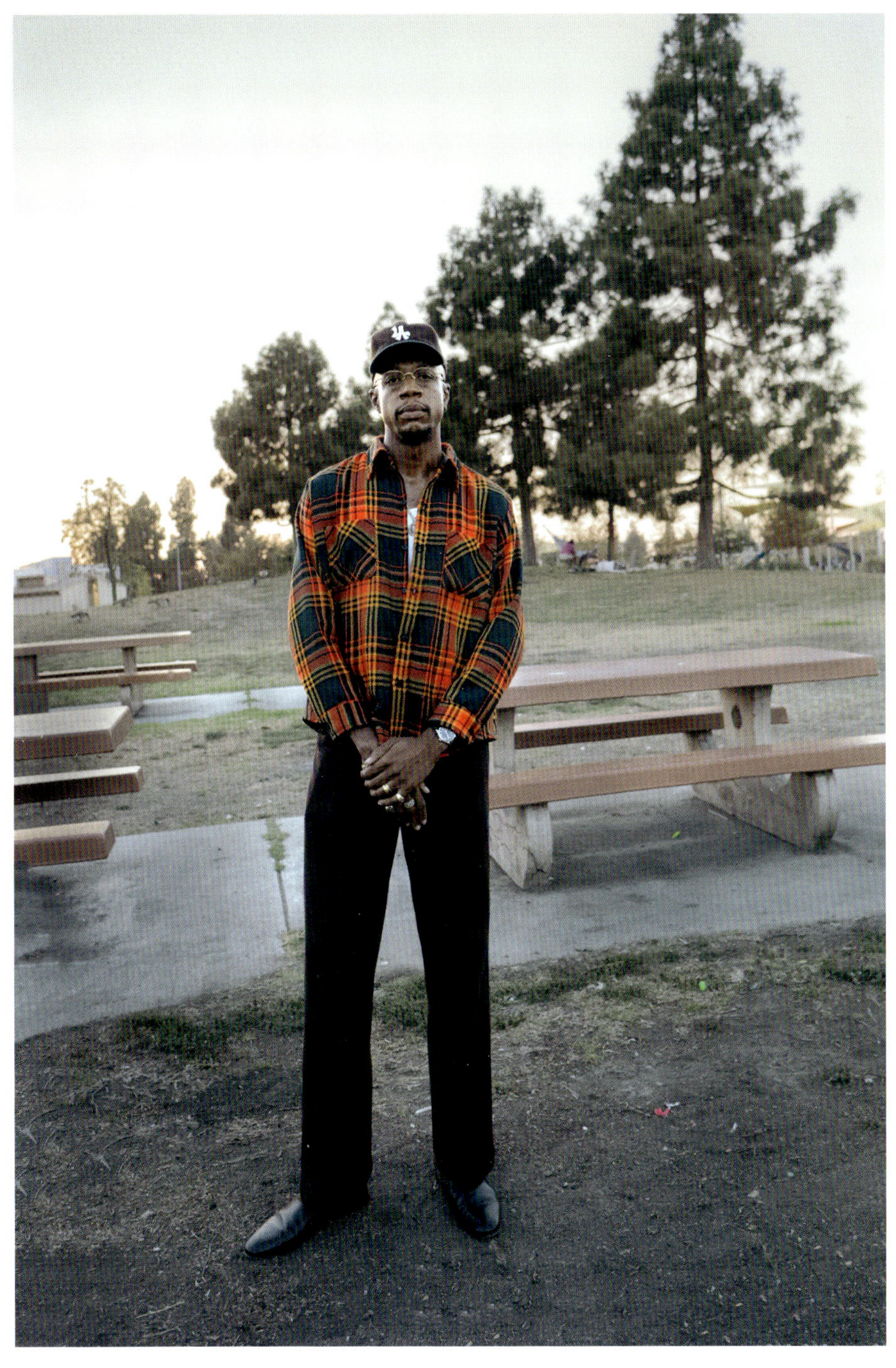

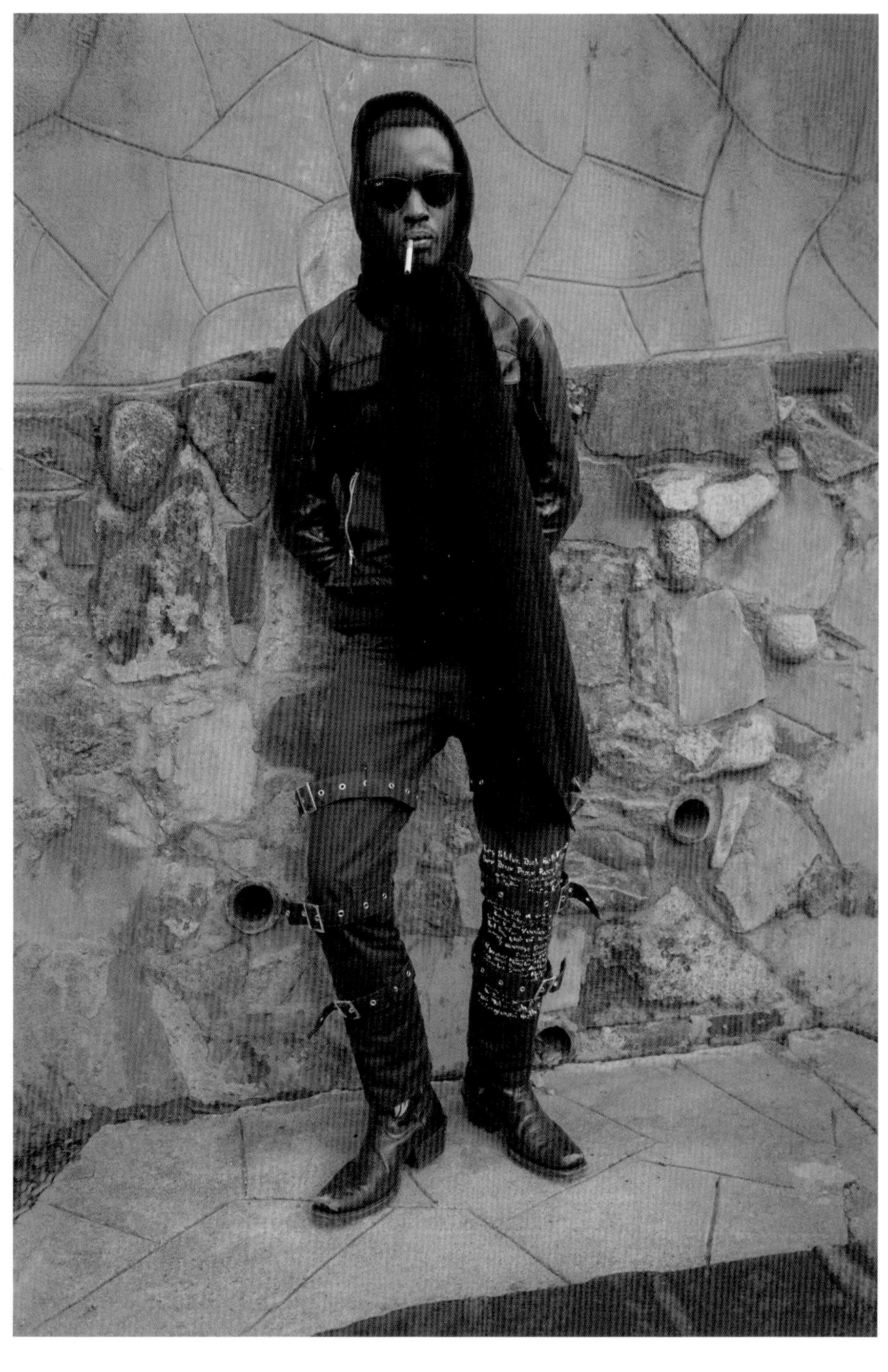

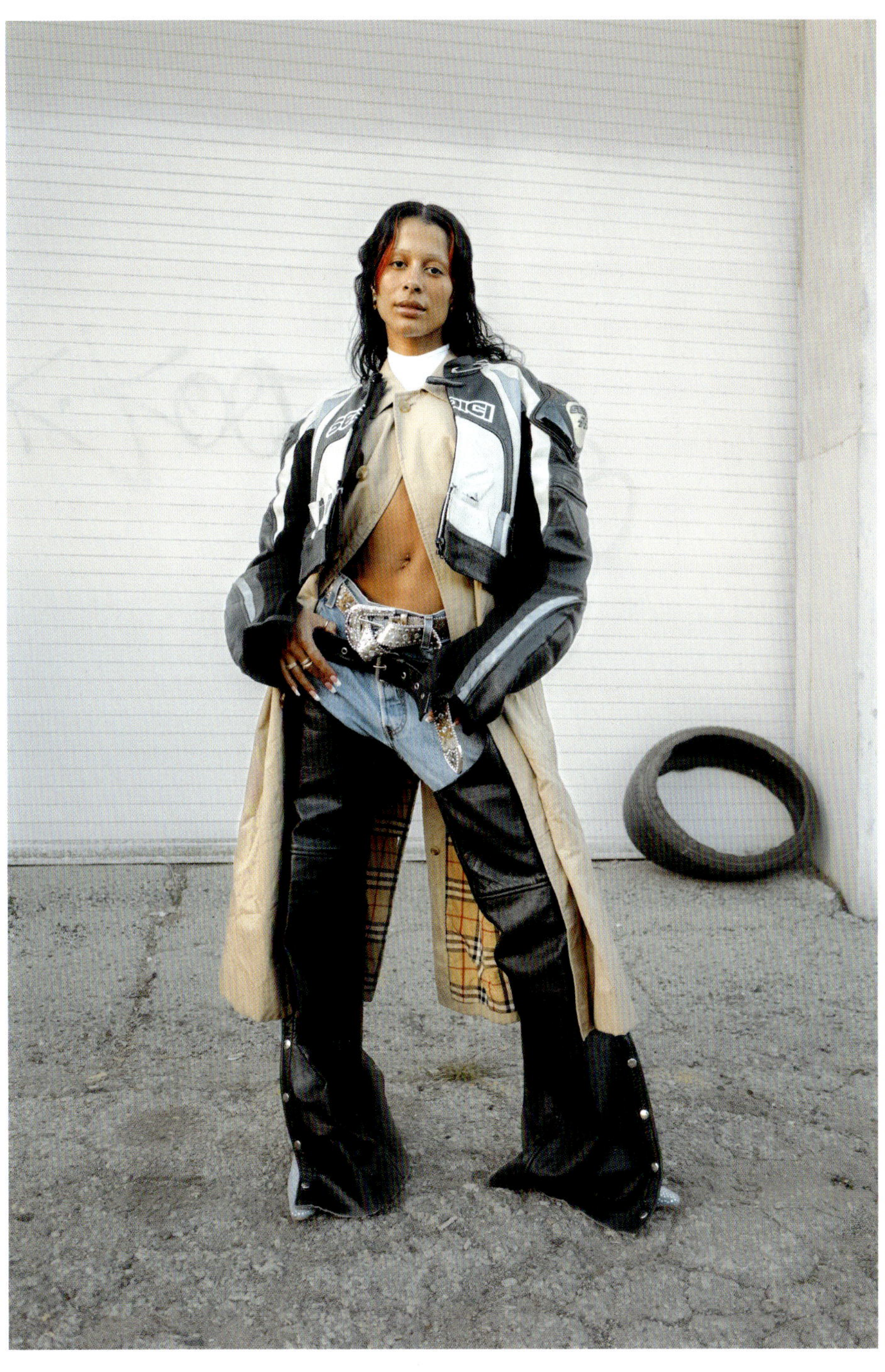

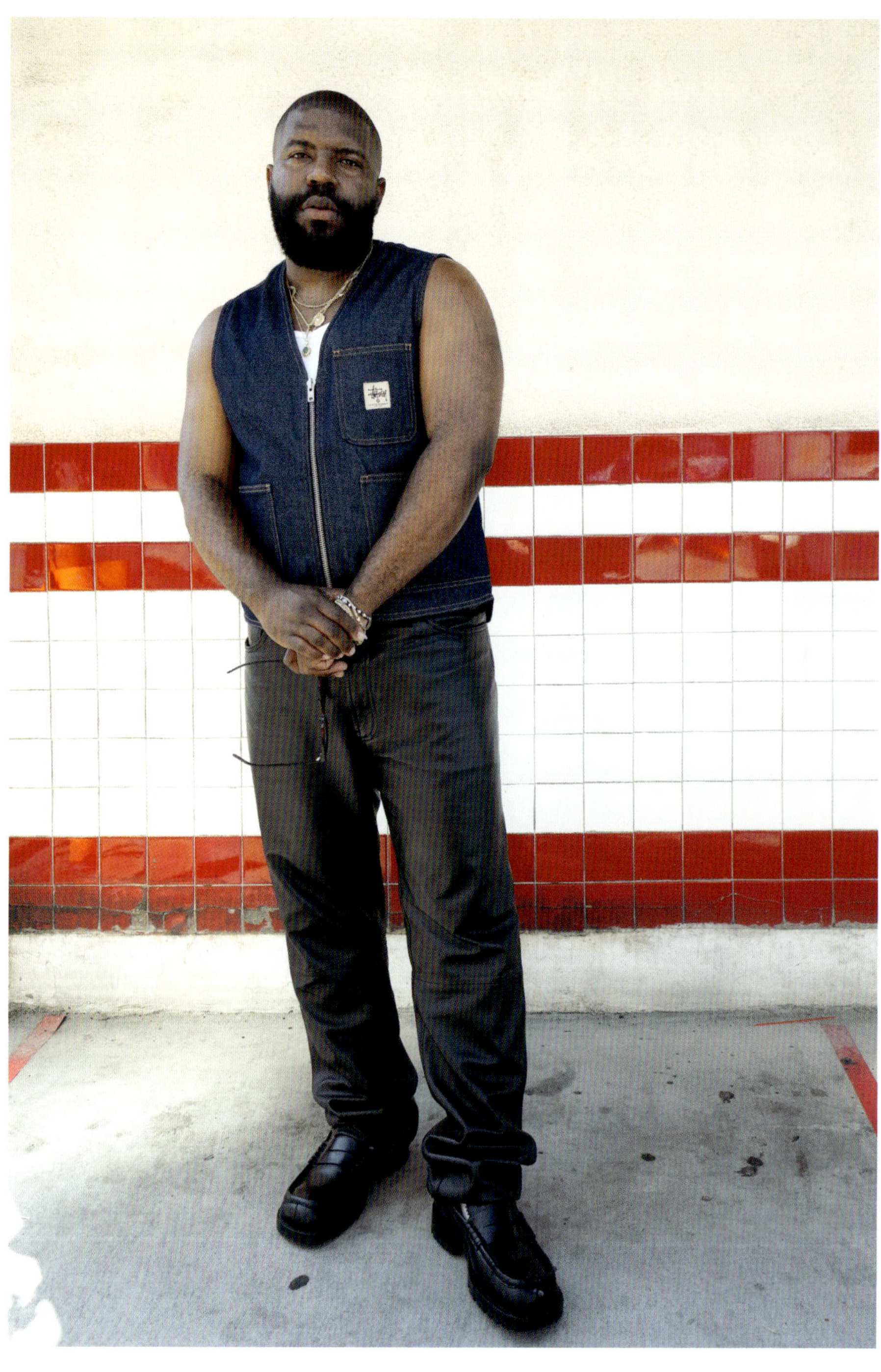

Marquise Miller
Stylist / Owner of MILLERSROOM
Hawthorne CA

Style Icon

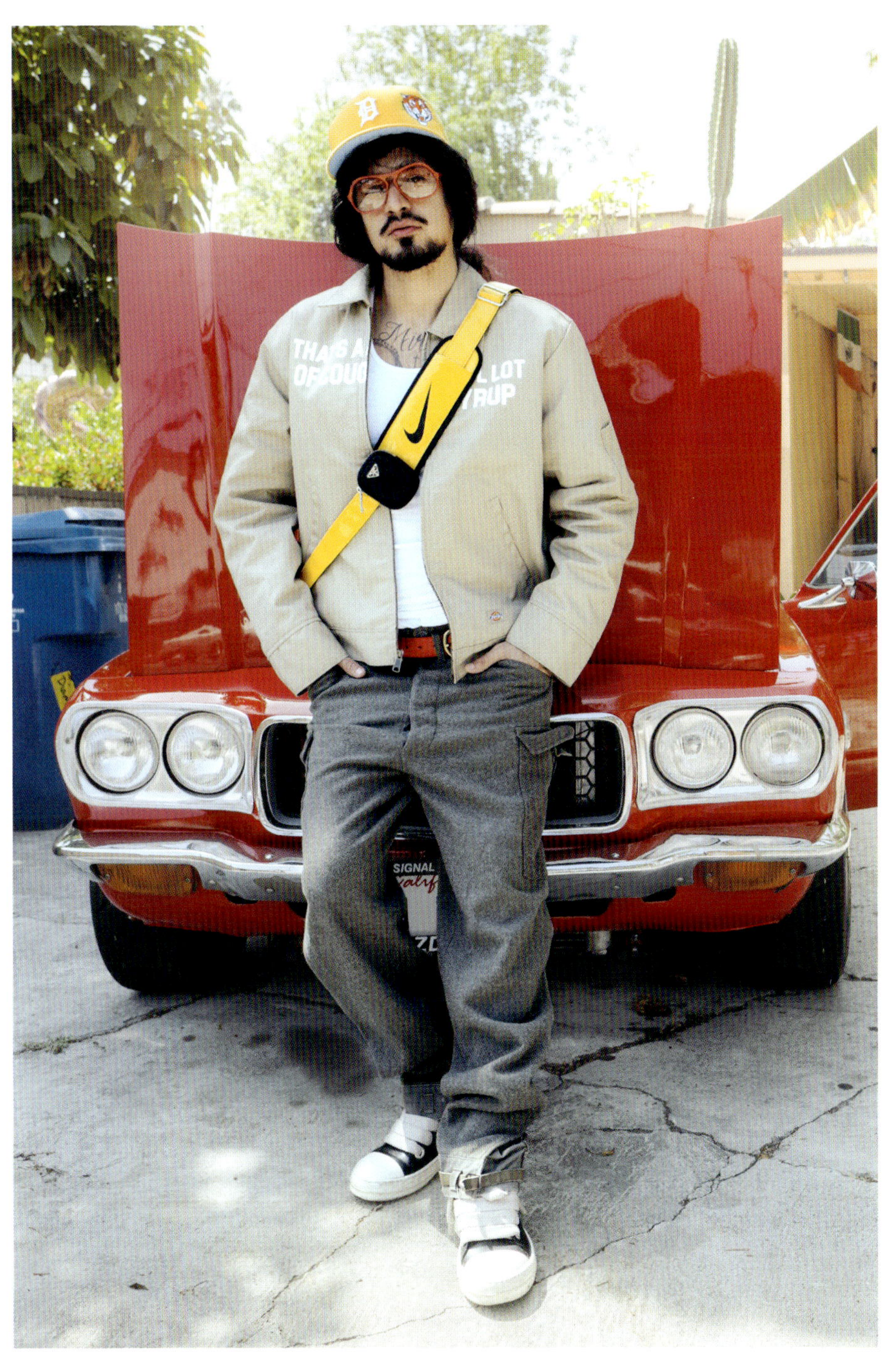

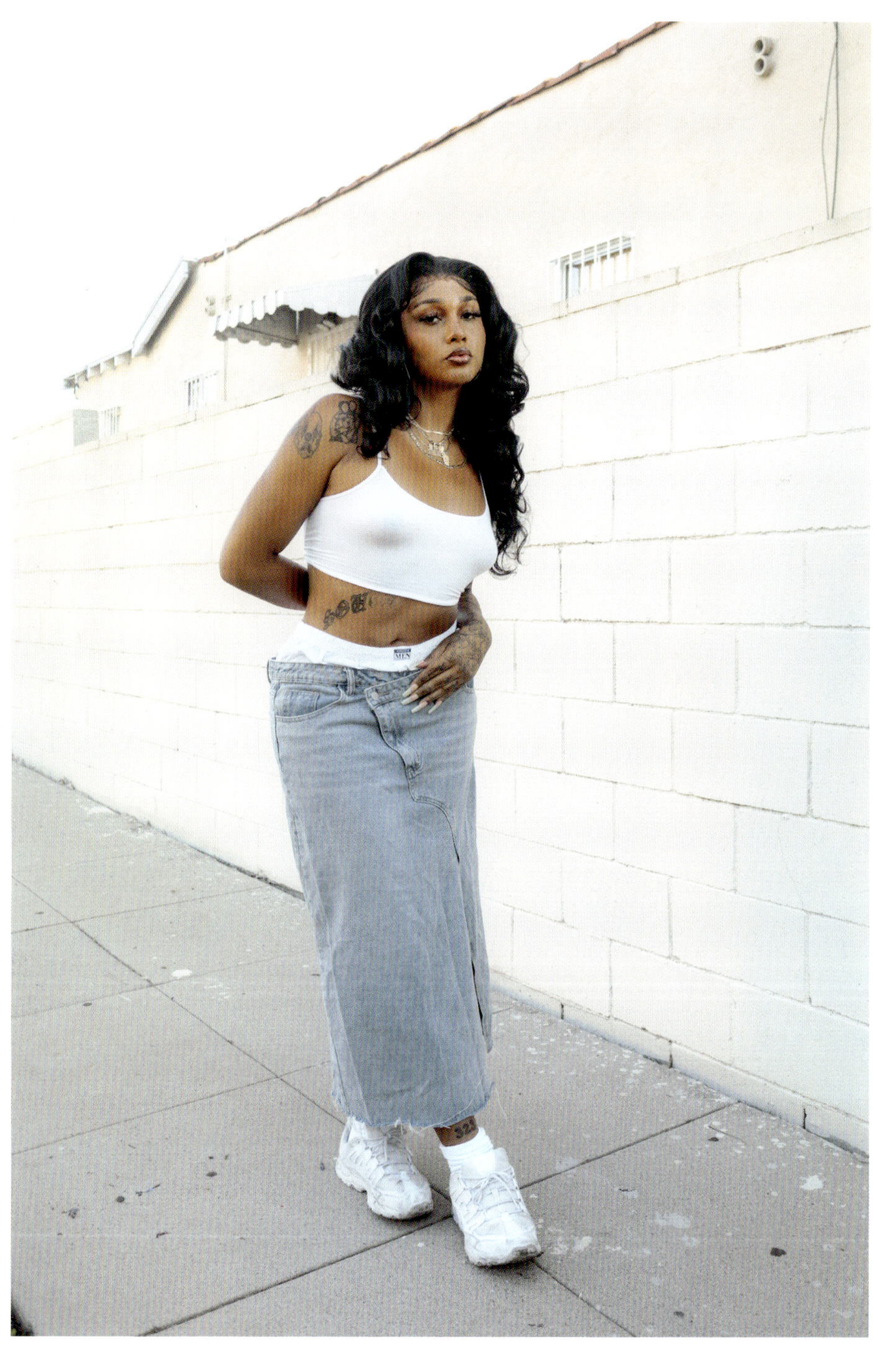

Activist / Model

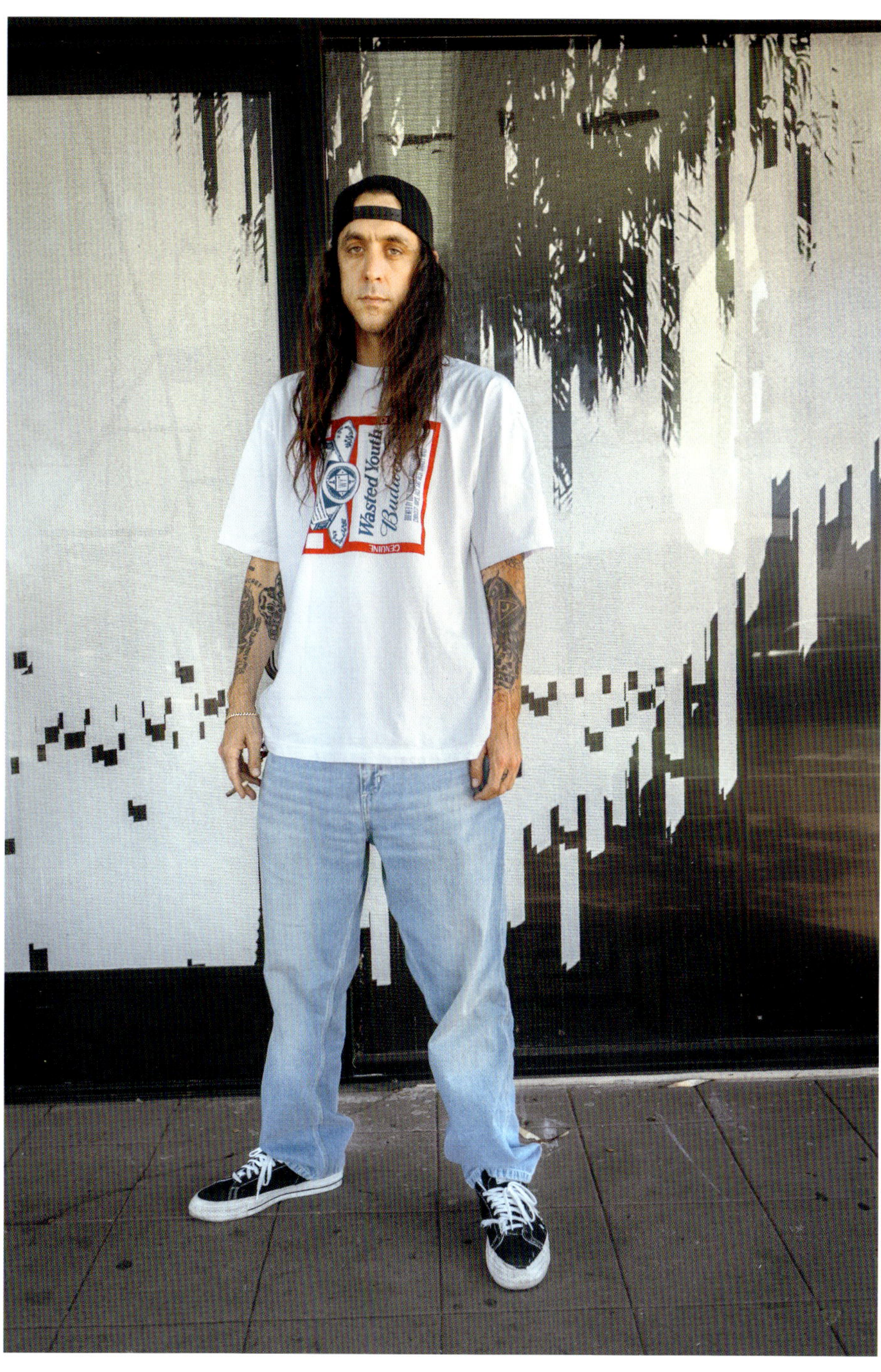

Trash Talk / Co-Founder Babylon Skate

Hollywood

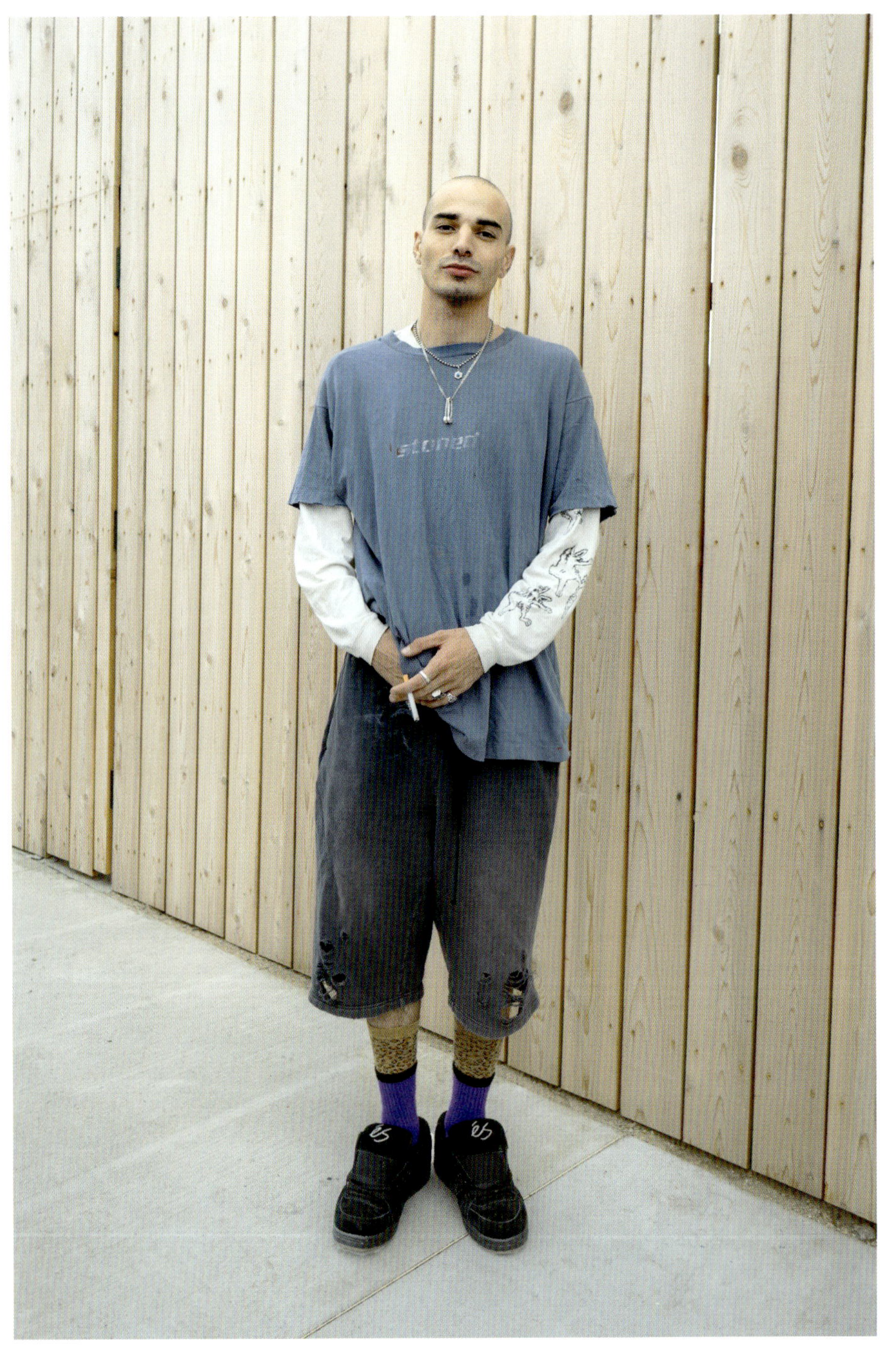

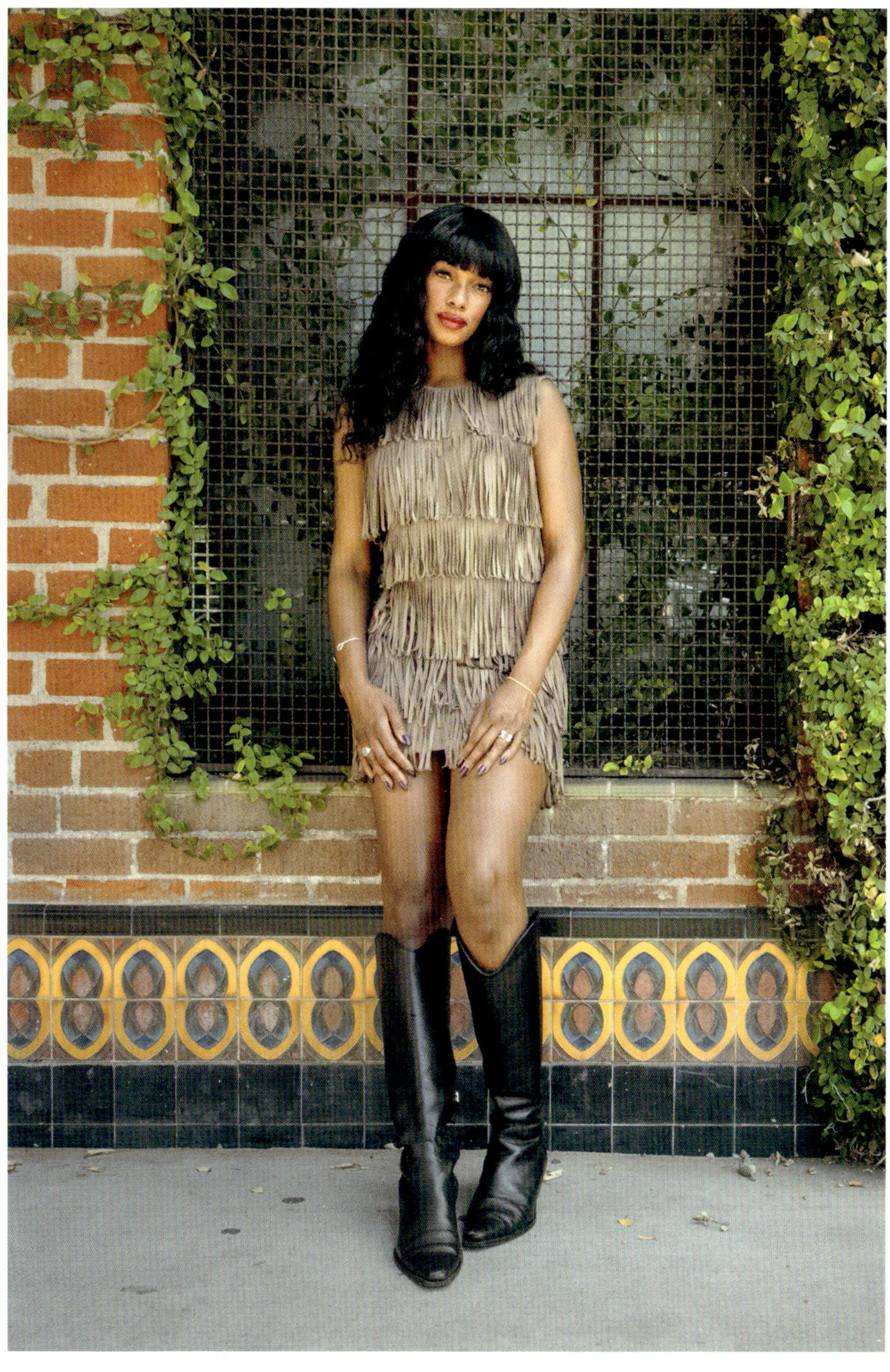

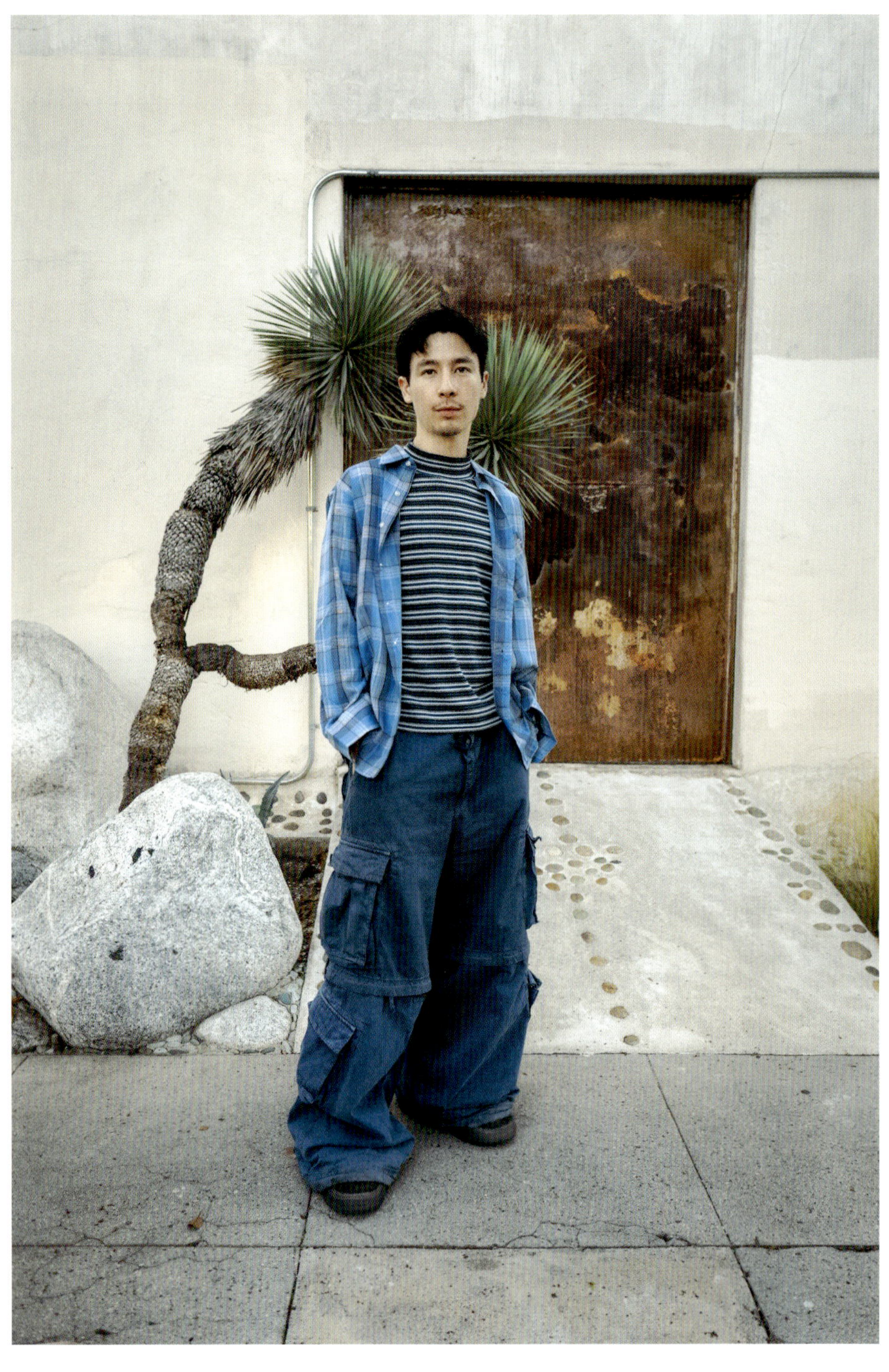

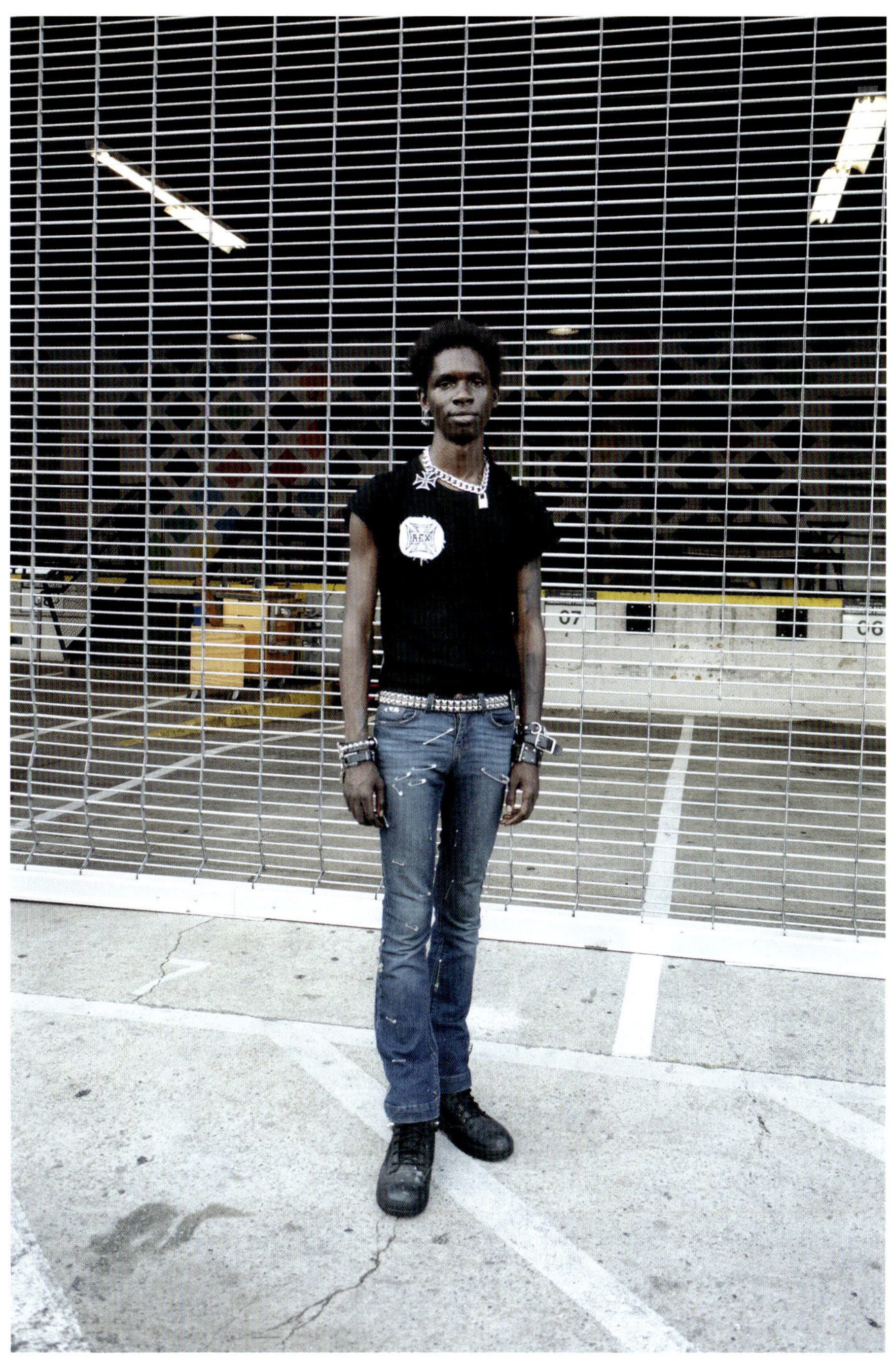

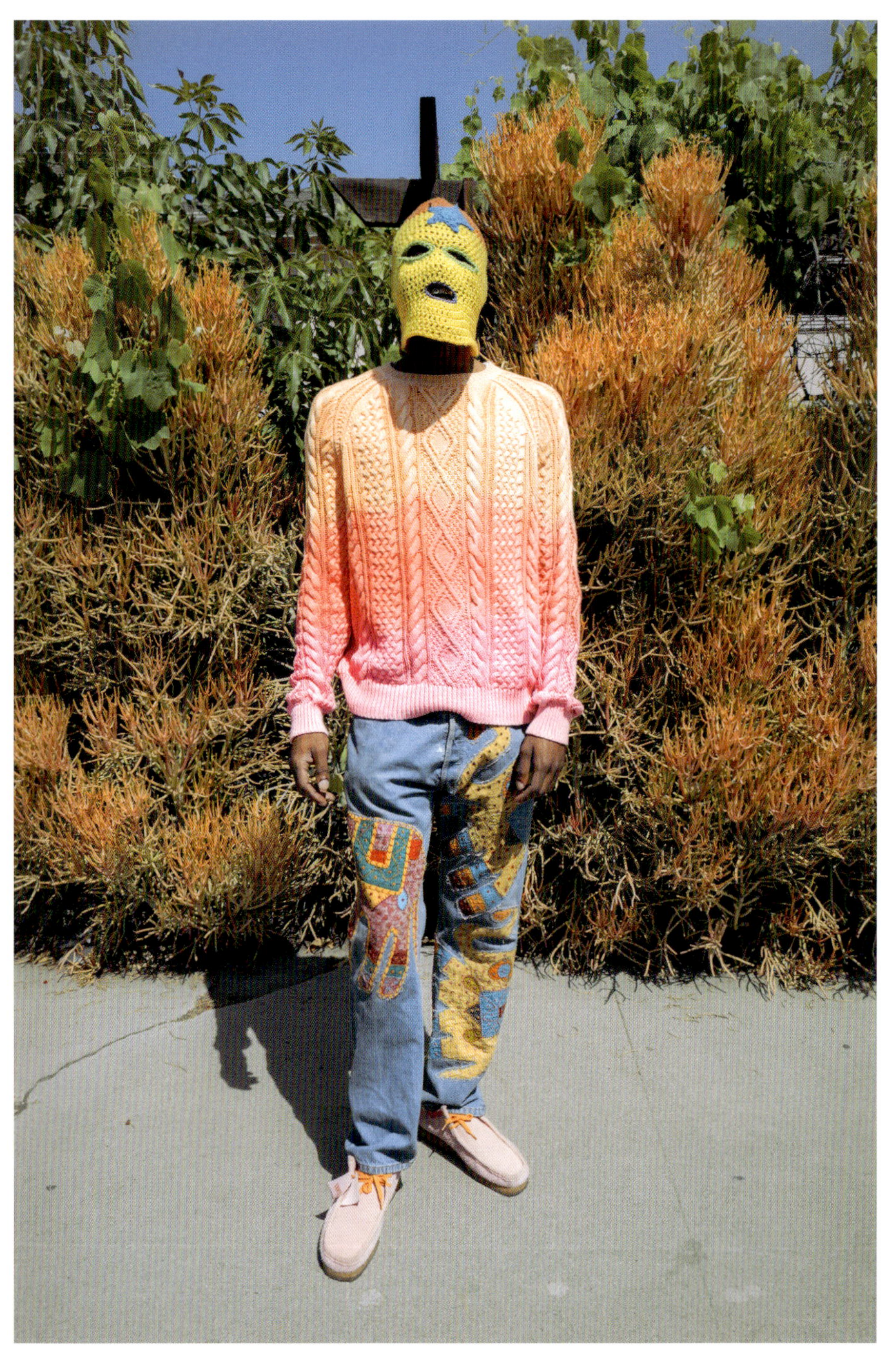

Music Producer

Mid City

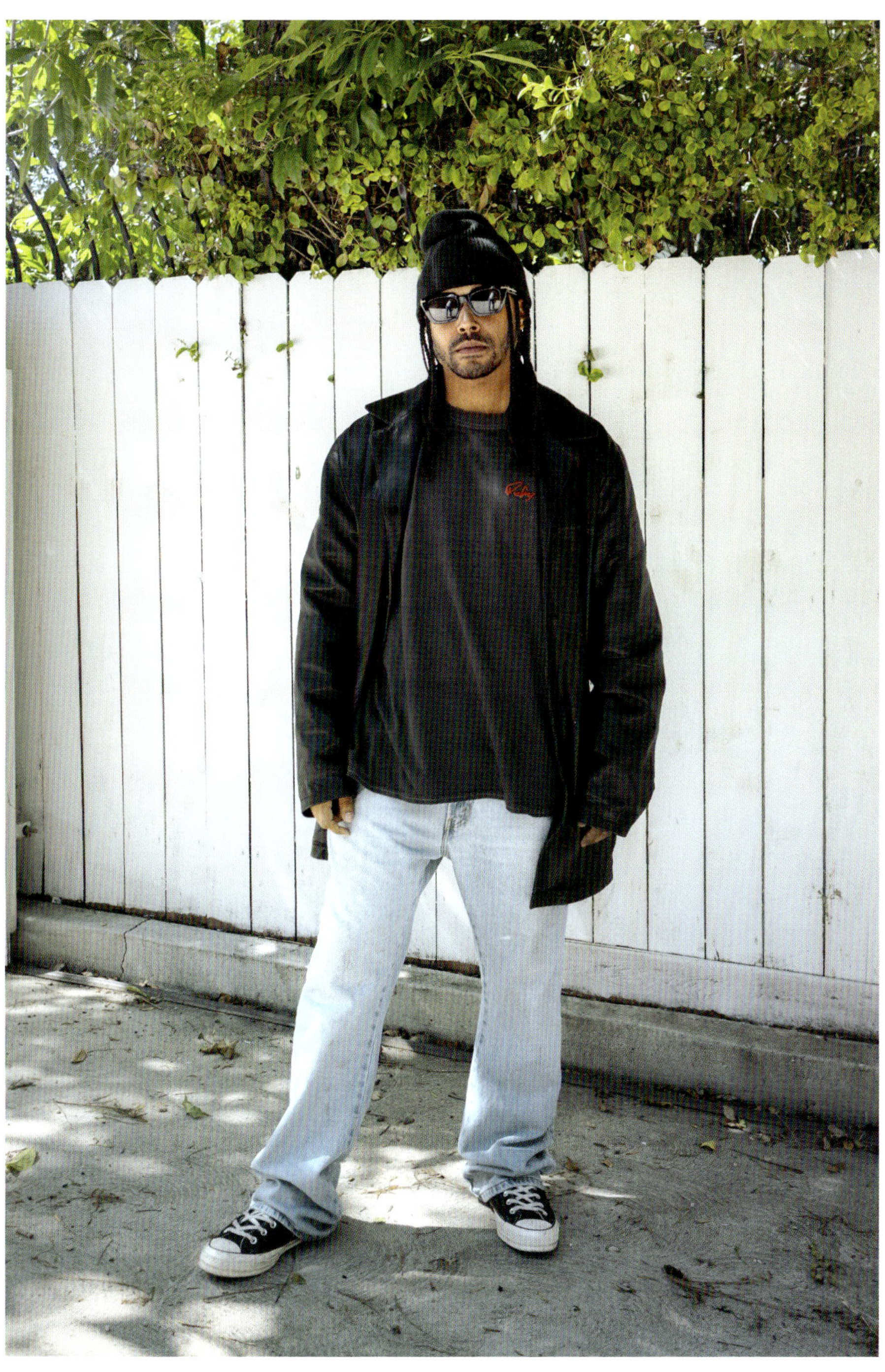

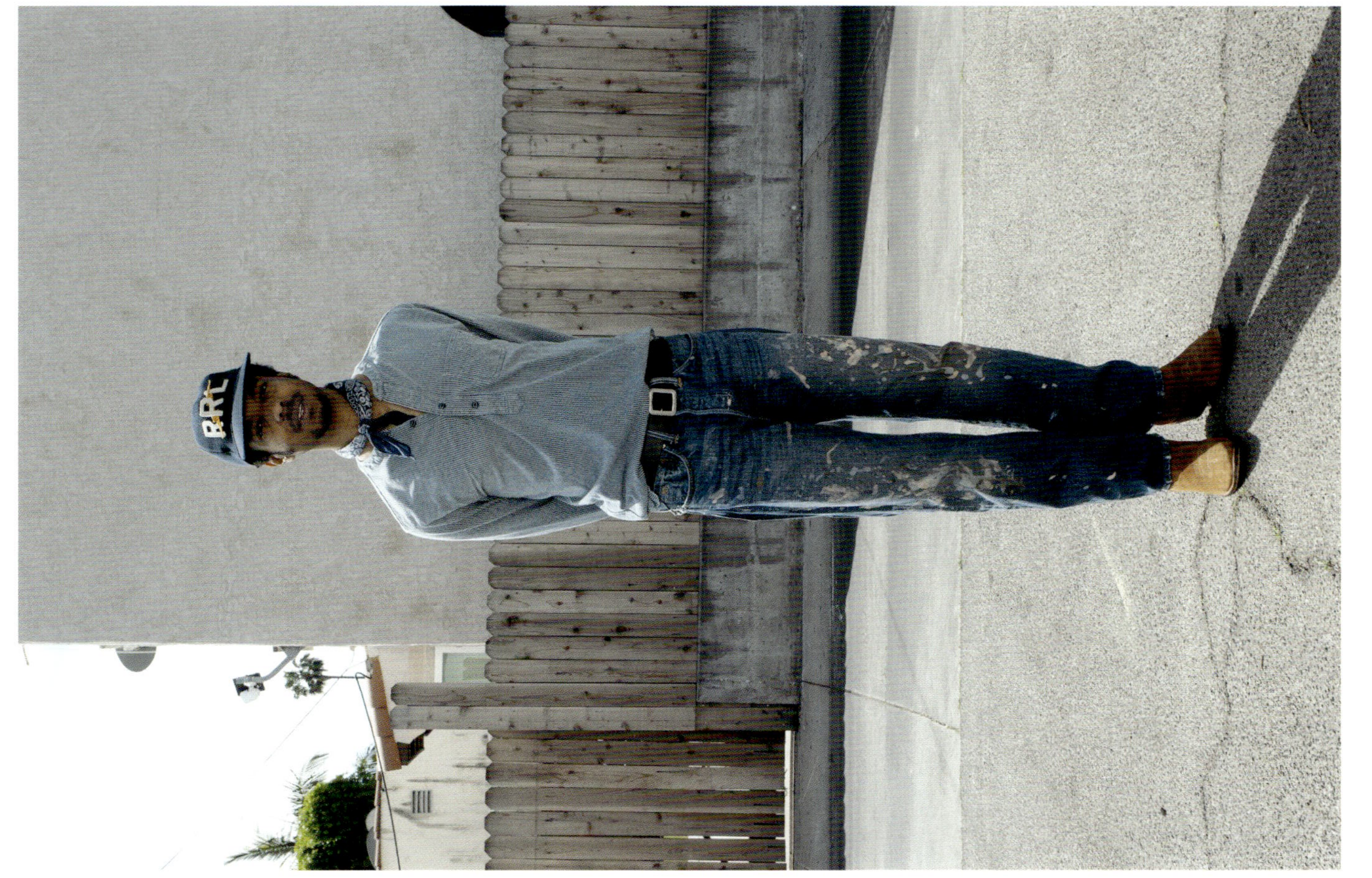

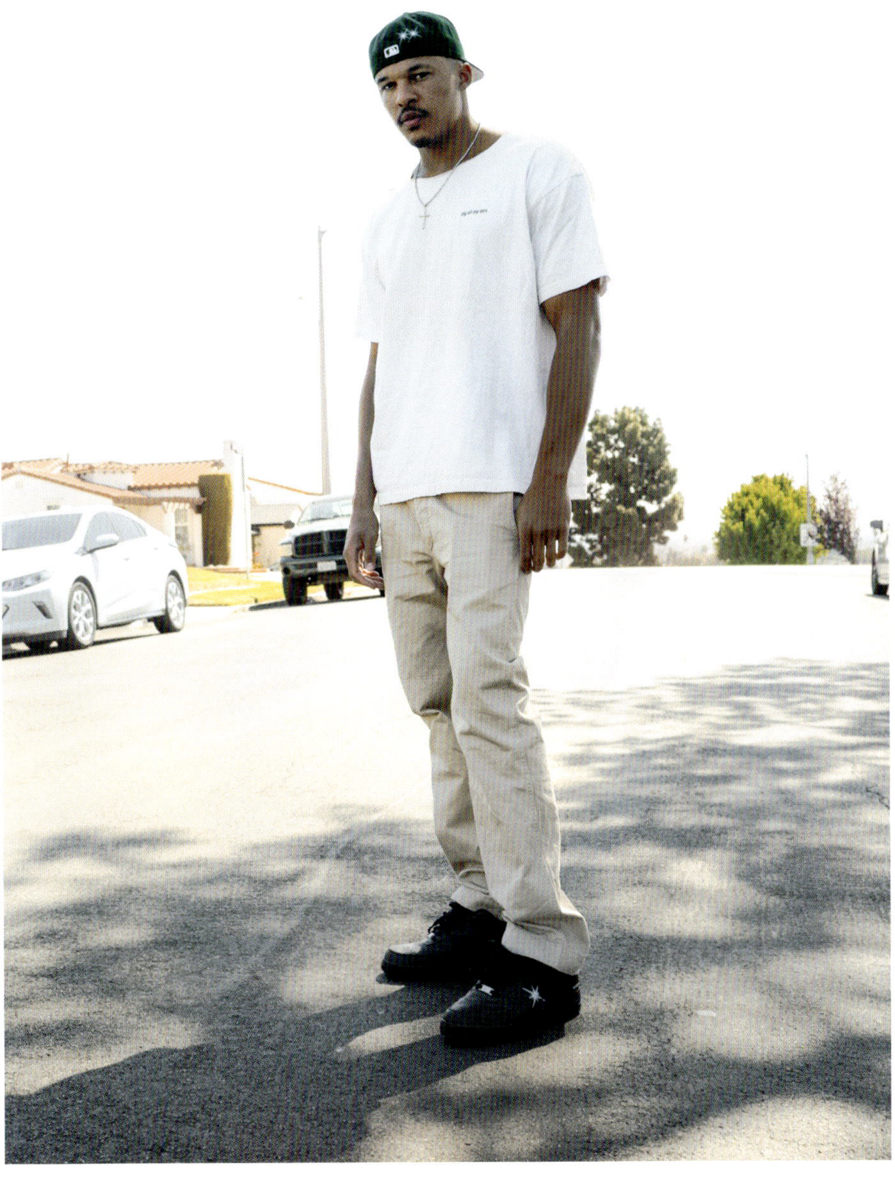

Model

Inglewood

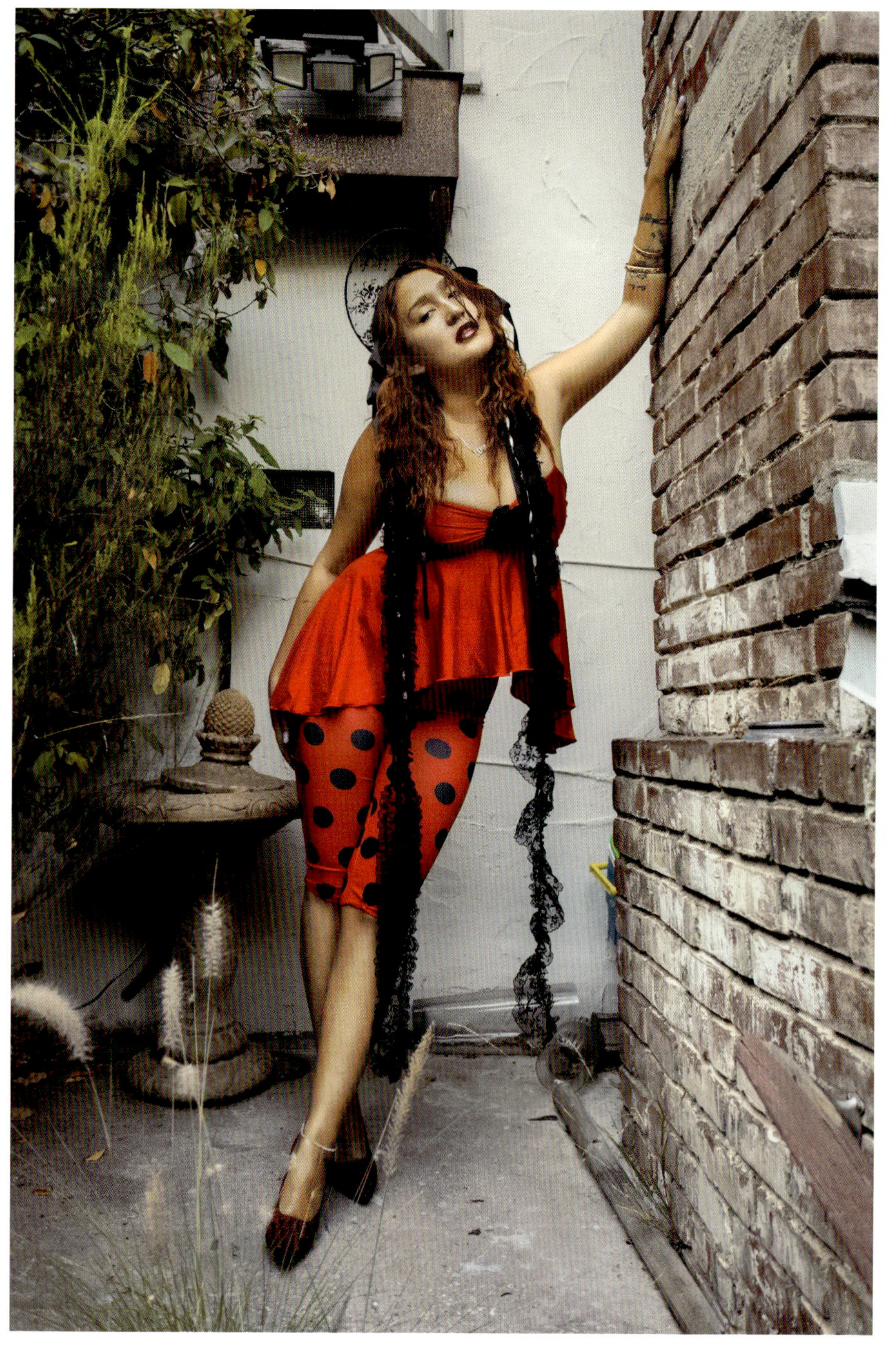

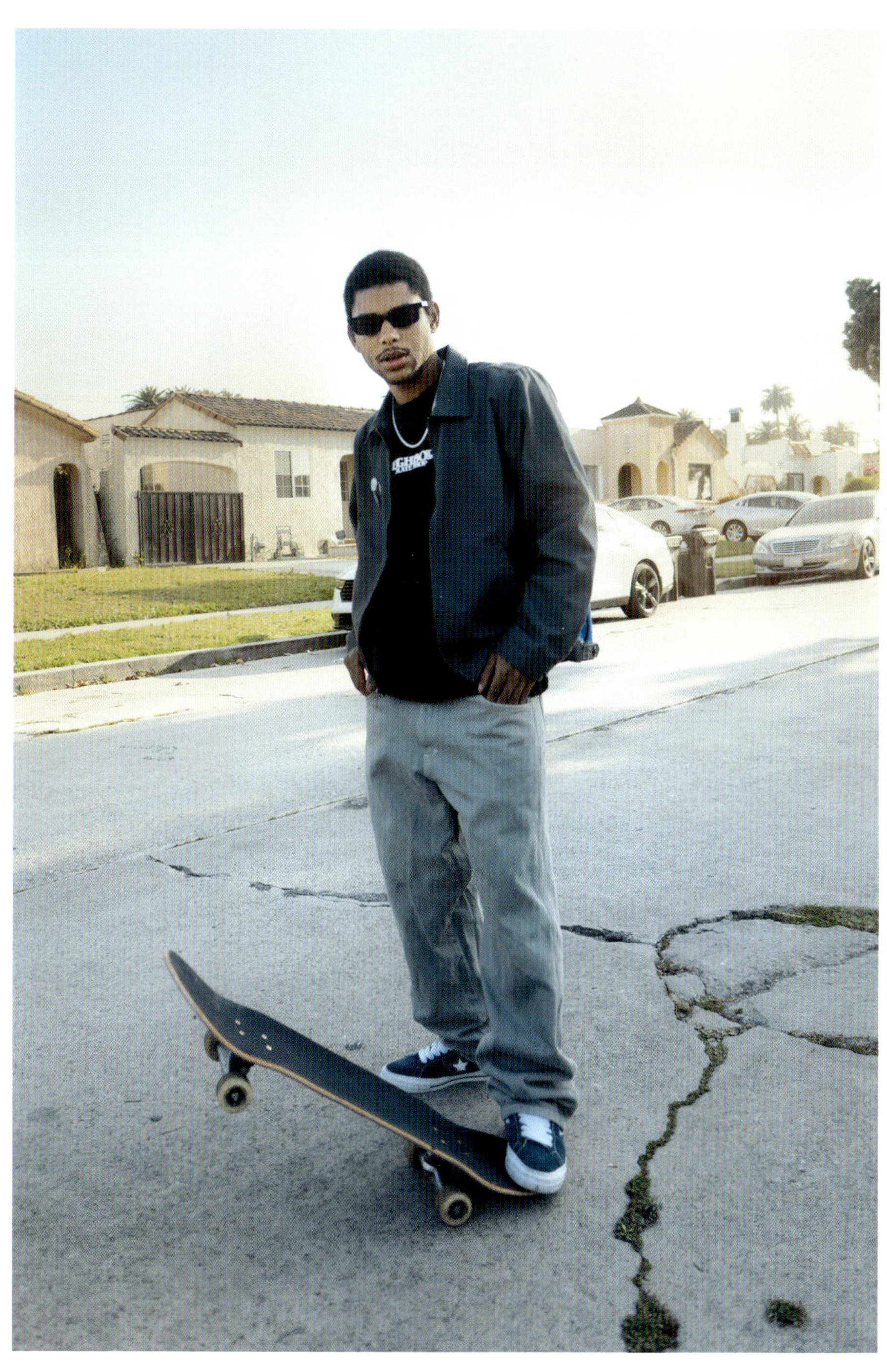

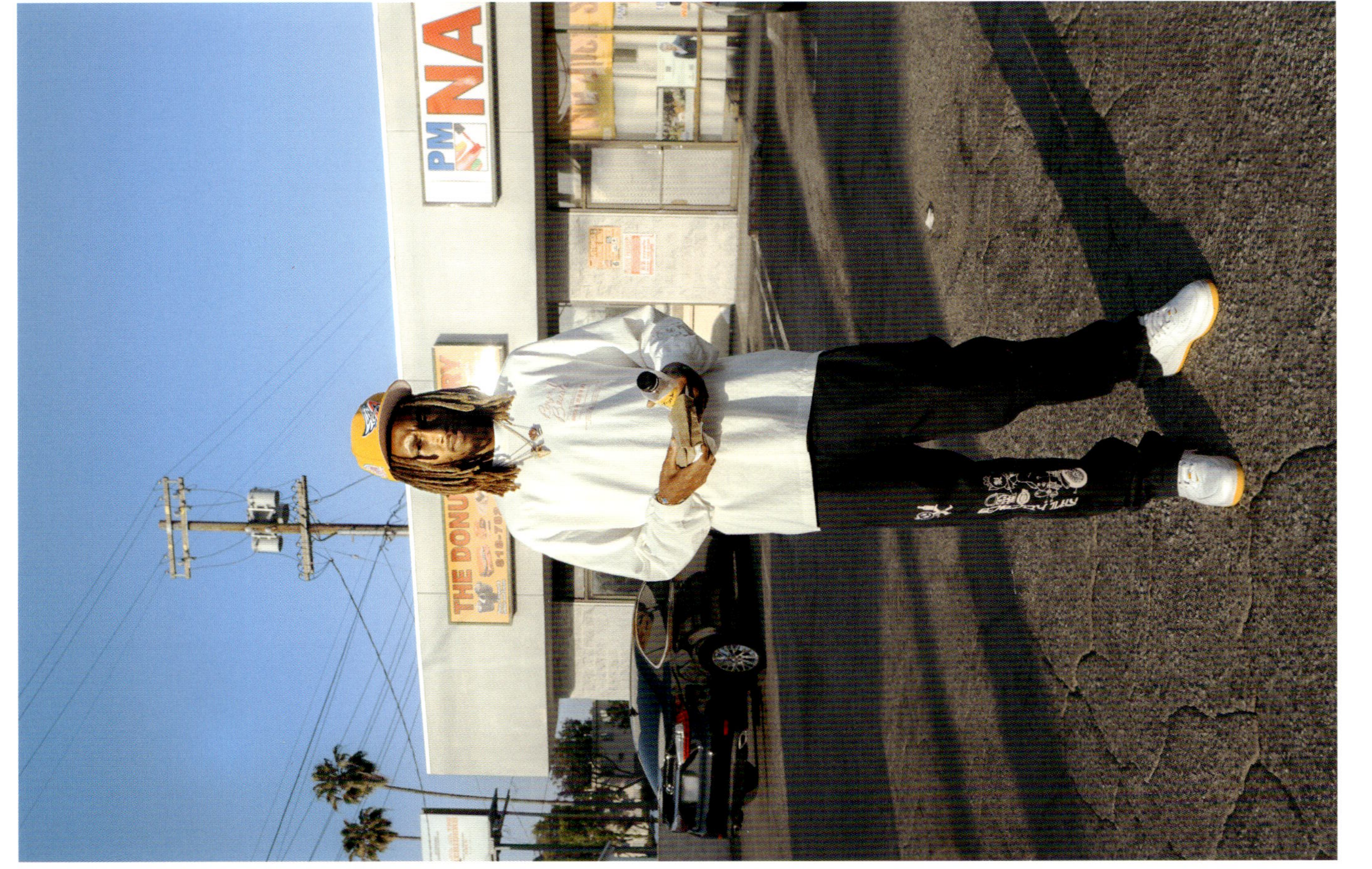
THE DONU
PM NA

Ace

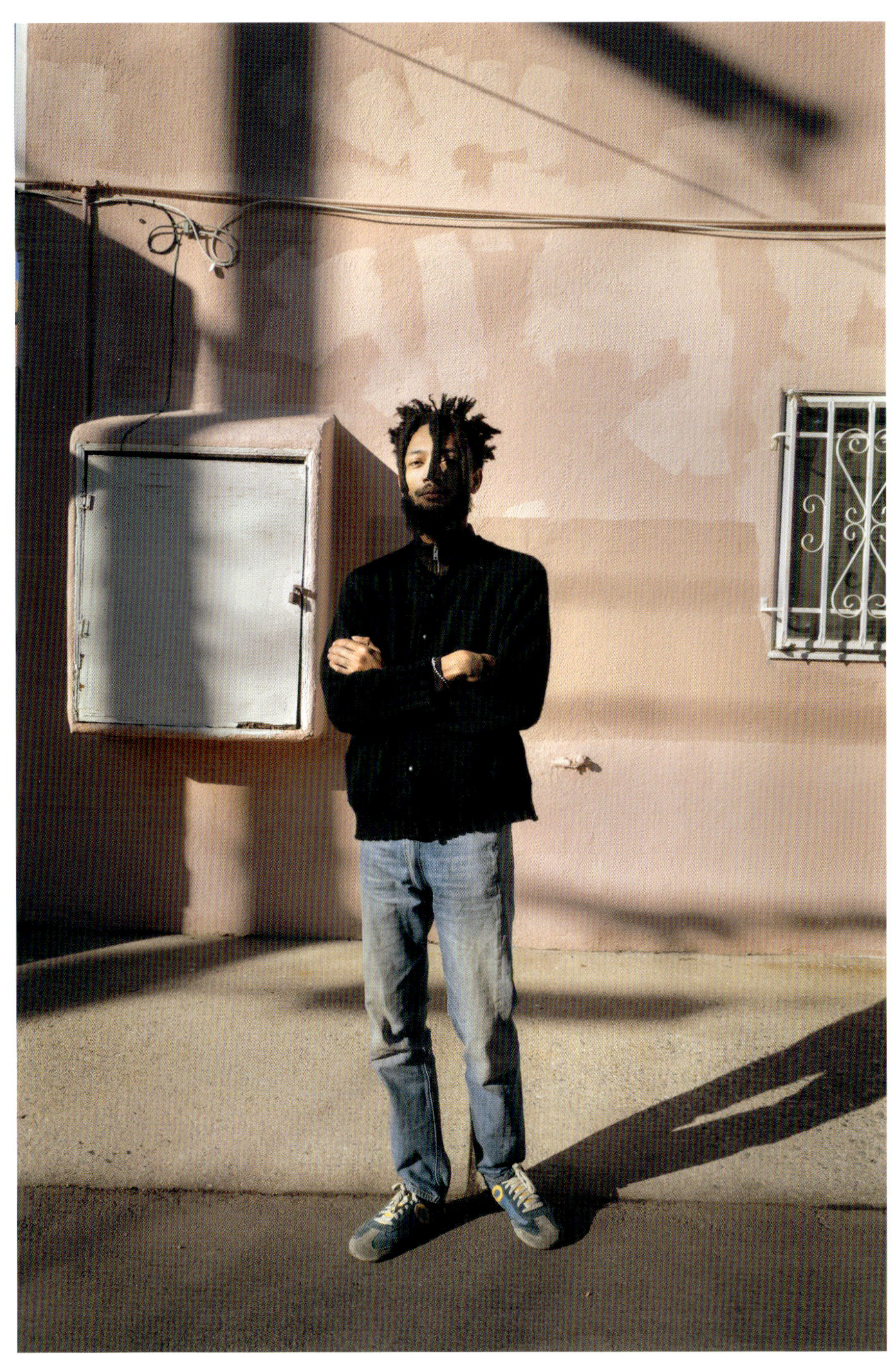

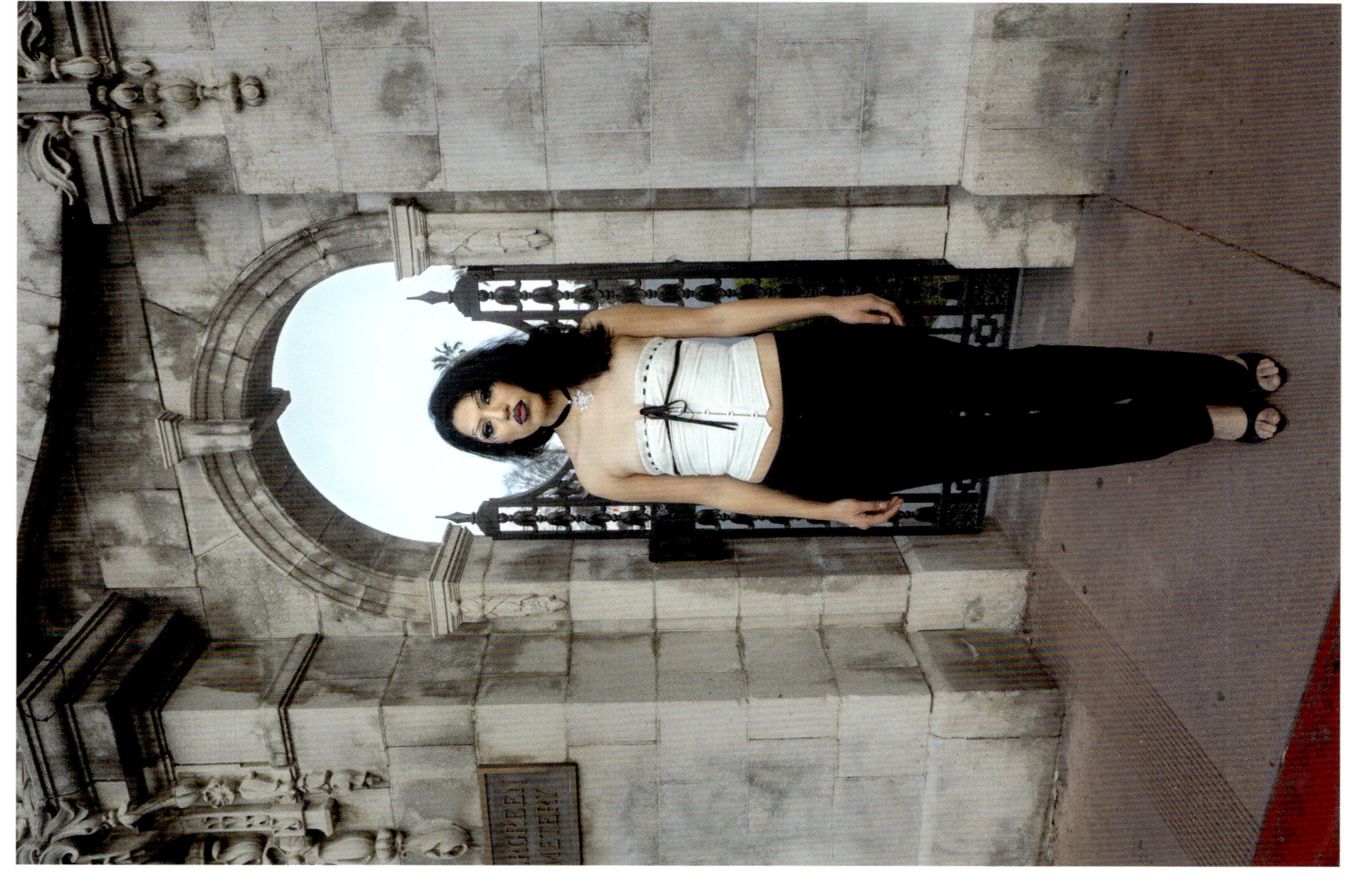

Kimberly Nolasco

Artist / Model / Barista

Boyle Heights

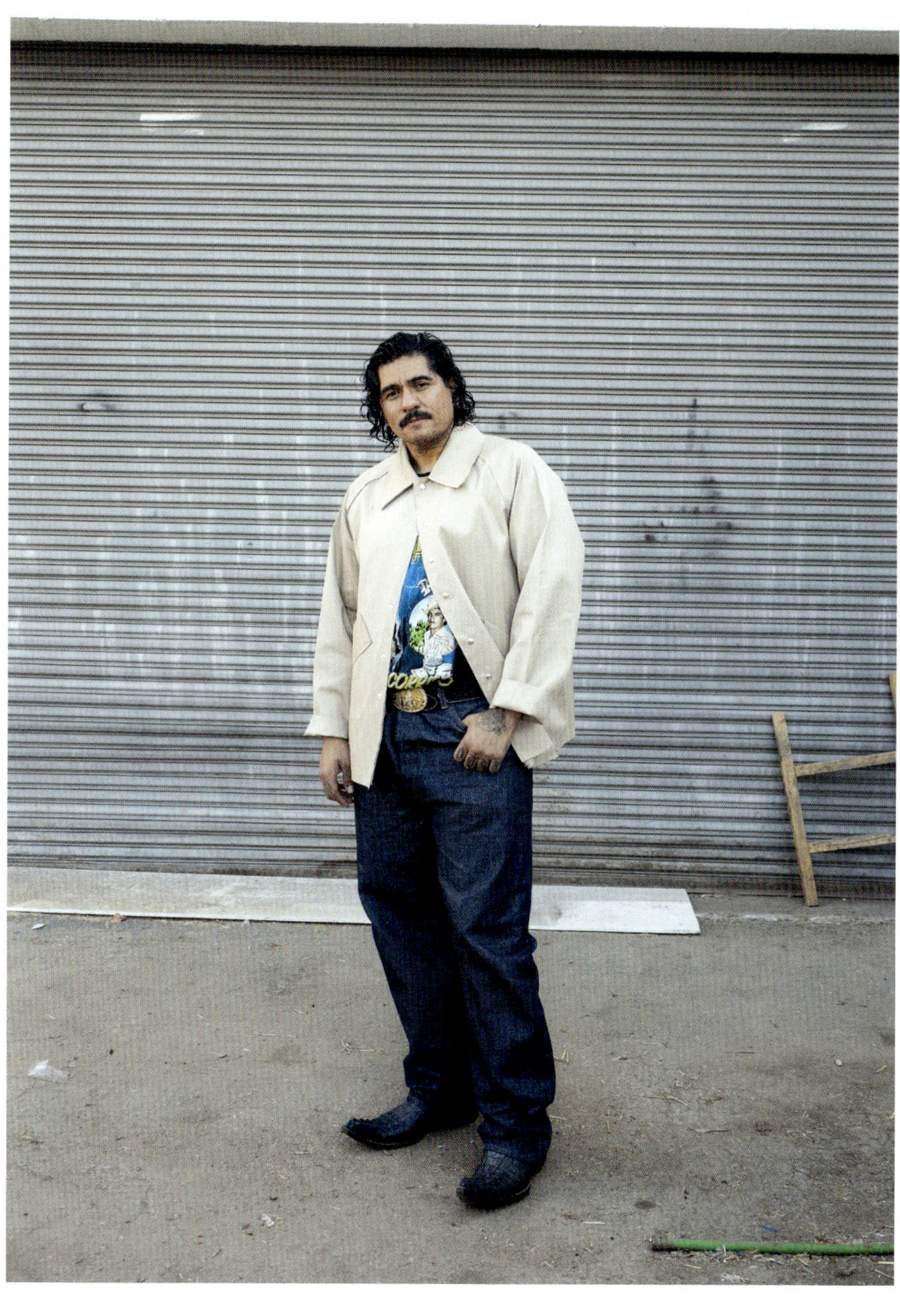

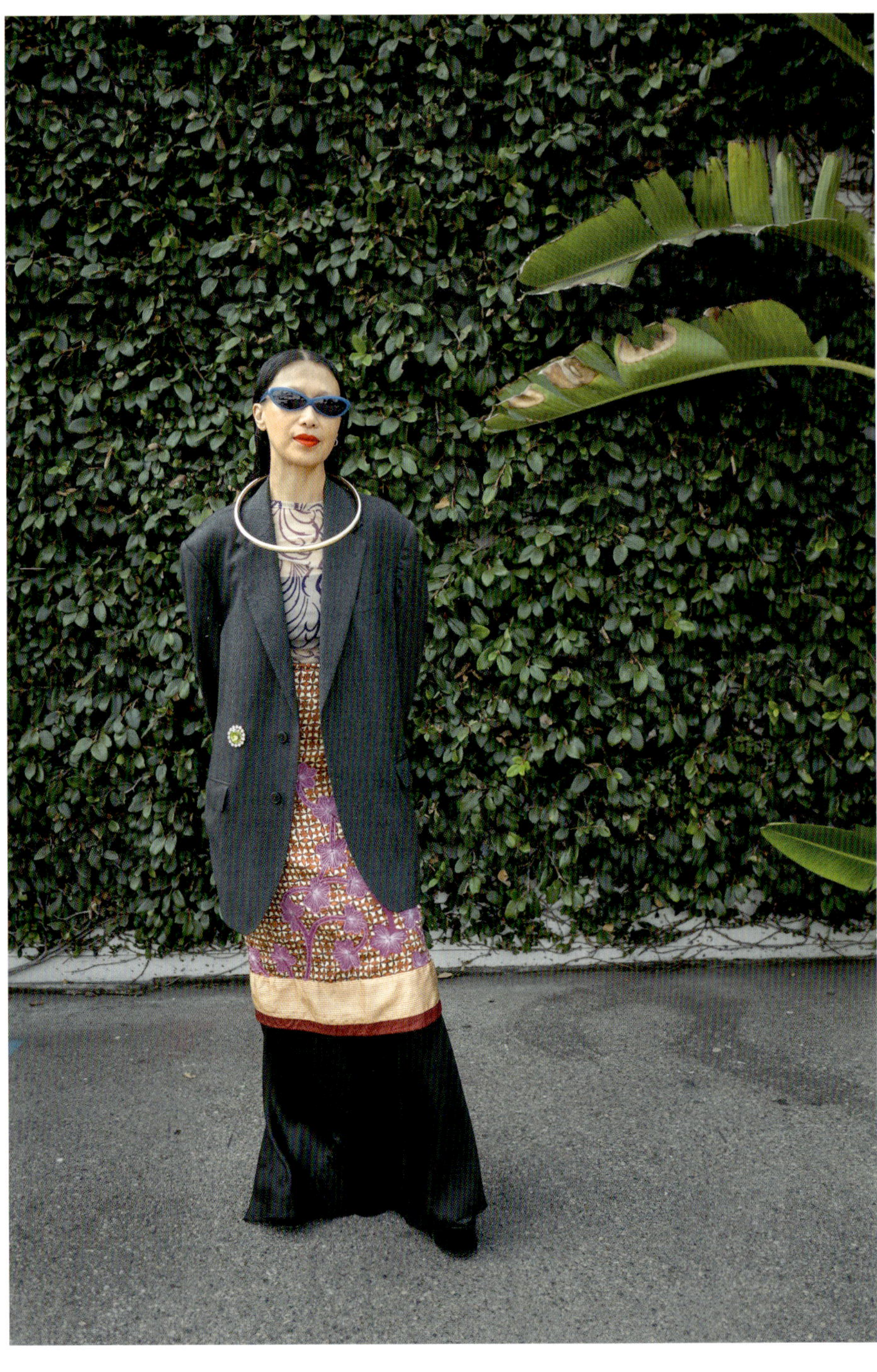

Creative

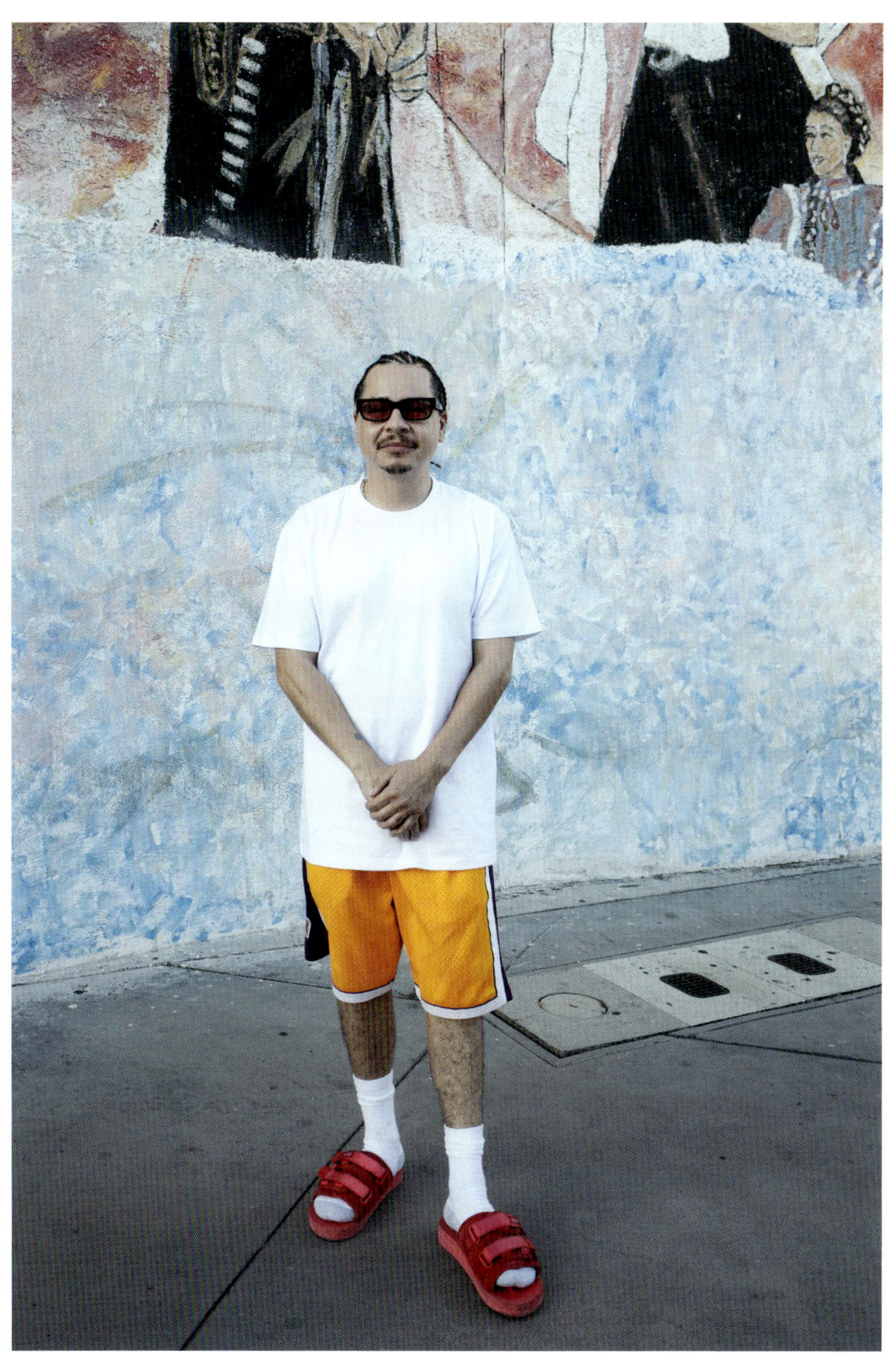

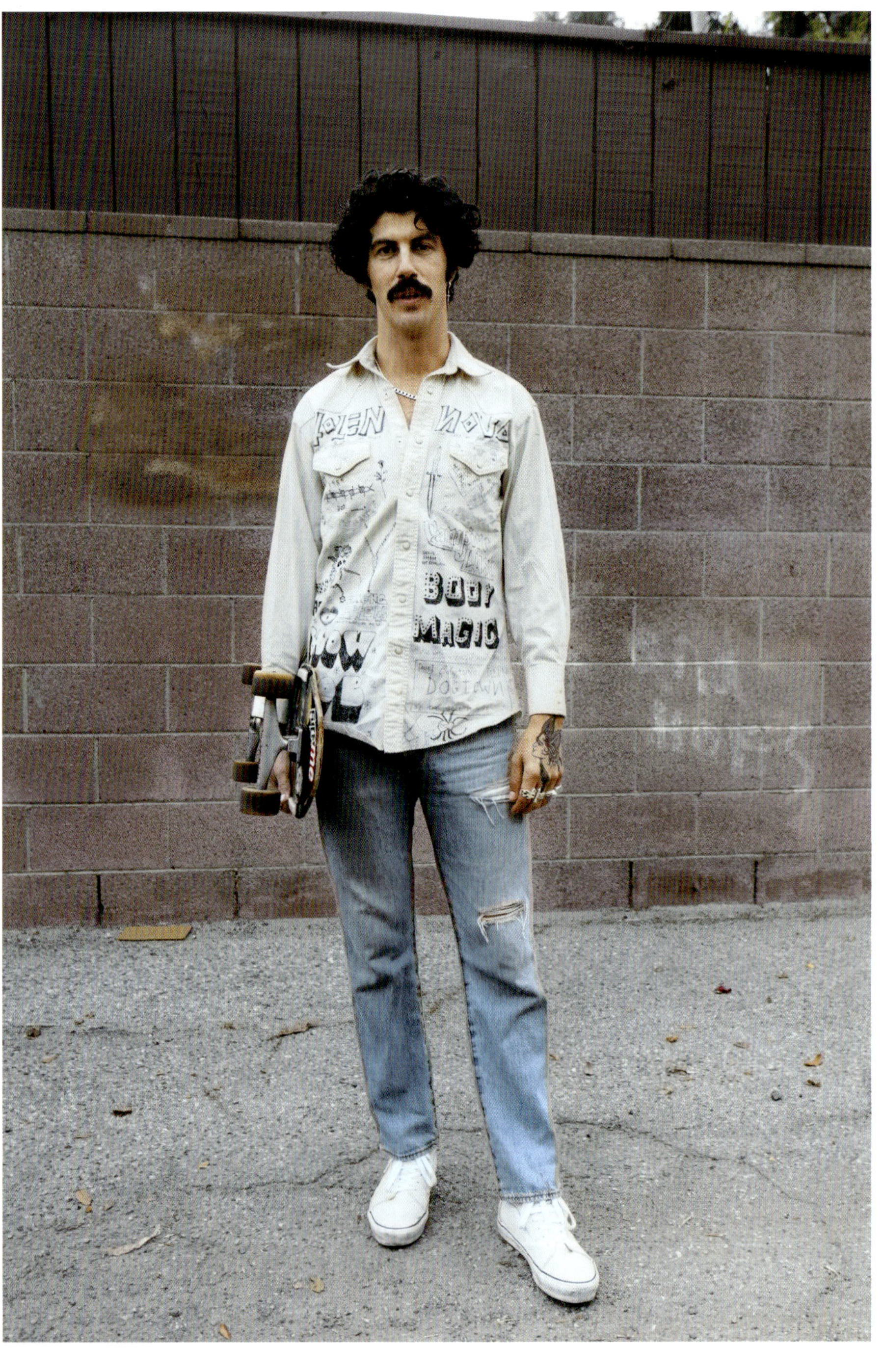

Musician in Stolen Nova

Venice

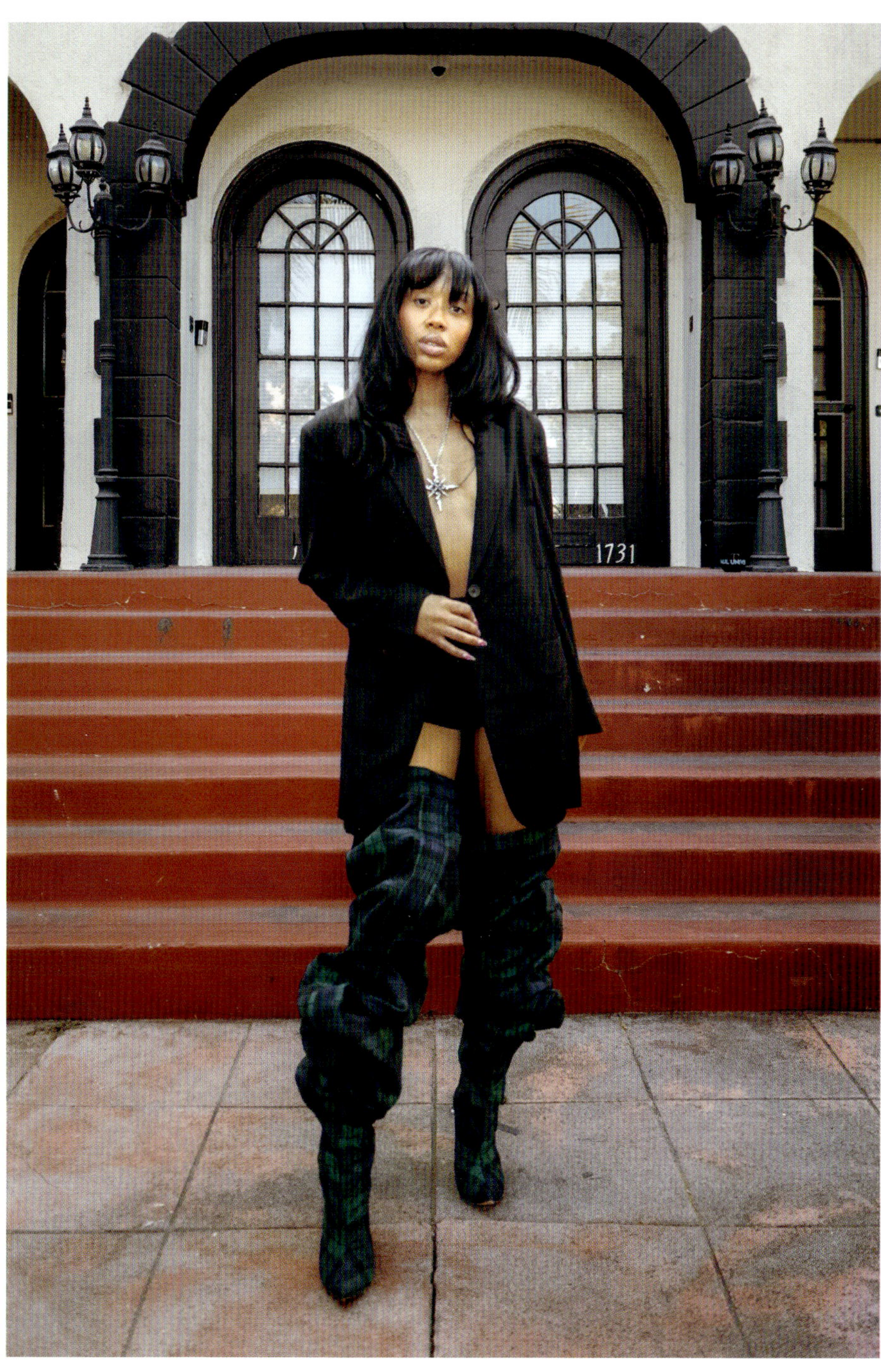

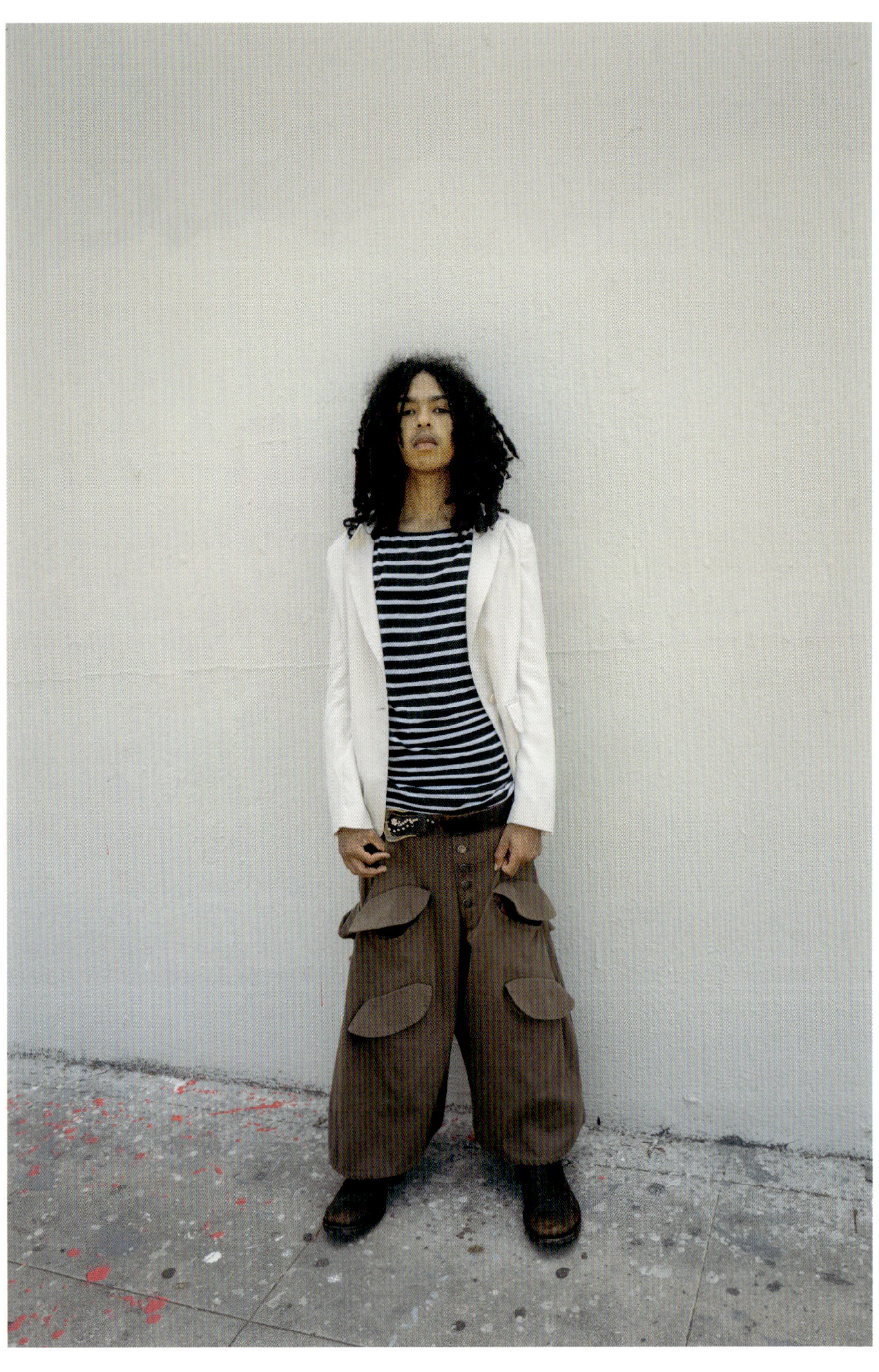

Producer / Filmmaker

Creative

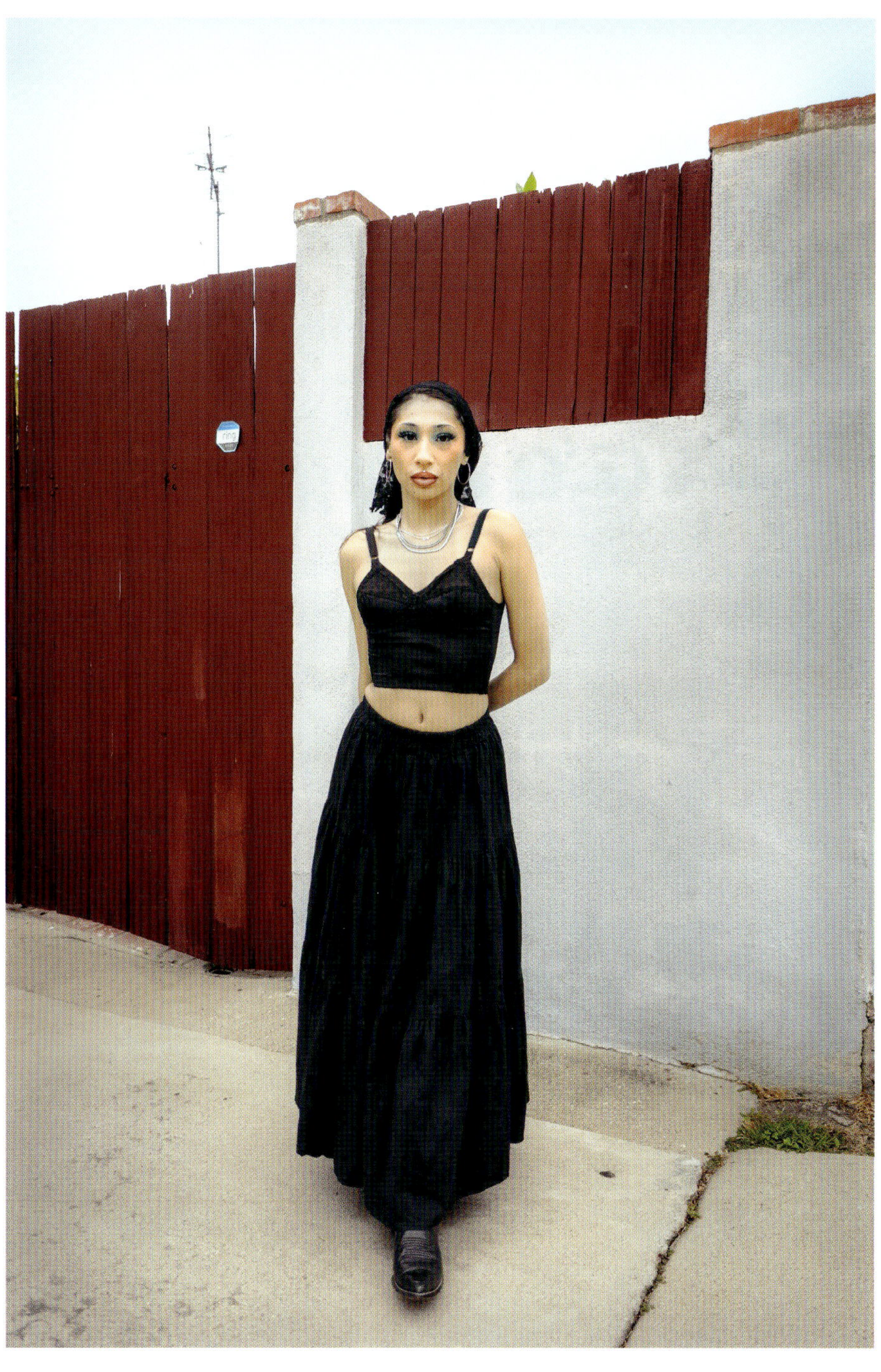

131

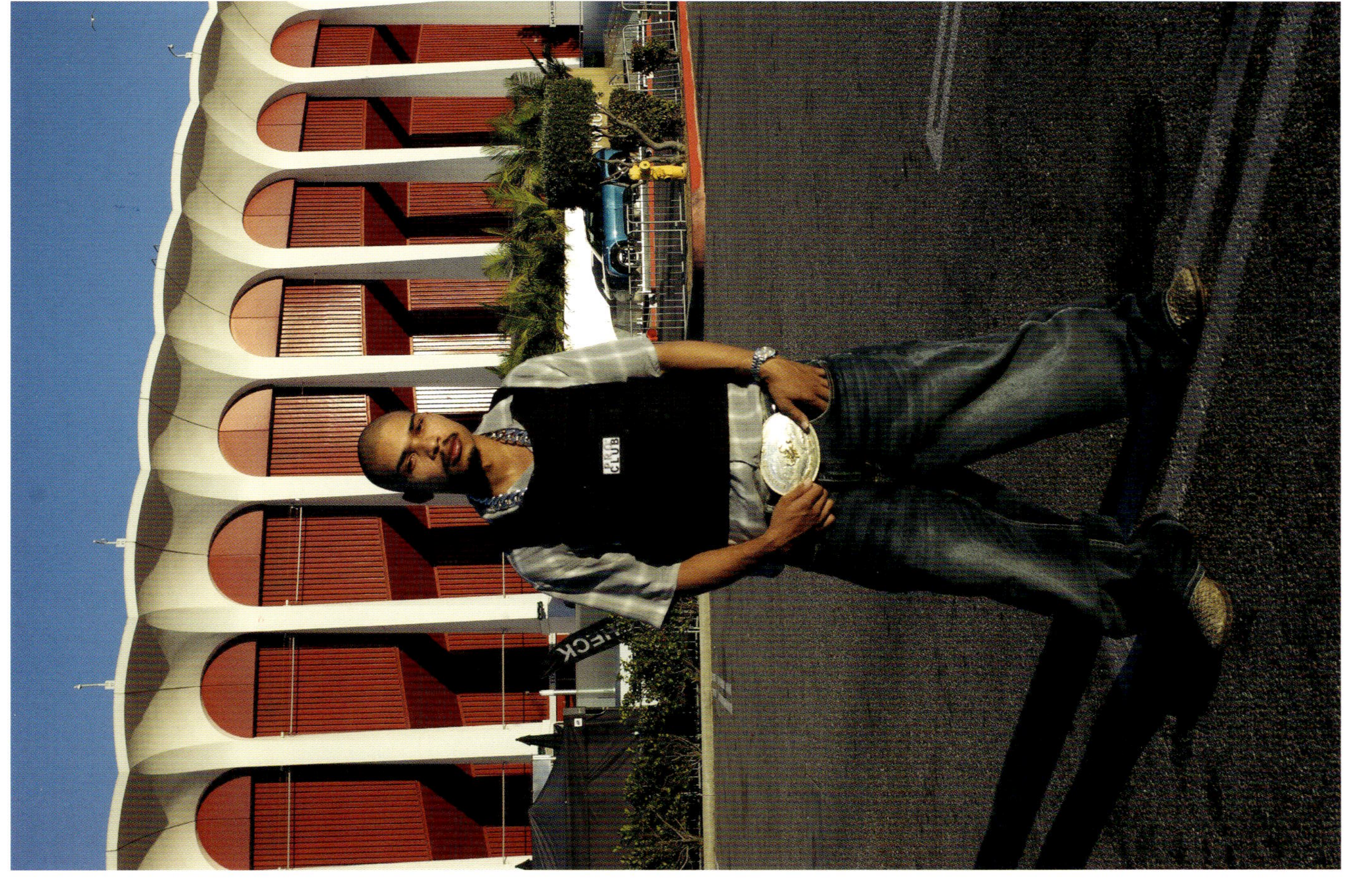

Apparel Designer

South Central

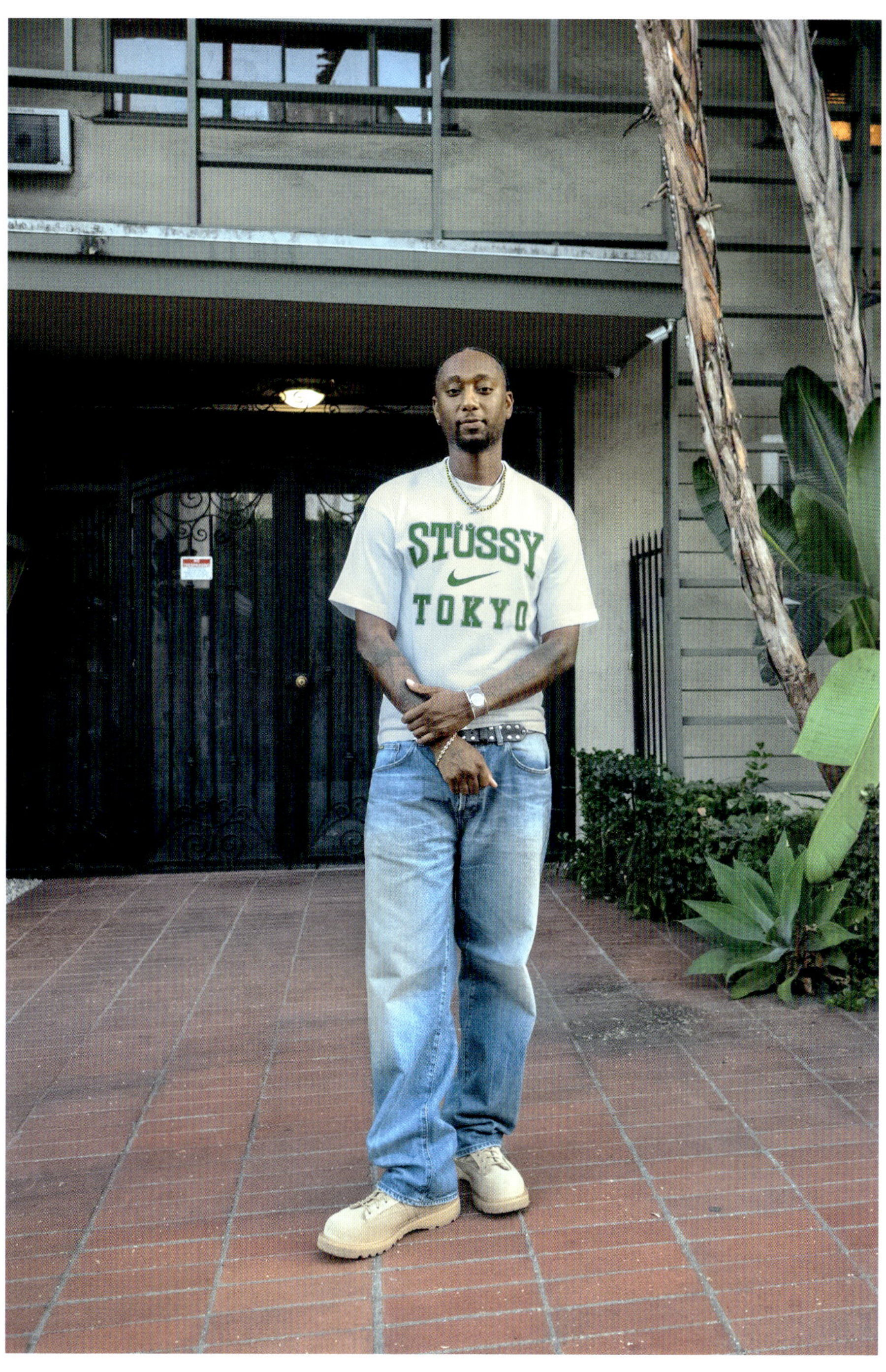

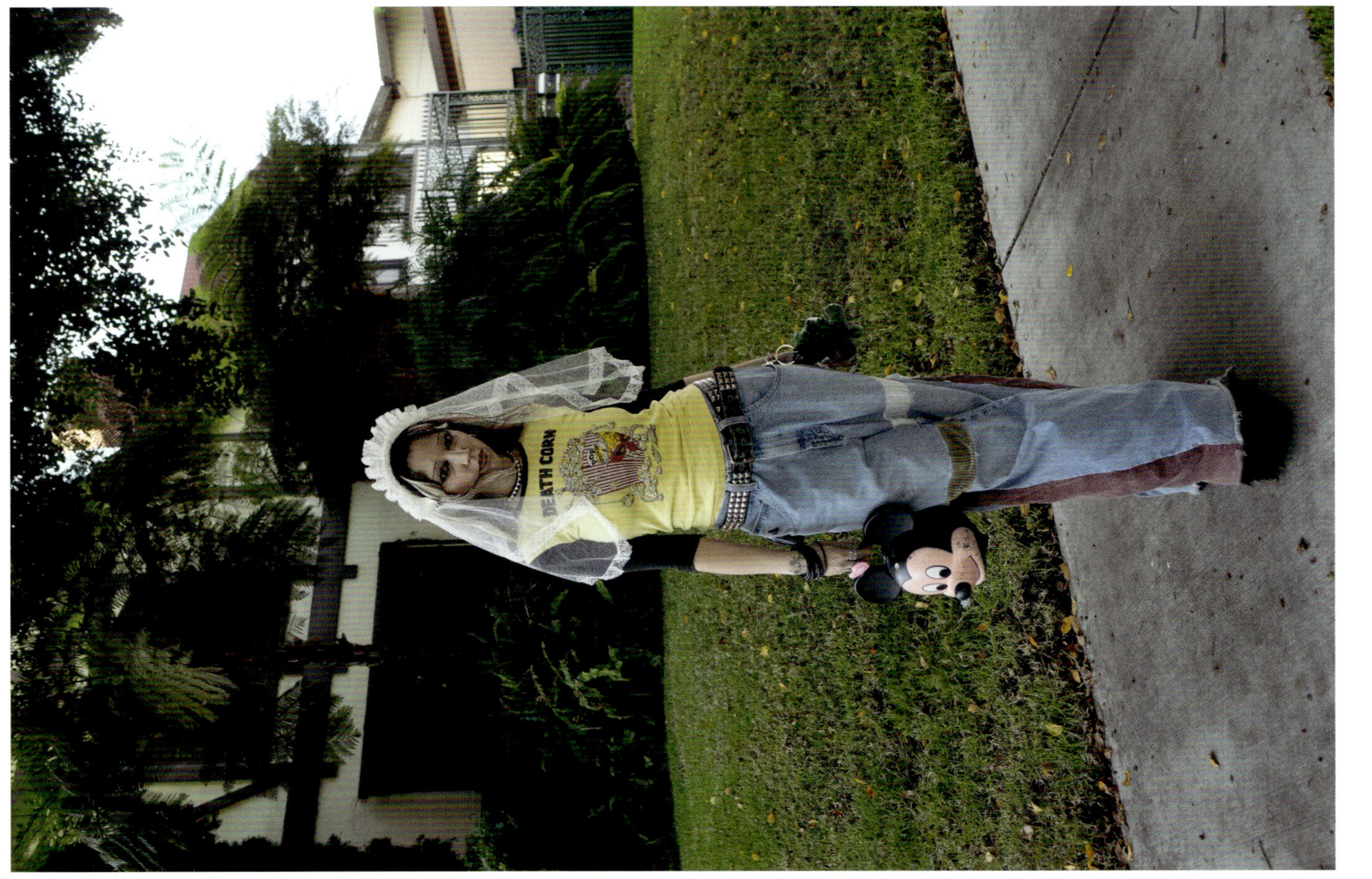

Shop Boy

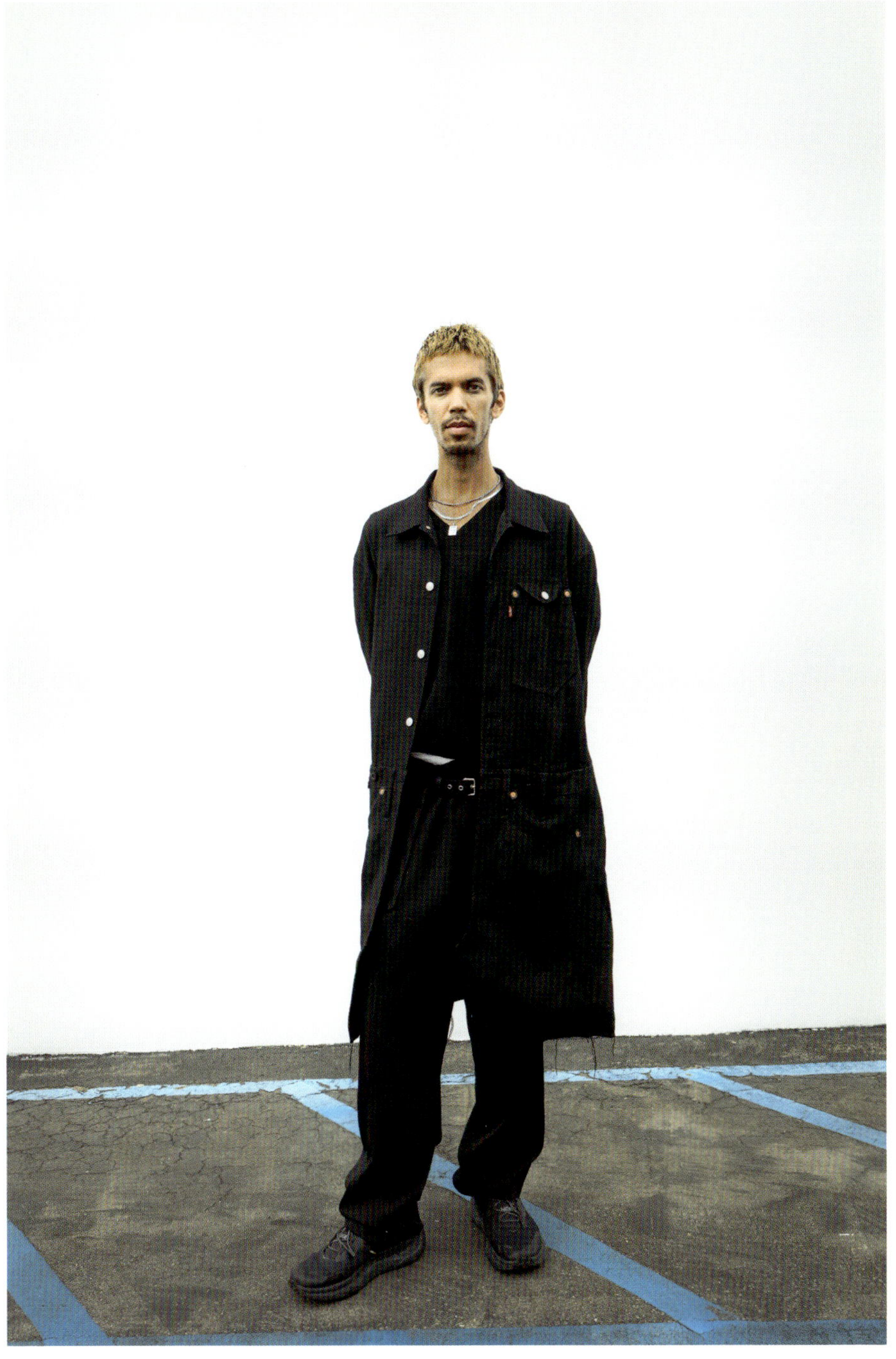

OC

Bass Player

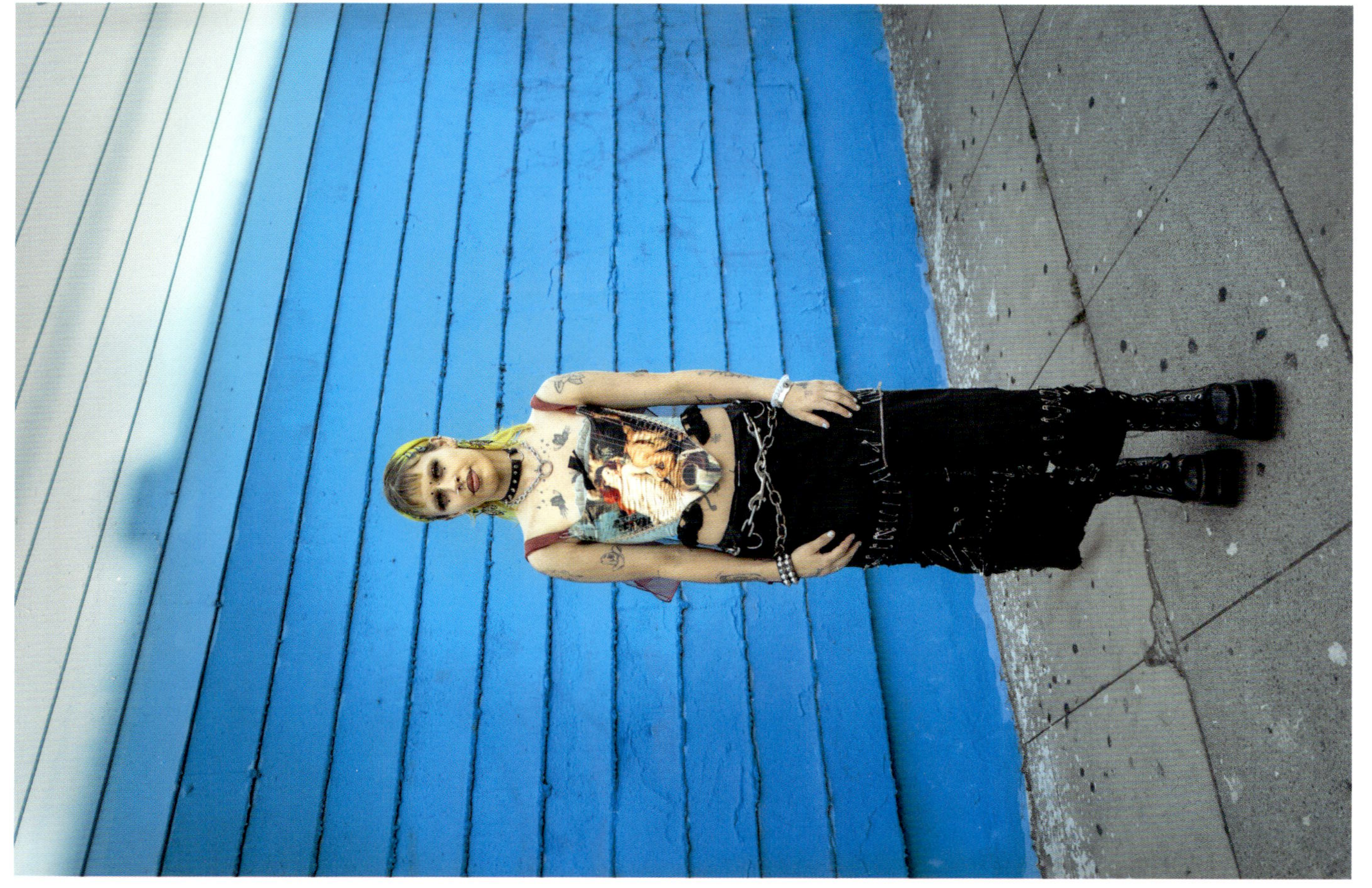

Model / Photographer

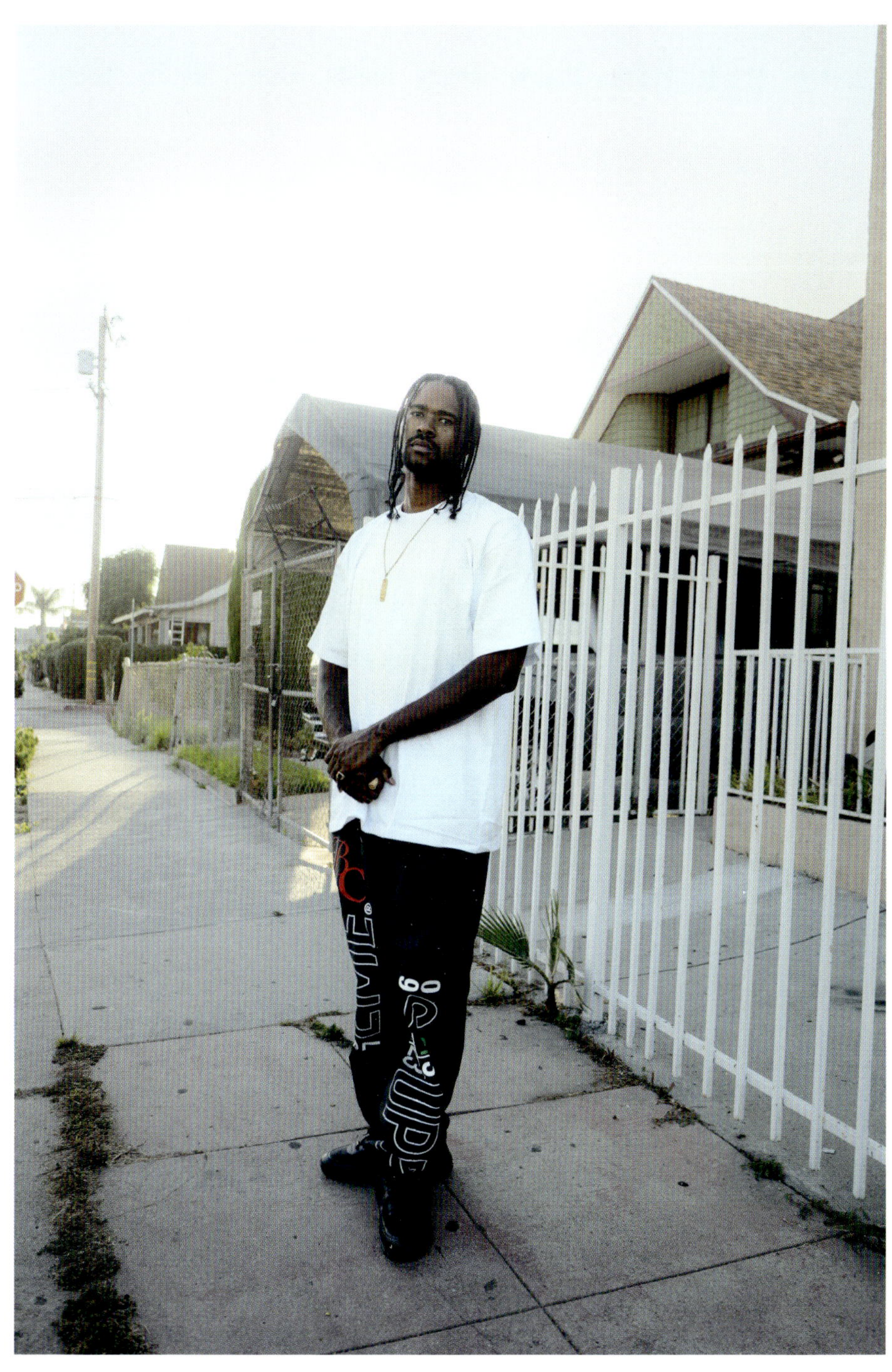

Model

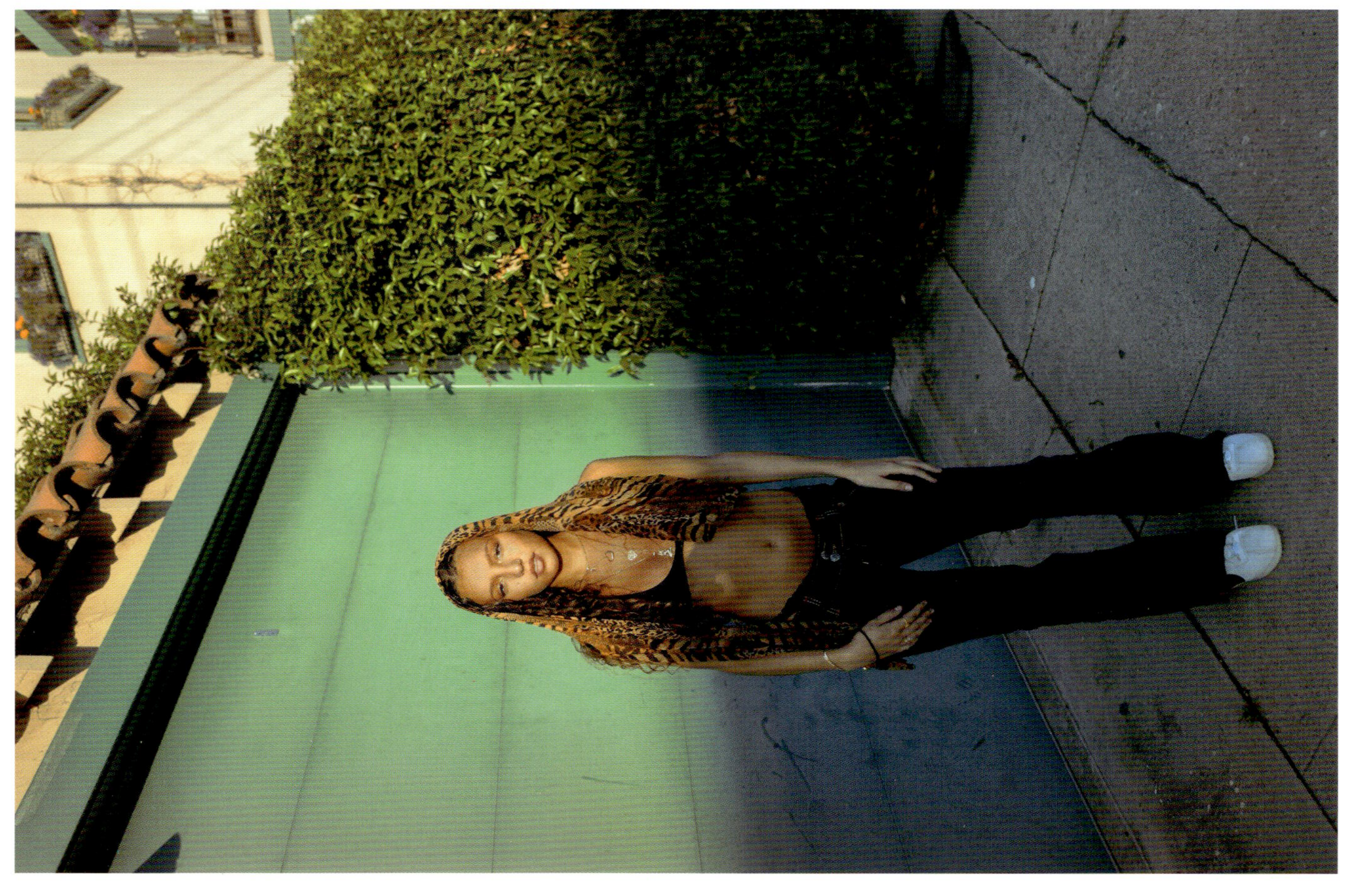

Model

Hollywood

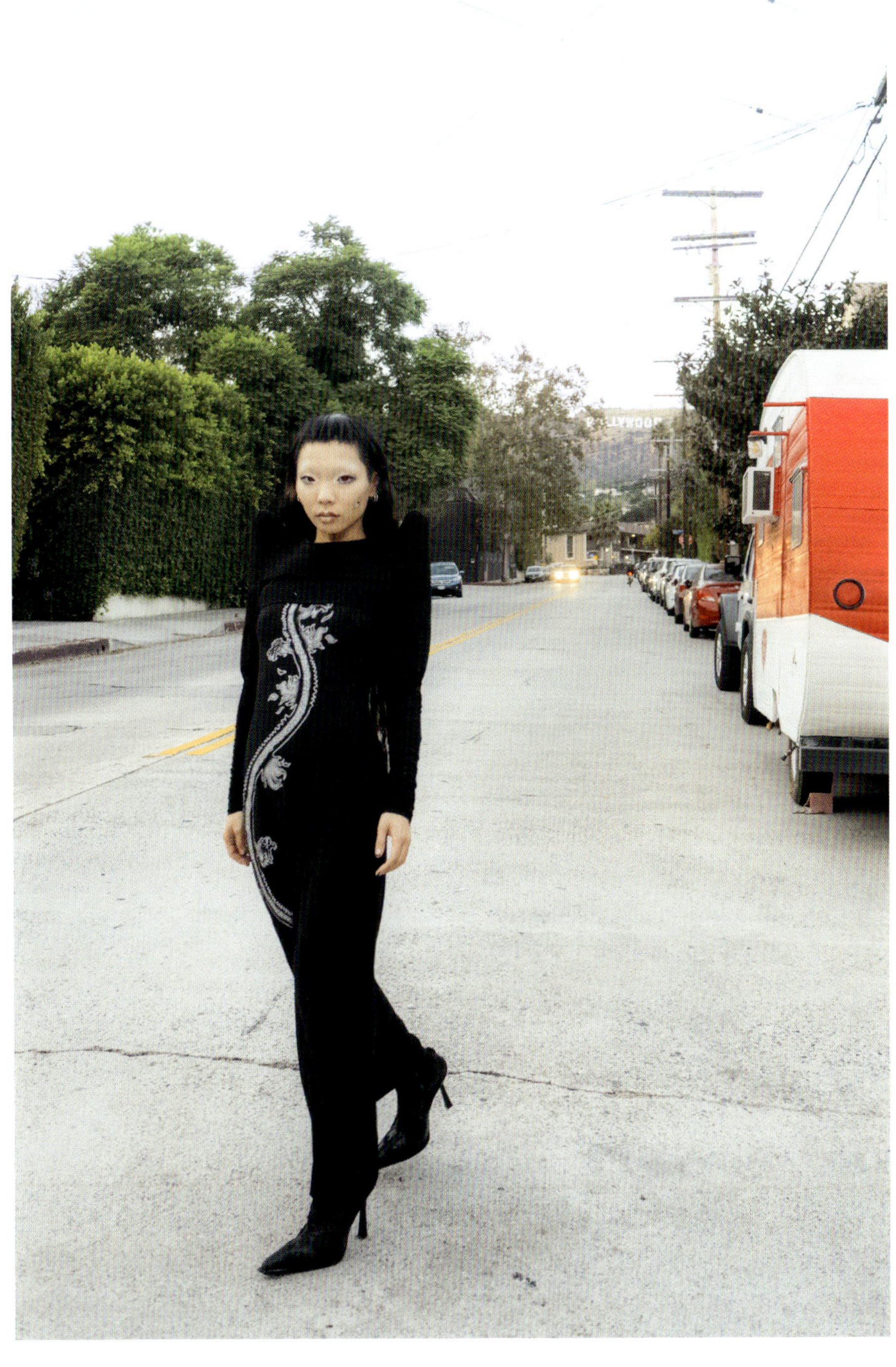

Pro Skater

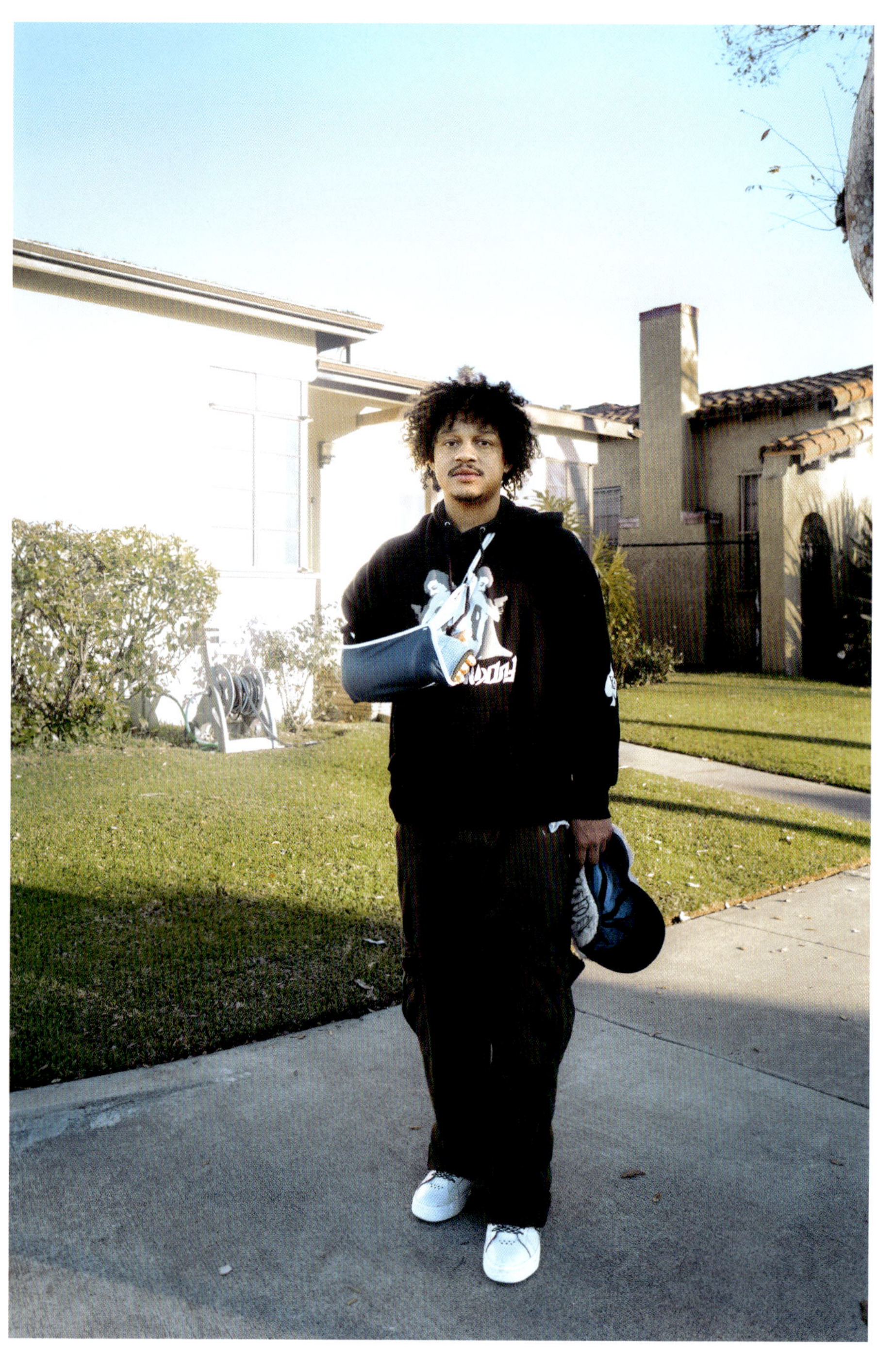

140

Vanessa Amaranto
Co-founder Art Community / Digital Content Creator
South Park

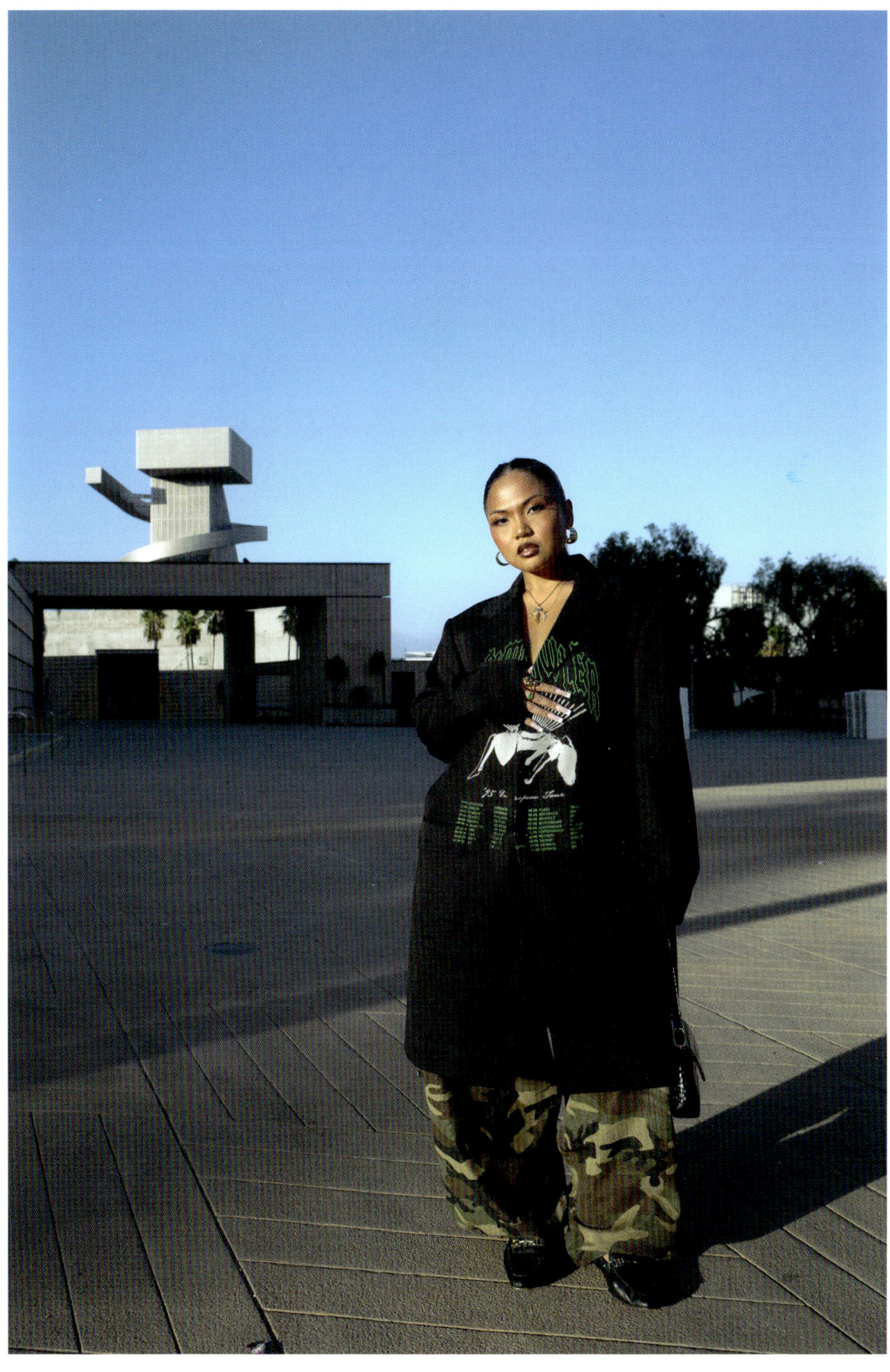

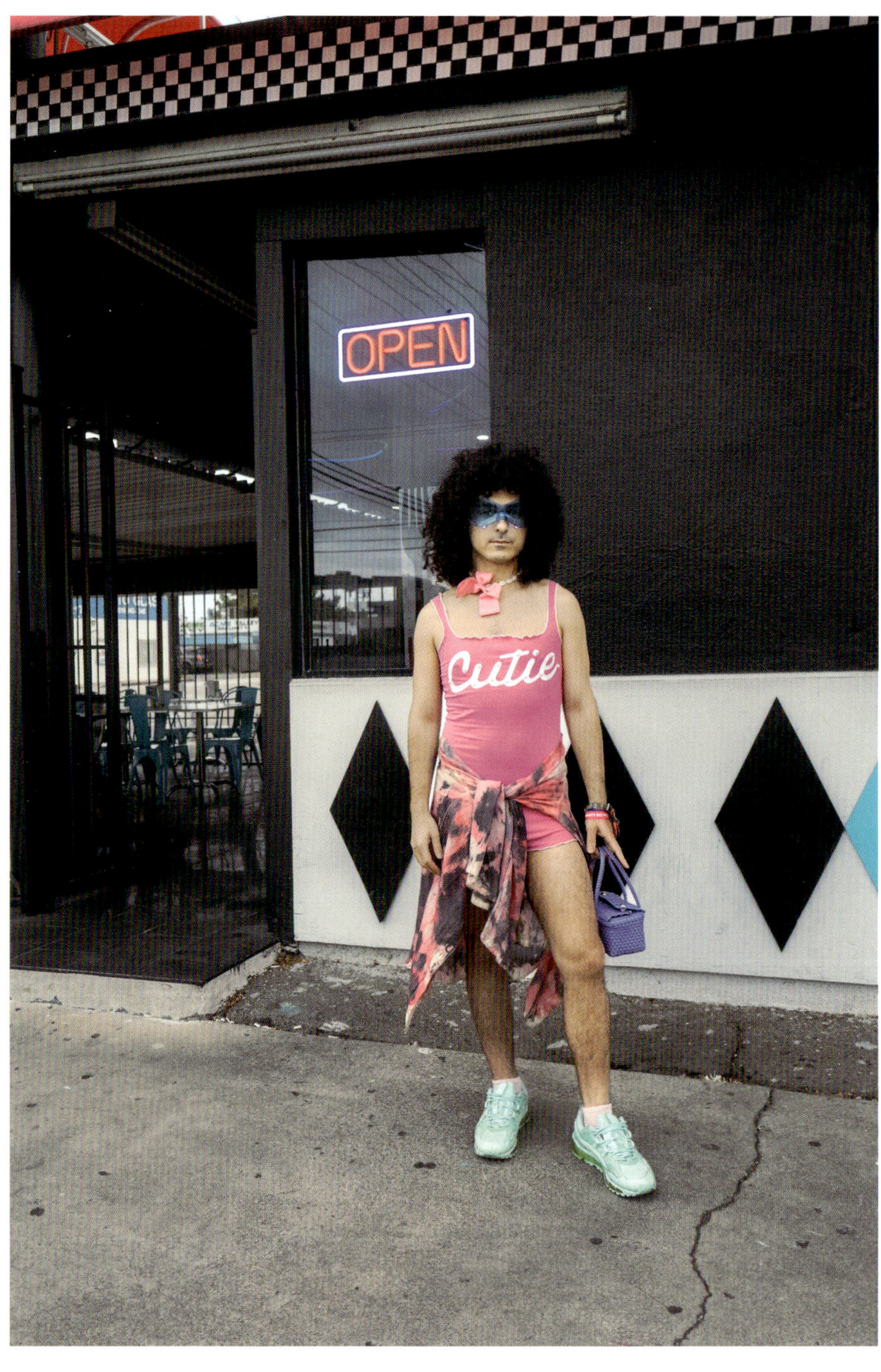

DJ / Photographer / Performer

The Valley

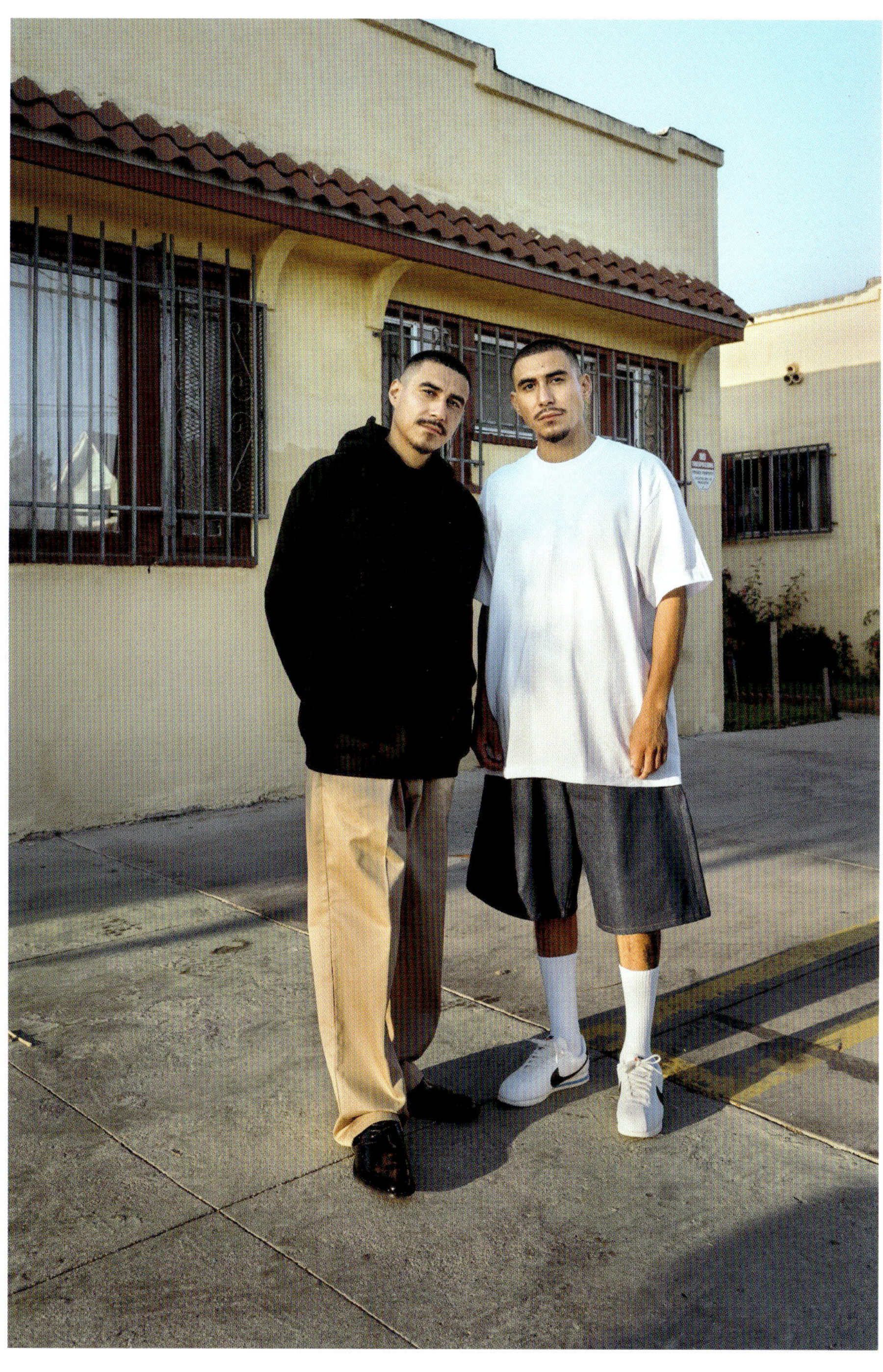

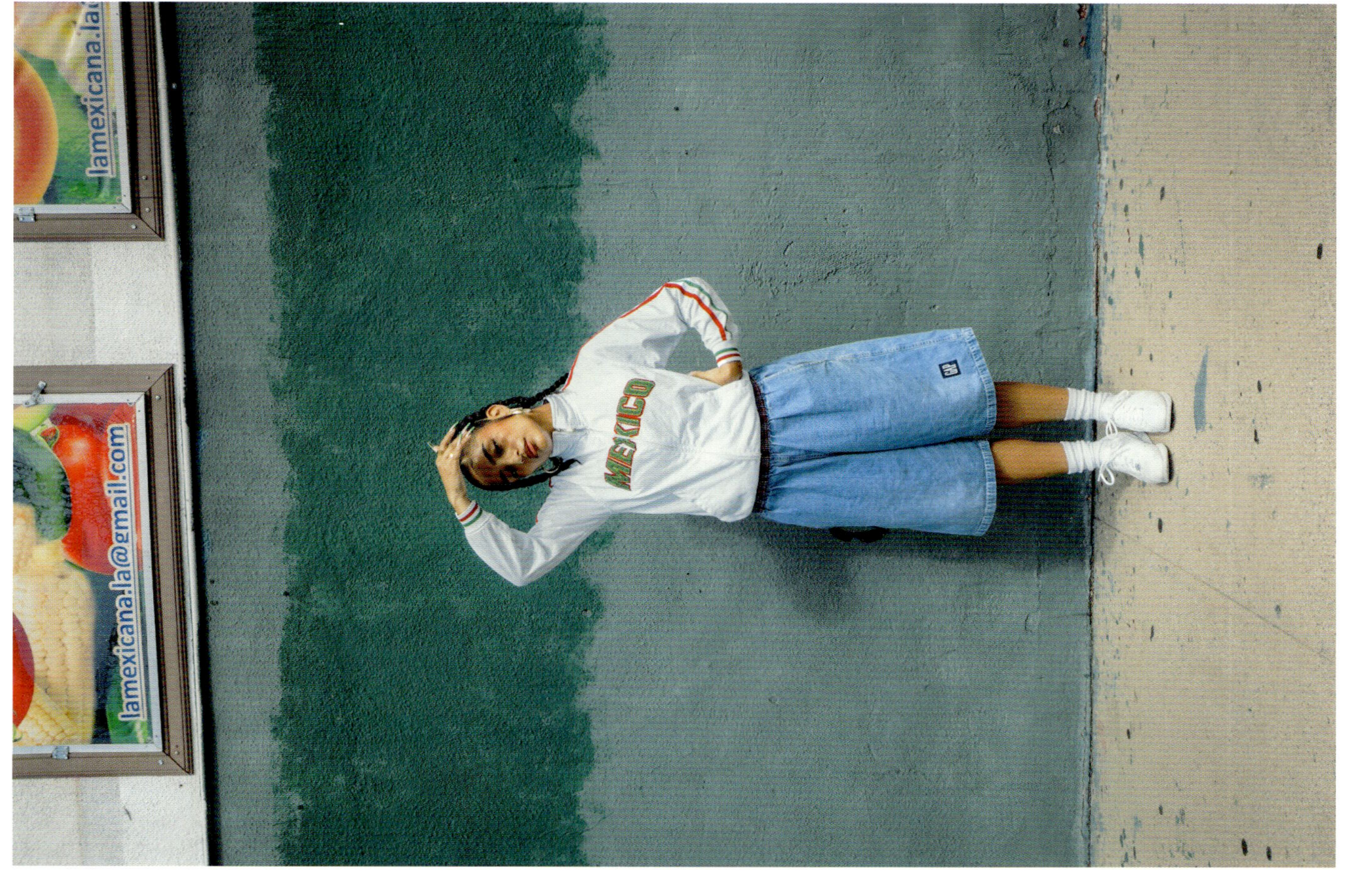
lamexicana.la
lamexicana.la@gmail.com
MEXICO

Rapper / Vegan Chef

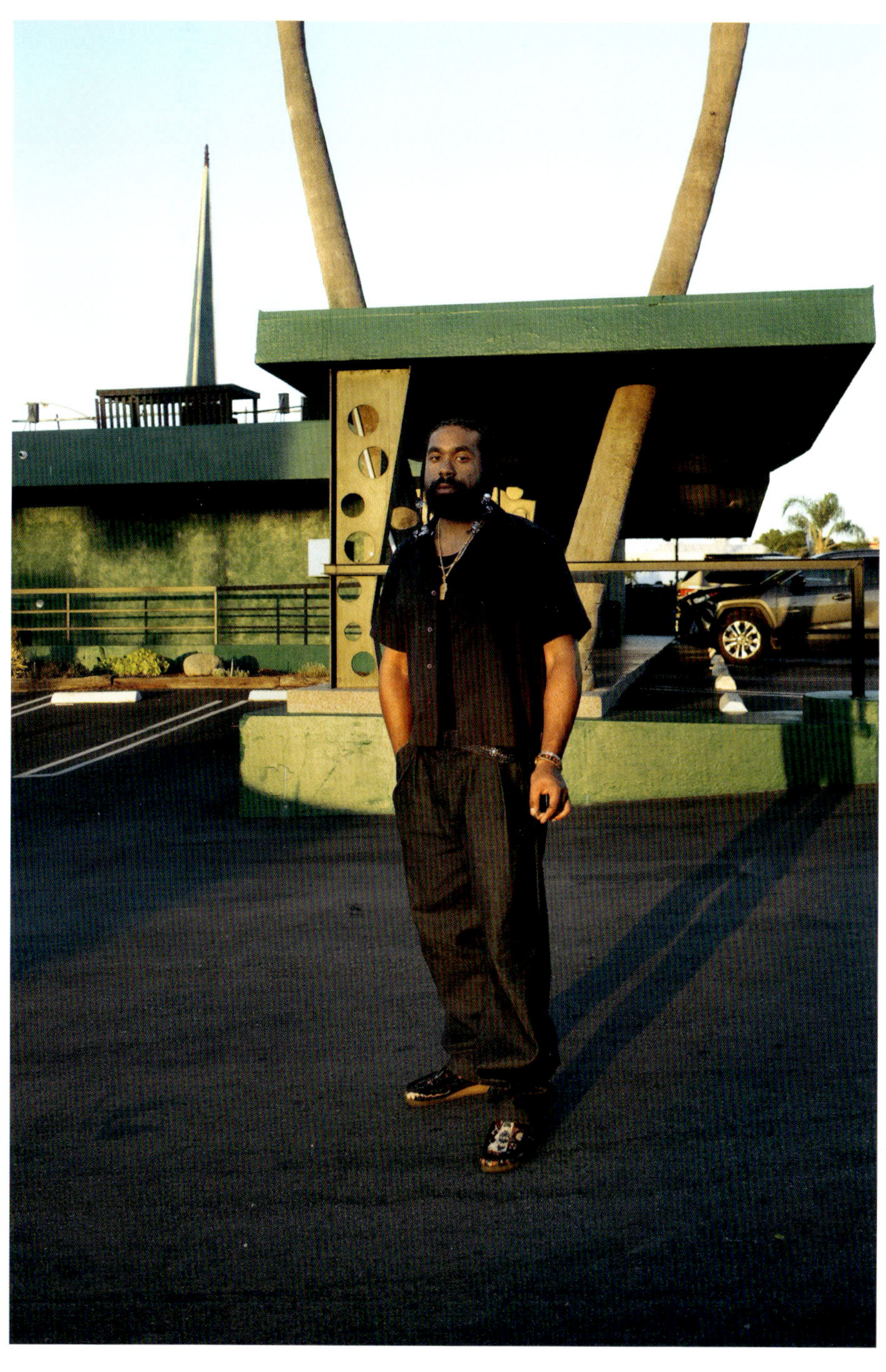

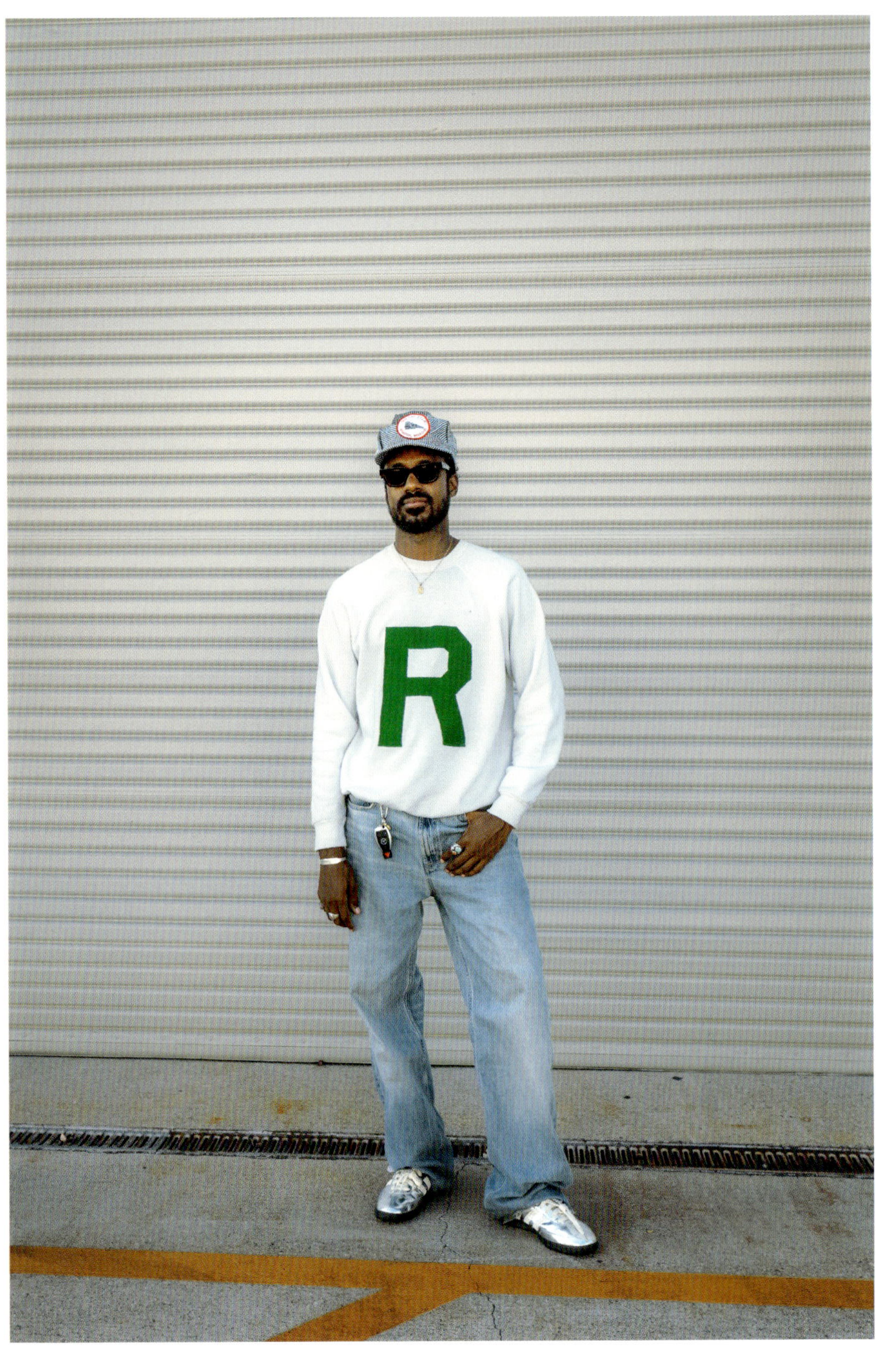

Artist

Inglewood

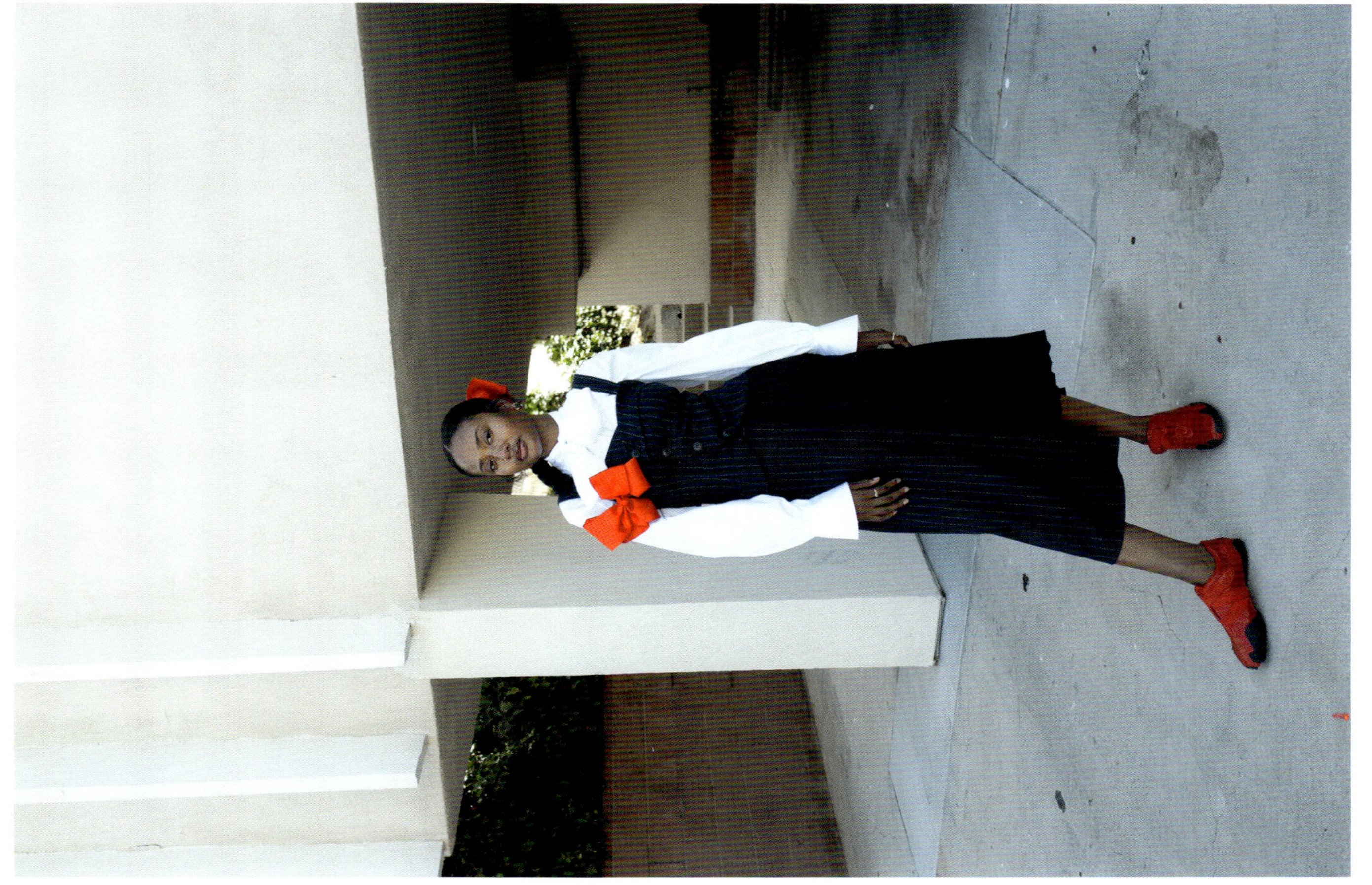

Akua Shabaka   Co-founder of House of Aama   Crenshaw District

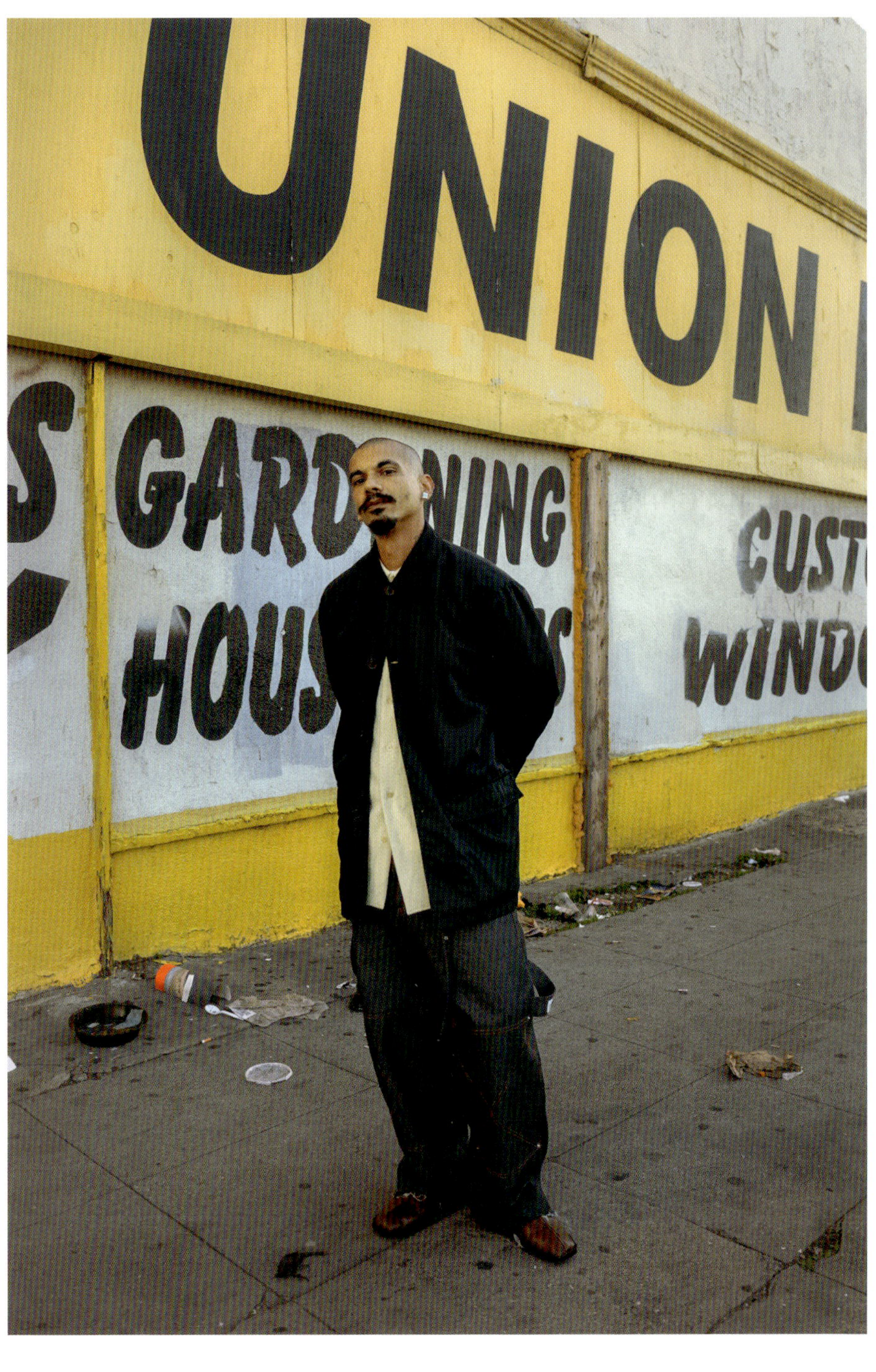

Designer

Venice

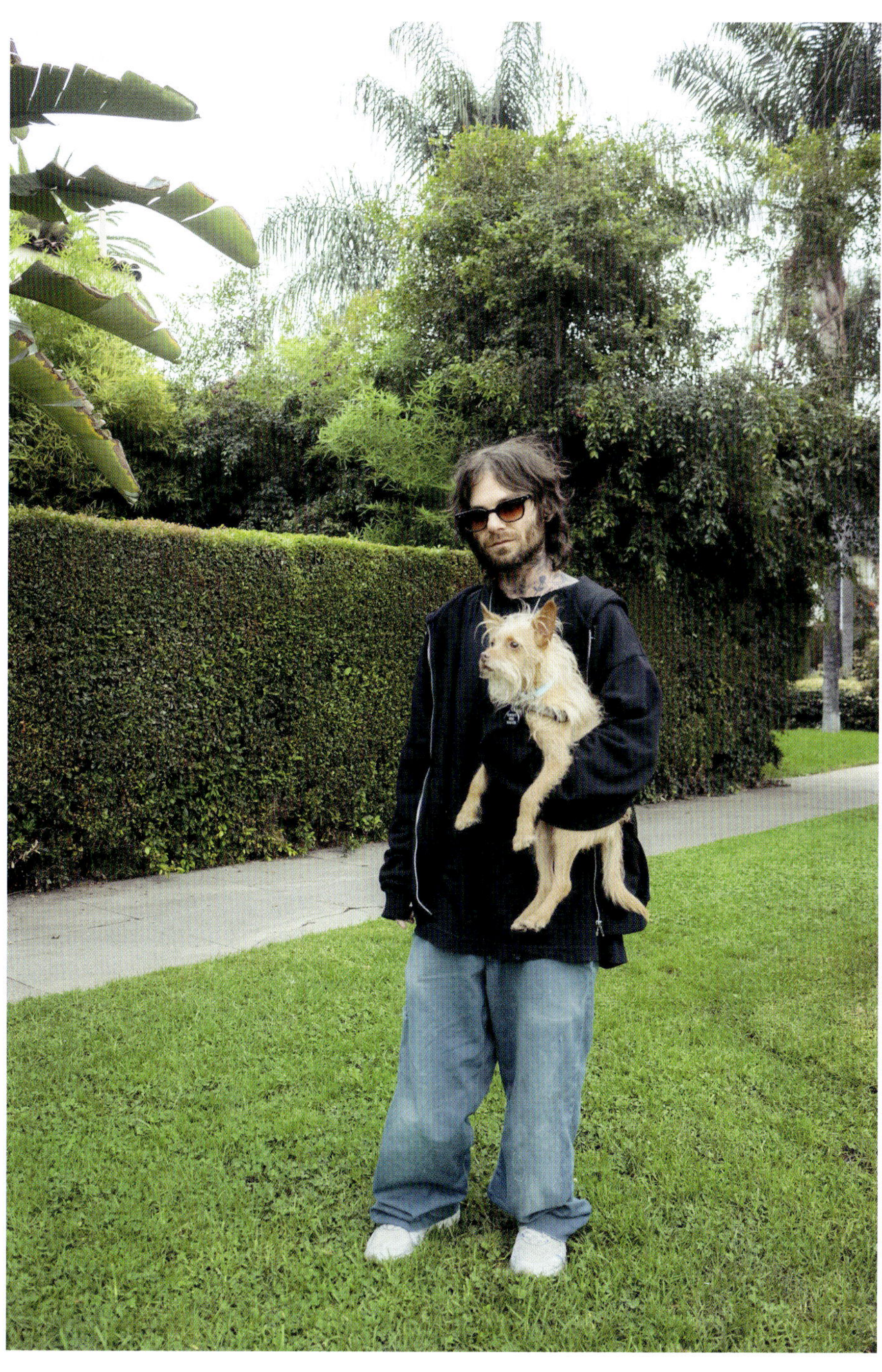

Morgan Freed

Co-Founder Emo Nite

Hollywood

149

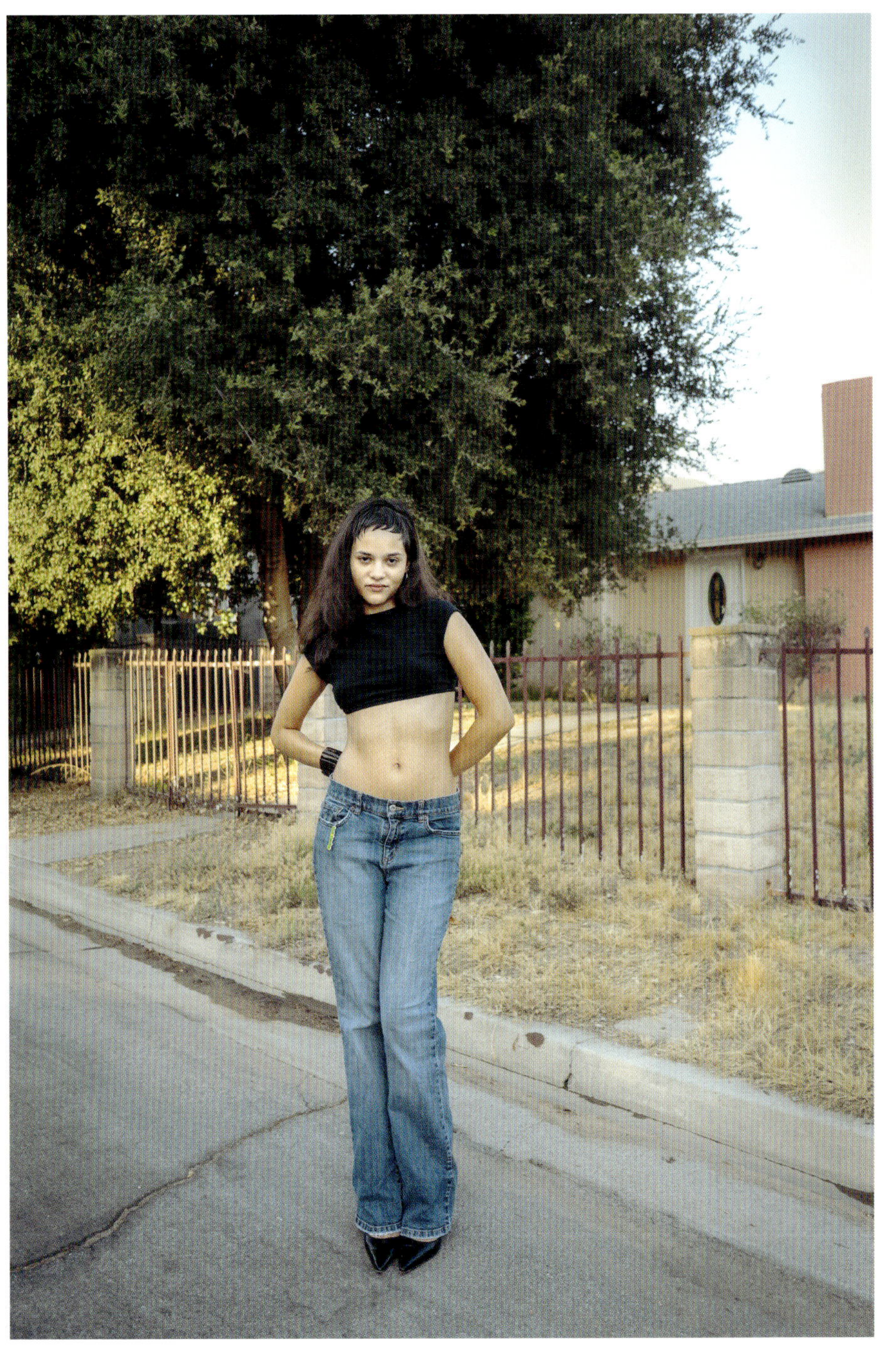

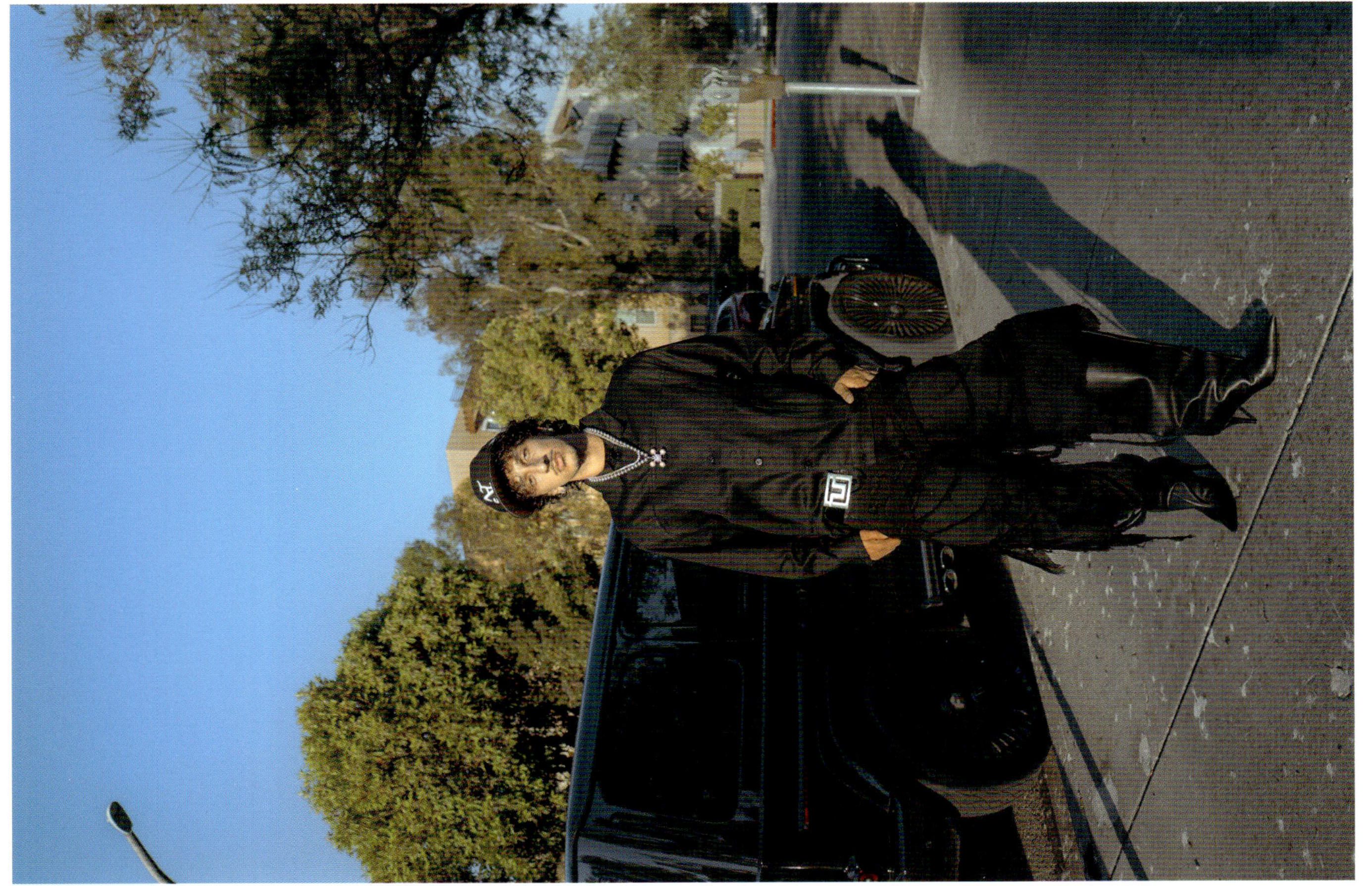

Stephane Mazumdar

Culver City

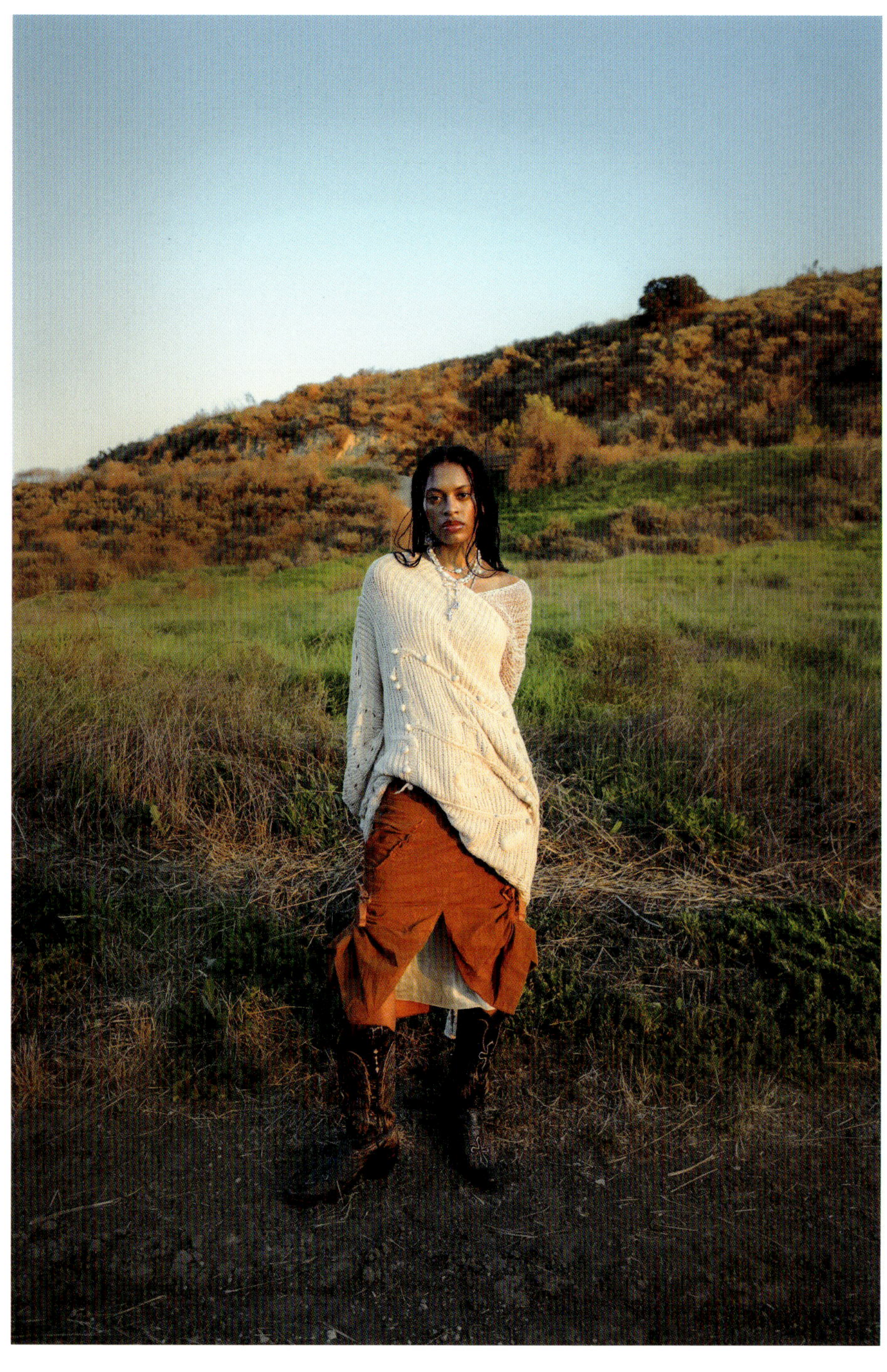

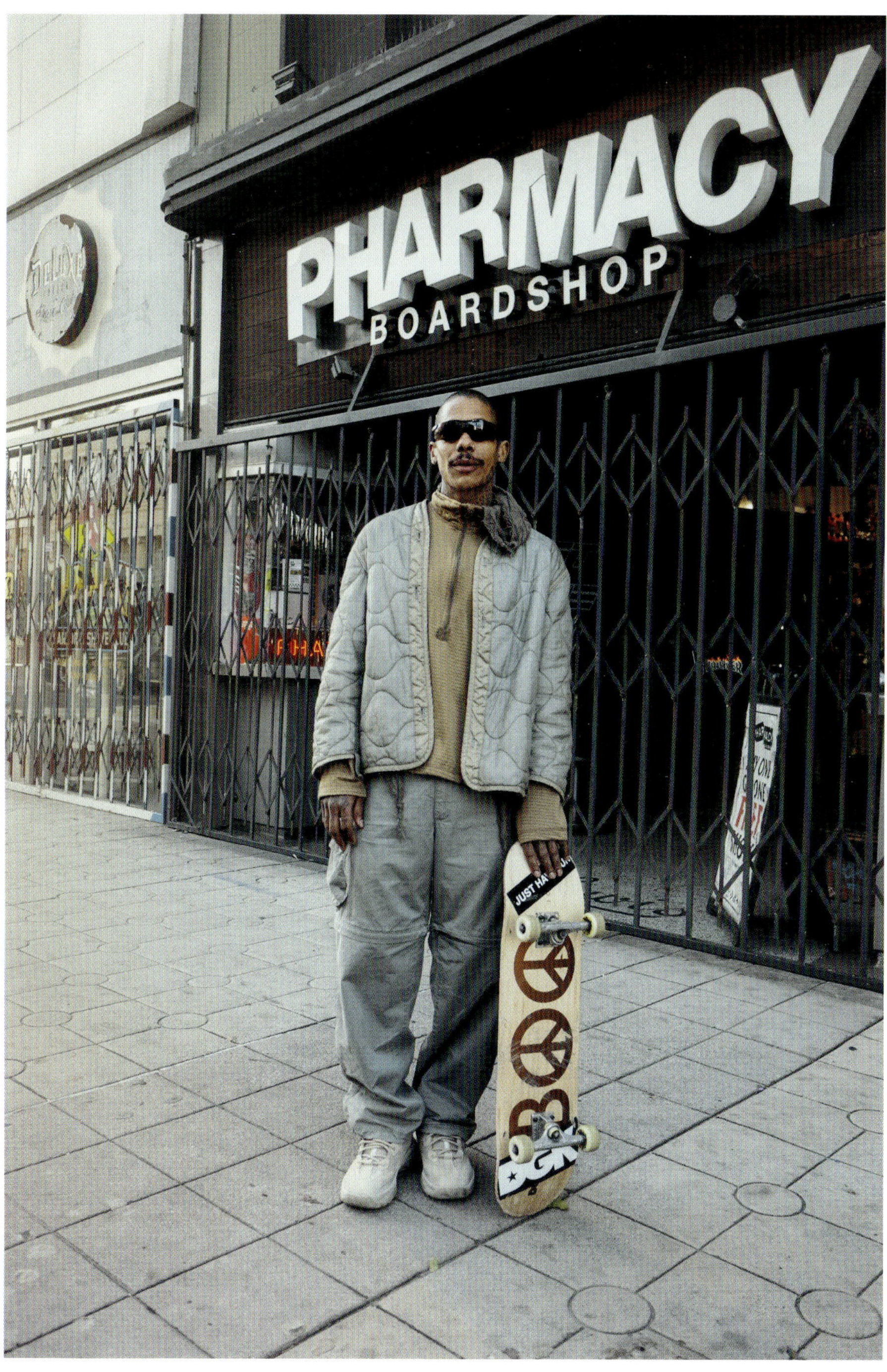
PHARMACY
BOARDSHOP
JUST HA
BO
DGK

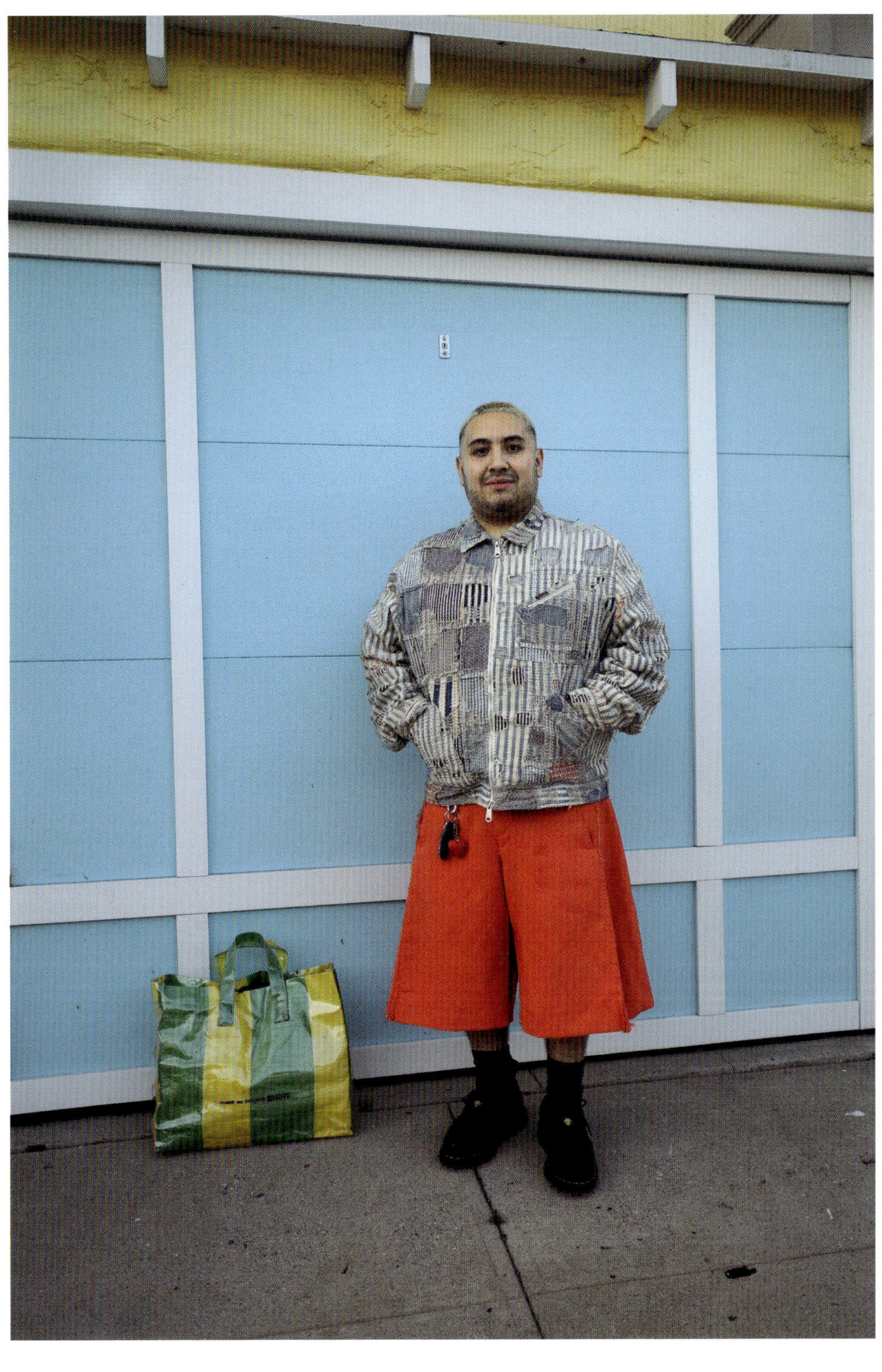

Creative

Miracle Mile

Photographer

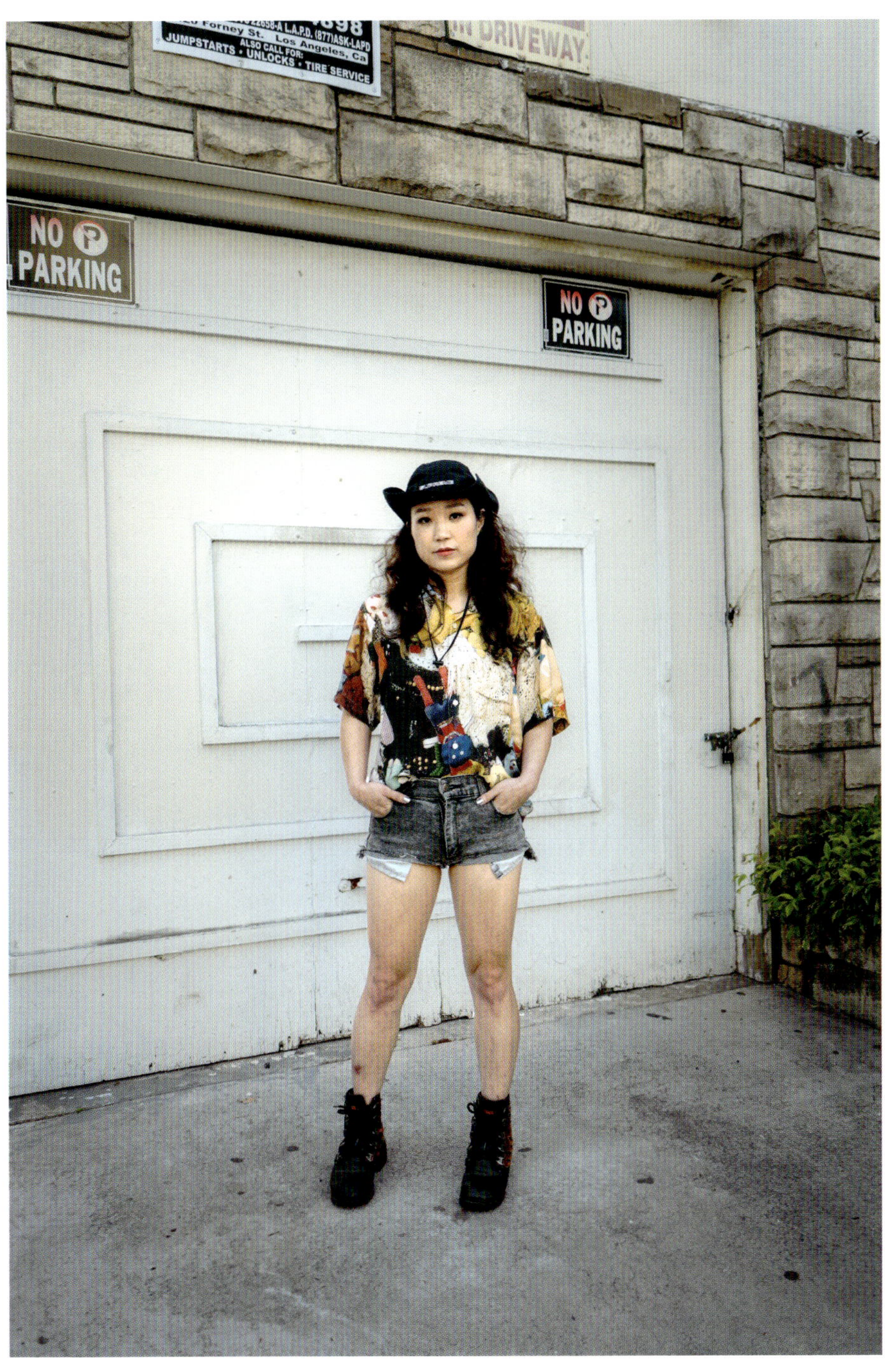

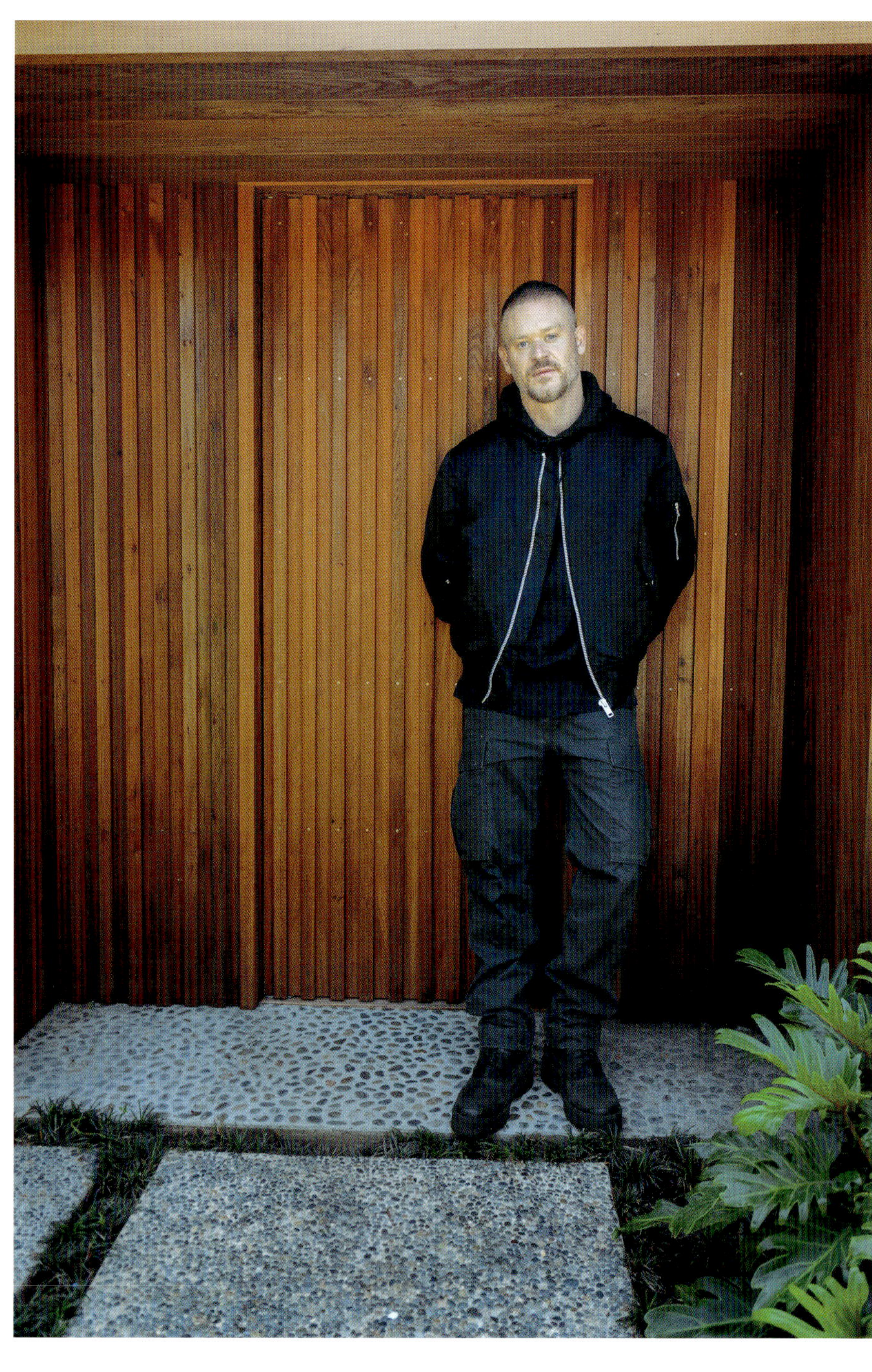

Model

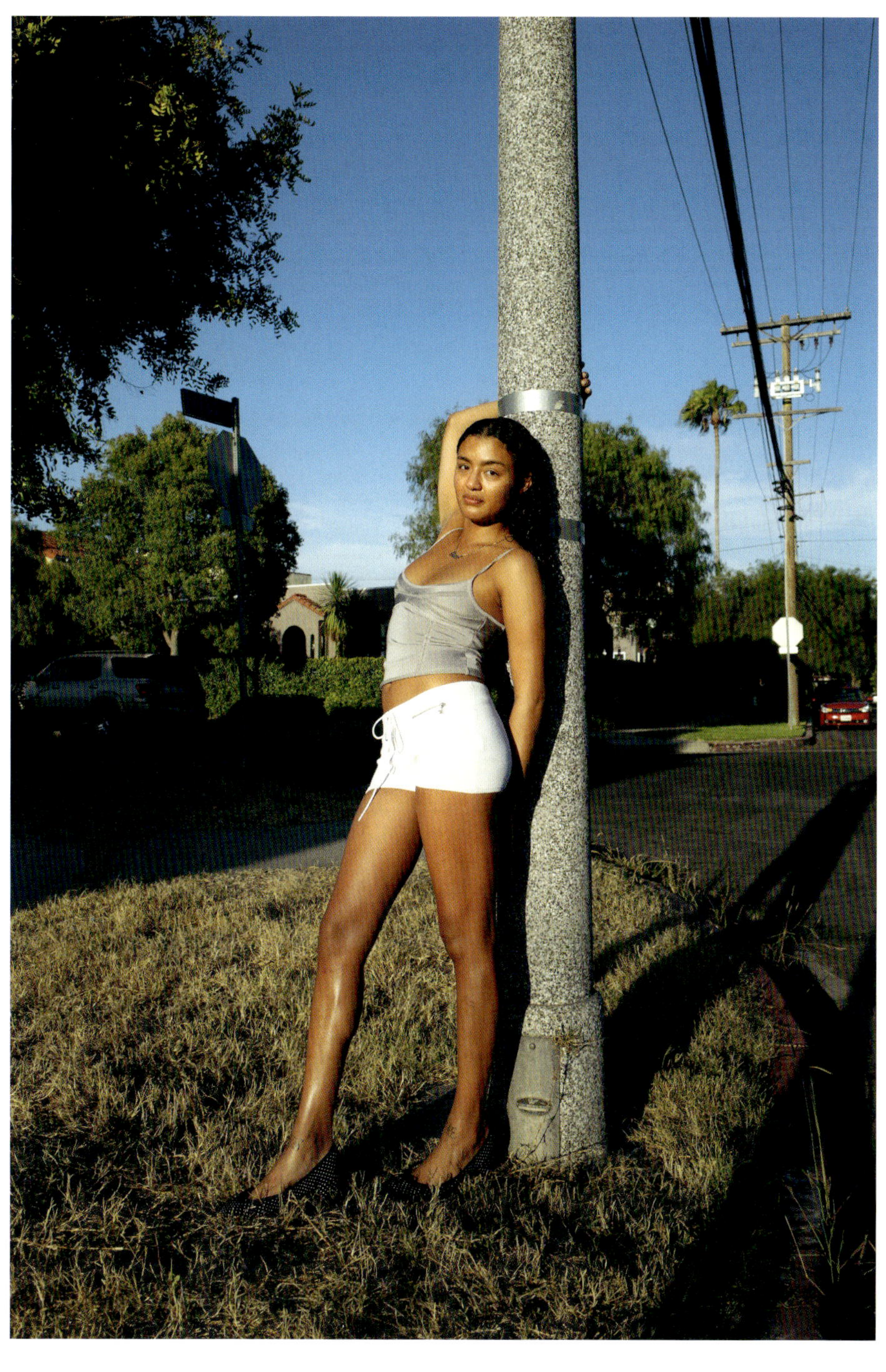

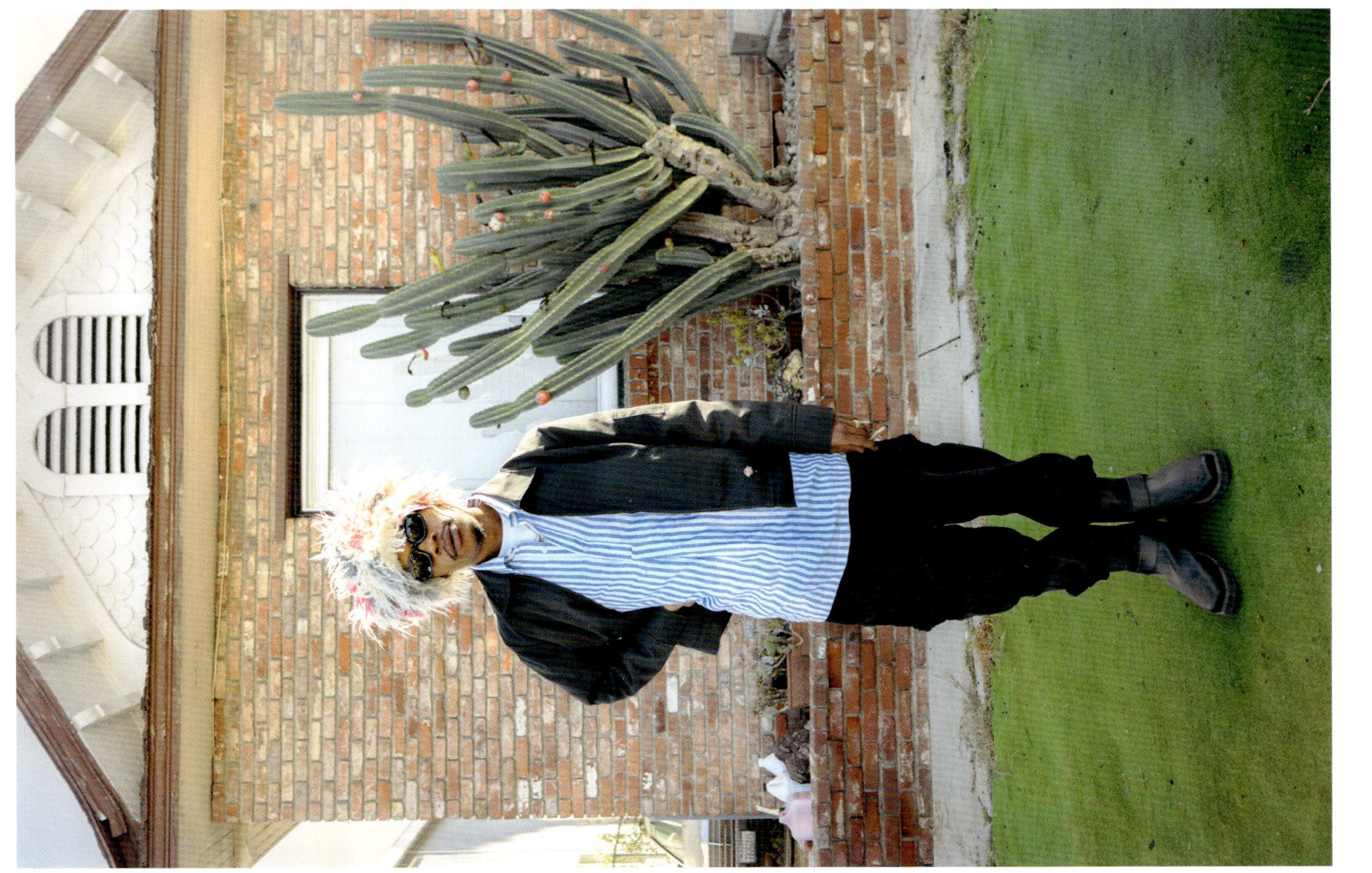

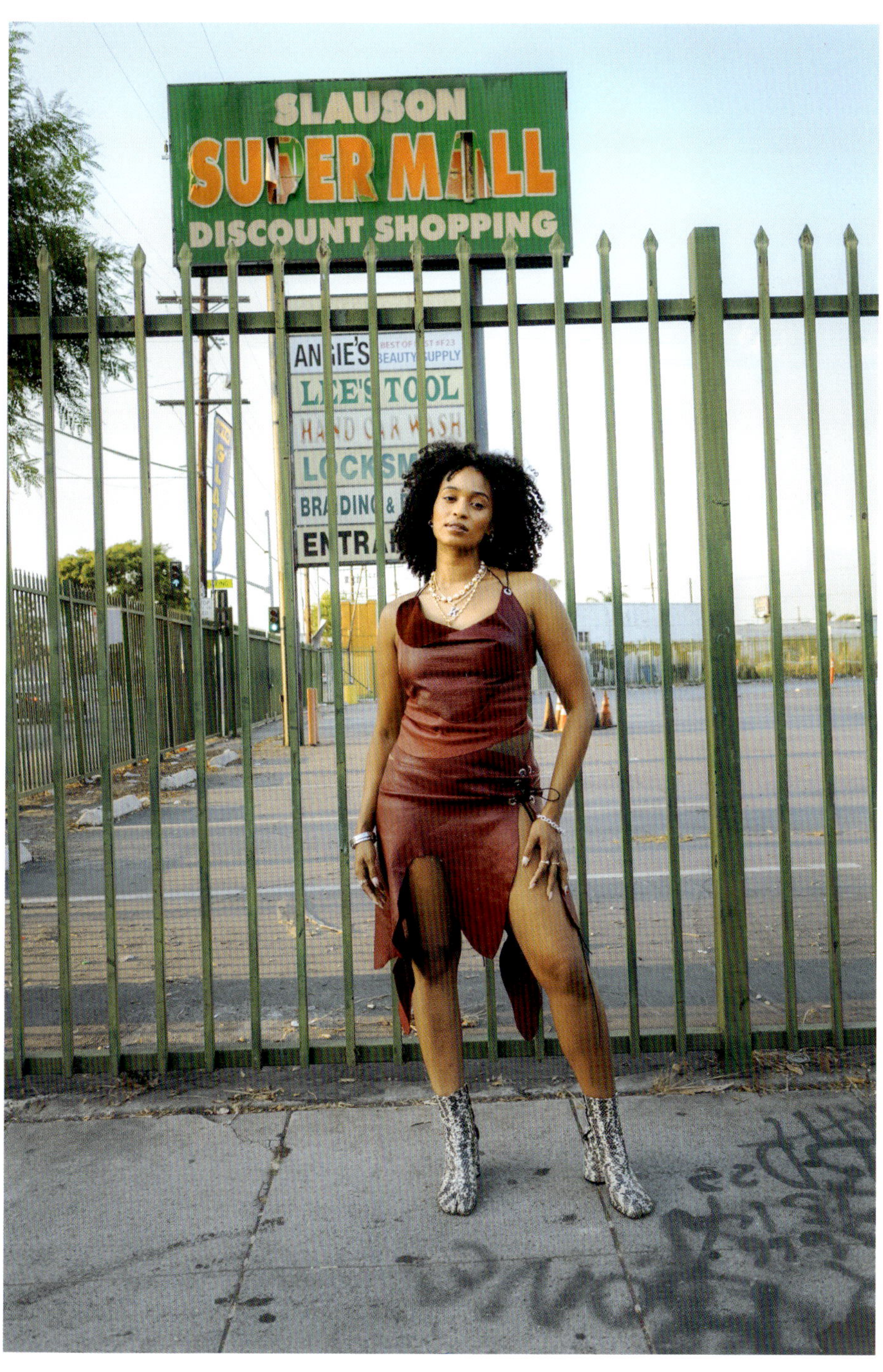
SLAUSON
SUPER MALL
DISCOUNT SHOPPING
ANGIE'S
BEST OF BELT #F23
BEAUTY SUPPLY
LEE'S TOOL
HAND CAR WASH
LOCKSM
BRAIDING &
ENTRA

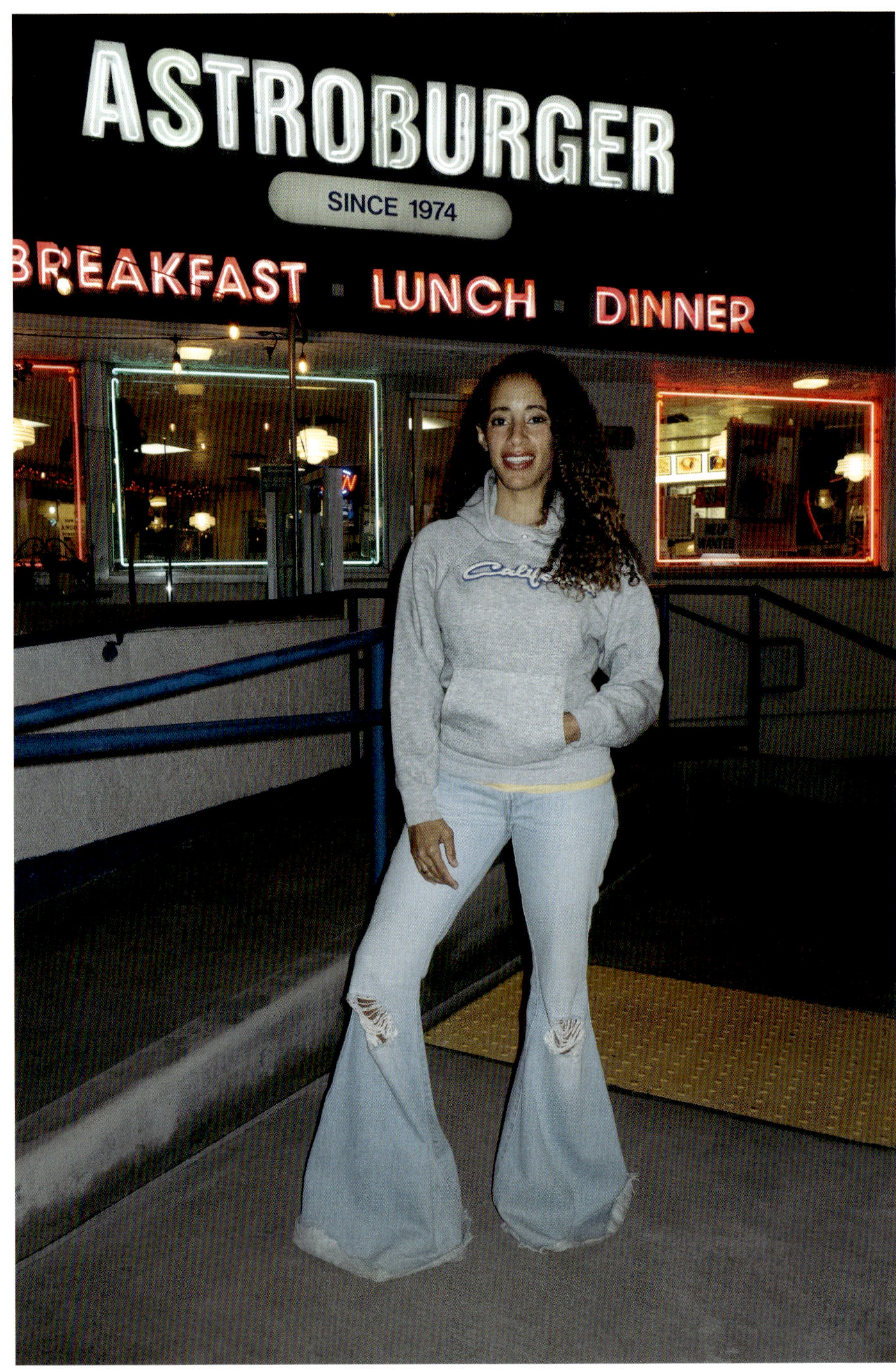

Stylist / Costume Designer / Author

NorCal / Hollywood

INDEX

Thank You

Jeffrey Deitch

Additional Thank You's

Chioma Nnadi, Brent Rollins, Tyler Gibney, Brian Roettinger, Kilo Kish, DJ Kitty Cash, Rob English, Adrian Miller, Acyde, Angelo Baque, Julie and Jay Lewis, Jenny Le, Jim Magen, Hype Williams, Ashley Fox, 2tone and Spanto, Alan the G, BJ Panda, Sandy Kim, Raven Diggs, Marquis Miller, Serena Morris, Dan Reagan, Stüssy, ERL, Yoyin, Carmen, Ian Reid, Sandy Kim, Jesse Acevedo, Emma Reeves, Fam Udeorji, Eve MacSweeney, Stella and My Ancestors. Every single person that trusted me to honor their style in my book.

Credits

Author Jasmine Benjamin **Photographer** Jasmine Benjamin **Intro** Hannah Bhuiya & Jasmine Benjamin **Foreword** Chioma Nnadi **Art Director** Kilo Kish **Graphic Design** Chance Medder **Map Illustrator** Issac Psalm Escoto **Retouching & Color Mastering** Trevor Parlo Clement **Editor** Sophia Dearborne **Proofreading** EdnaSarah Fortuné **Author's Photo by** Malik Levi Berlin

Executive Producers
Jeffrey Deitch, Ade 'Acyde' Odunlami